Doing Business in China

Doing Business in China

Getting Ready for the Asian Century

Jane Menzies
Mona Chung
Stuart Orr

Doing Business in China: Getting Ready for the Asian Century
Copyright © Business Expert Press, 2012.

First published in 2012 by
Business Expert Press, LLC
222 East 46th Street, New York, NY 10017
www.businessexpertpress.com

ISBN-13: 978-1-60649-344-1 (paperback)

ISBN-13: 978-1-60649-345-8 (e-book)

DOI 10.4128/9781606493458

Business Expert Press International Business collection

Collection ISSN: 1948-2752 (print)
Collection ISSN: 1948-2760 (electronic)

Cover design by Jonathan Pennell
Interior design by Exeter Premedia Services Private Ltd.,
Chennai, India

First edition: 2012

10 9 8 7 6 5 4 3 2 1

Printed in the United States of America.

From Jane Menzies: To John
From Mona Chung: To Holly
From Stuart Orr: To Rose

Abstract

The Asian Century will bring many changes to world trade and to the global economy. It is predicted that China will be the largest single economy in this new economic era; understanding how business operates in China will hence be central to success in the Asian Century. This book will be of particular interest to researchers, managers, and anyone interested in international business in China. It examines the experiences of a wide range of Australian businesses that have internationalized to China, including planning for, establishing and operating a business in China, staff selection and management, the trade and investment environment, legal practices and regulations, politics, corruption and intellectual property protection. Australian businesses were selected for this project because of Australia's strong economic connection with China and the stability of the Chinese economy over the last 20 years, including during the GFC. China has been Australia's top trading partner since 2007. The consistency of the Chinese economy and the long-term commitment of Australian businesses to operations in China provided a valuable perspective from which to examine foreign business operations in China. Over the last 20 years, the Chinese economy grew tenfold, to become the second largest in the world. The longitudinal perspective of many of the participants over this period of change enabled them to offer insightful observations regarding the fundamental drivers of business practices in China. The findings presented in this book are based on interviews collected from 40 organizations, ranging from global mining and banking organizations to small manufacturing or service companies, covering a range of industries, and entry modes.

This book examines the process of preparing for successful operations in China, the opportunities offered by the Chinese market, and the obstacles to establishing and maintaining business operations in China. The research utilizes a number of frameworks to consider business in China, including foreign direct investment and trade, cultural, political and legal, intellectual property, strategy, market entry, and human resource management frameworks. The findings presented in this book are based on a rich and well-considered collection of observations provided by senior executives with long-term experience of operating businesses in

China. This book provides generalized findings that can be transferred to other developed country contexts and evaluates the appropriateness of international business and trade frameworks for the Chinese context.

Keywords

Australian business internationalization, China, doing business in China

Contents

Acknowledgments

The authors would like to acknowledge the assistance provided by the Australia China Business Council (ACBC)—Victoria Branch for their active support in completing the project. They would like to thank the members and other individuals who gave us their time and talked with us about their business activities in China. They would also like to acknowledge the financial assistance provided by the Faculty of Business and Law, Deakin University, to complete the project. The authors would like to acknowledge the copy editor, Lynn Spray. Dr. Menzies would like to acknowledge the support provided by Dr. Ilan Alon and The China Center, at Rollins College, Winter Park, Florida, who hosted Dr. Menzies as part of her sabbatical, which enabled her to devote considerable time to writing this publication to book.

Foreword

China's popularity as a research topic for both inward and outward trade and investment has increased steadily in the past two decades. Understanding the interactions of different countries with China is a vitally important dimension of internationalization, as different contexts can result in a different interplay between home and host country variables, such as politics, culture, economics, resource base, legal factors, among many others.

Australia is similar, on many levels, to other Western Anglo-Saxon countries such as the United States or the United Kingdom, though it has a much smaller population (22.6 million people) and its organizations tend to be smaller, have fewer resources, and are less international than their American or European counterparts. Despite the reduced access to resources, Australian organizations have been successful in the Chinese market across many sectors, including natural resources, automotive, education, engineering, building and construction, heavy industries and banking to name a few, all of which are discussed in this book.

This book presents research describing the abilities, choices, and mind-sets of managers from Australian organizations when they internationalize to China, from a number of theoretical perspectives. In particular, this book focuses on the motivations, strategies, and entry mode choices that organizations select. This book also presents a variety of managers' perceptions on the frameworks pertaining to trade and investment, culture, politics, law, and intellectual property rights. The human resource management issues that these organizations face are also explored.

This book makes a unique contribution to a small, but growing, literature on Australian companies in China. The authors should be commended on an enjoyable, informative, and absorbing read on entry into the world's second largest economy—China, the Middle Kingdom.

Dr. Ilan Alon[1]
Department of International Business
Rollins College
Winter Park, Florida

List of Abbreviations

ACBC	Australia China Business Council
BSA	Business Software Alliance
CCOIC	Arbitration Court of the China Chamber of International Commerce
CIETAC	China International Economic Trade Arbitration Commission
CIT	Corporate Income Tax
CJV	Cooperative Joint Venture
CPC	Chinese Communist Party
DFAT	Department of Foreign Affairs and Trade
EJV	Equity Joint Venture
FDI	Foreign Direct Investment
FESCO	Foreign Enterprise Service Company
FIEs	Foreign Invested Enterprises
FIRB	Foreign Investment Review Board
FTA	Free Trade Agreement
GATS	General Agreement on Trade in Services
GATT	General Agreement on Tariffs and Trade
GDP	Gross Domestic Product
GDP PPP	Gross Domestic Product Purchasing Power Parity
GFC	Global Financial Crisis
HCNs	Host Country Nationals
HR	Human Resources
HRM	Human Resource Management
IP	Intellectual Property
JV	Joint Venture
M&A	Merger and Acquisition
MNE	Multinational Enterprise
NPC	National People's Congress
OECD	Organization for Economic Cooperation and Development
PBSC	Politburo Standing Committee

PCNs	Parent Country Nationals
PCT	Patent Cooperation Treaty
PRC	People's Republic of China
R&D	Research and Development
RMB	Renminbi
RBV	Resource-based View
SEZs	Special Economic Zones
SIPO	State Intellectual Property Office
SME	Small to Medium Enterprise
SOE	State-owned Enterprise
T&D	Training and Development
TCNs	Third Country Nationals
TM	Talent Management
TRIMS	Trade-related Investment Measures
TRIPS	Trade-related Aspects of Intellectual Property Rights
WIPO	World Intellectual Property Organization
WOFE	Wholly-owned Foreign Entity
WTO	World Trade Organization

CHAPTER 1

Introduction

China, also known as the Middle Kingdom or *Zhōngguó*, has been an attractive emerging market for international businesses that can be expected to offer new opportunities, well into the future. It is predicted that China will grow and flourish until it is the world's largest economy in 2016. Along with its own rapid growth, China offers many foreign companies great potential for their future growth. Despite the attractiveness of this country, it is difficult to understand how it operates, and there are many minefields waiting for the unwary. An understanding of the context, the drawbacks, and issues associated with internationalization to China, will assist with understanding how entry decisions should be made for this unique market. The purpose of this book is to provide an overview of the Chinese business environment, and present the findings from research, conducted with Australian managers who either are involved in their organization's international activities in China or have had the experience of internationalizing their business to China. These viewpoints are invaluable in understanding the dynamics of this market for researchers, would-be investors, and those interested in exporting or participating in international trade.

China has experienced stunning double-digit growth rates in gross domestic product (GDP) for over two decades and, as of 2010, it is the second largest economy in the world.[1] It is predicted that China's economy will surpass that of the United States by 2016 in GDP purchasing power parity (PPP).[2] This is just one dimension of China's economic success; however, it is predicted that it may take another 30 years or so for China to "catch up" and become the largest economy in real terms. This prediction, however, has changed dramatically since the Global Financial Crisis (GFC). China will have to develop and maintain a range of economic fundamentals in order to reach this goal. However, serious "Black Swan" events,[3] such as the recent GFC and European Debt Crises, may impede China's future growth.

The Context of China

China's entry onto the world economic stage occurred in 1978, with the implementation of Deng Xiaoping's "this Open Door Policy."[4] Since then China has opened its borders and economy to commercialism, industrialization, foreign direct investment (FDI) (now both inwards and outwards), and international trade. China's economic growth has been astonishing in the past 30 years; and its move from a closed-door, communist, centrally planned economy to a "socialist market economy," or what has been termed by others as "the world's largest capitalist economy" with such success, has been even more astounding. Along with these economic developments, numerous changes have been made on a social, cultural, political, and legal front. As a result, the Chinese people have seen a positive effect on the economy, country, standard of living, quality of life, and security in China.[5]

Culture is a pervasive issue for foreign business in China and is not well understood by foreign managers. For this reason, the theme of Chinese business culture runs throughout this book. Understanding the deeper cultural values is often the key to creating a successful business in China.

In the past, China has been perceived as the "factory of the world" due to its low-cost, endless supply of hardworking labor. China's comparative advantage as a low-cost manufacturing nation is currently being eroded by increasing wage levels (wage inflation has ranged between 7% and 25% per annum in recent years)[6] and greater worker protection, which increase business costs. In response to this, the government is working to develop the innovation-based segment of the economy, investing in education, a strong patent system/patent portfolios, and an emphasis on research and development. In fact, the focus of China's 12th five-year plan is the development of an innovation economy.[7] Only time will tell whether China will be successful in this respect. Considering its past success in developing other parts of its economy and the power of the government, China is likely to be successful in this endeavor as well. A common saying in the Chinese business community is, *"things get done in China, but it is not always easy."*[8]

The Context of Australia–China Business Relations

China's growth has been the single largest contributor to global growth over the past 5 years, and this is expected to continue until, at least, 2016.[9] In 2011, China accounted for 45.1% of the world's crude steel output[10] and 58.6% of the world's pig iron output.[11] As a major global minerals supplier located close to Asia, Australia has taken advantage of the economic development in China. Today, Australia enjoys a mineral boom because of its supplier relationship with China.[12] In 2010, Australia represented China's 6th principal import source, with 4.1% of trade imported from Australia.[13]

China is not only a resources market for Australia; other Australian companies have been pursuing the Chinese market since the introduction of the Open Door Policy in 1978.[14] Overall, however, the results of this pursuit have been somewhat inconsistent. Some Australian companies have unquestionably had success in China. For example, the ANZ Bank has one of the most developed Chinese operations of the Australian banks operating in China. It has managed to open a number of branches throughout China and has progressed successfully through the stages, as specified by government regulations, to become an incorporated bank in China in 2010.[15] Other Australian organizations have not been so successful and have had to withdraw from China. For example, the large Australian beer manufacturer, the Foster's Group, was unable to make a profit from their Chinese operations and pulled out of China in 2006.[16]

China is now Australia's largest trading partner,[17] and its importance to the Australian economy has grown alongside China's increasing economic, political, and strategic influence in the Asia-Pacific region and in the global economy.[18] In 2011, Australian investment in China amounted to A\$16.9 billion,[19] making it Australia's 11th largest investment destination.[20]

In terms of trade, 3,245 Australian companies were exporting to China in 2006.[21] Currently, major areas of opportunity include mining and energy; agribusiness; manufacturing; construction; technology; management; consultancy; regional development; and financial, legal, education, engineering, and architectural services.[22] Major exports from Australia to China include iron ore, wool, copper ores, and coal.[23] In the area of services, Australia's major exports to China are education and education-related travel and personal travel (e.g., Chinese visitors to Australia). There are approximately 1,000 Australian exporters entering the Chinese market each year,[24] with about 400 Australian businesses operating in China; most of them engaged in manufacturing, property, business services, finance, insurance, education, mineral exploration, and information services.[25] Recognizing the significance of these business relationships, Australia and China began negotiations for a Free Trade Agreement (FTA) in 2005.[26] The FTA aims to facilitate Australian exporters and businesses in gaining greater and smoother access to the Chinese market.

Australian-Chinese business relationships are important to Australia, mainly due to China's demand for resources. However, many other sectors of Australian industry have been successful in China, such as the food and beverage, education, and manufacturing industries. Australian organizations have actively participated in China-related activities, but little is known about how these organizations internationalize to China. Hence, it is important to develop our understanding of how they do business in China.

This book presents the findings of this research into Australian organizations' entry strategies into China. It provides an explanation of and insights into how Australian organizations make decisions when entering the Chinese market place and the factors influencing those decisions. Forty Australian organizations with business activities in China participated in the research. Senior executives, directors, managers, and consultants familiar with their international business activities in China were interviewed to collect the data. In order to illustrate the predominant factors and their impact, a business strategy model was developed for entering the Chinese market. This model incorporates all the factors, which were identified as having an impact on an organization's decision-making process (Figure 1.1). Each aspect of this model will be considered in detail in Chapters 2–9.

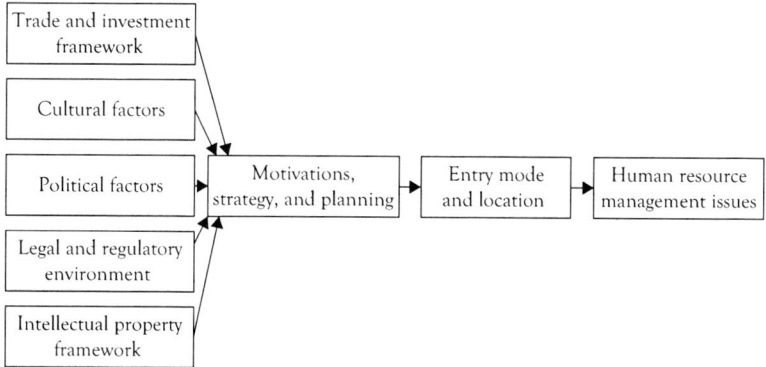

Figure 1.1. Business strategy model for entering the Chinese market.

The Study

To conduct the study, initially support from the Australia China Business Council (ACBC) was gained by approaching The Honorable Jim Short, who then approached ACBC's board for their support of the project. The board gave the researchers approval to contact ACBC members to participate in the study—invitations were e-mailed to all members of the Victoria branch. Nonrespondents were followed up with telephone calls to encourage participation. In addition, the research team members' personal contacts were used to select companies who were not members of ACBC. The snowballing method[27] of participant recruitment was also used to increase participant numbers. This involved asking the interviewees to identify potential interviewees from other companies they thought would be suitable and available to participate in the study.

Once the participants had agreed to be involved in the research, the aims and background of the study were explained, and confidentiality and anonymity were assured. An appointment was then made to conduct the interview. The interviews mainly took place at the participants' offices. Most interviews lasted approximately an hour, and the interviews were recorded and transcribed by a professional transcriber. One participant did not want a recording to be made at the interview and notes were taken instead. The interview transcripts were then analyzed using a thematic methodology, which identified the major themes representing the viewpoints of the participants. A total of 43 interviews were conducted for the 40 Australian organizations (in some cases, more than one partici-pant was interviewed from the organization). To conduct this research, a grant worth $12,000 was provided by Deakin University. The ACBC, Victoria branch, supported the research in kind.

The Organizations Involved in the Study

The descriptive features of the organizations represented by the partici-pants, including industry, entry mode(s), business activity in China, year started in China, and location(s), are presented in Table 1.1. The partici-pants are represented by pseudonyms, which highlight their key features.

The largest sector in the sample consisted of organizations in the manufacturing industry (10 out of 40). Other industries investigated in the study were business and property services (5); building, construction, and engineering (3); education (4); agriculture, forestry, and fishing (4); and finance and insurance (3). There were a small selection of organiza-tions that were scattered across various industries, such as accommoda-tion, restaurants and cafés, mining, publishing, information technology, government, administration and defense, and health and community services.

Several types of entry modes were represented in the data, with some firms utilizing multiple entry modes. For example, one firm engaged in both acquisition and greenfield modes. The modes identified in the research data included the following: fly-in-fly-out mode (8); using representative offices (2) or a registered office (1); joint ventures (6); using agents and partner-ships to source customers, or, in the case of education institutions, sourcing students (5); wholly-owned foreign entities (WOFE) (13); licensing (1); supplier relationships (1); exporting (6); and exporting assistance (1).

The popular internationalization locations in China amongst the par-ticipants included Shanghai (24), Beijing (15), Guangzhou (9), Shenzhen (4), and Tianjin (6). Various other locations are shown in Table 1.1. The organizations represented in the data had participated in China over very different periods of time. One organization established its business rela-tionships in China in the late 1890s, whilst another organization had established its operations there in 2007. The majority of companies in the study had internationalized to China in the early 1990s.

Table 1.1. Characteristics of the Organizations Involved in the Study

Case	Pseudonym	Industry type[28]	Entry mode(s)	Key activities in China	Year started in China	Location in China
1	Lab Co	Business and property services	Fly in fly out	Business consulting to organizations wishing to do business in China in the biotechnology industry	—	Eastern seaboard of China
2	Bank Co 1	Finance and insurance	Wholly-owned Foreign Entity (WOFE) and 2X acquisition (20%)	Local and foreign banking. Corporate banking, commodity and trade finance, markets and consumer, and corporate services	1980s	Beijing, Shanghai, Tianjin, Chongqing, and Guangzhou
3	Architect Co	Building, construction, and engineering	WOFE	Architectural design works in China	2004	Registered office in Tianjin and branch office in Shanghai
4	Parcel Co	Transport and logistics	Joint venture (49% Parcel Co, 51% Chinese partner)	Provide logistics services in China and internationally including to Australia	2005	Shanghai, Hong Kong, and Shenzhen
5	Hotel Co	Accommodation, cafés, and restaurants	Agents	Uses wholesale travel agents in China to recruit tourists/customers for their Australian hotel	—	North China, Southern China, and Taiwan
6	Resources Co 1	Mining	Exporting, joint ventures with partners and WOFE.	Exports resources to China	1890s	Shanghai, Beijing, and other locations

(Continued)

Table 1.1. Characteristics of the Organizations Involved in the Study (Continued)

Case	Pseudonym	Industry type[28]	Entry mode(s)	Key activities in China	Year started in China	Location in China
7	Metal Co	Manufacturing	WOFE	Manufacturing facilities and sales offices across China	2000s	Shanghai, Suzhou, Guangzhou, Beijing, Tianjin, and Chengdu
8	Vat Co	Manufacturing	WOFE (2001; originally a joint venture, 1995)	Manufactures metal vats in China, for sales in China, and exports to Australia and other international markets	1995	Changzhou, Jiangsu Province
9	Marketing Co	Business and property services	Fly in fly out, with a registered office	Provides marketing consulting services in China	2005	Hong Kong based, contacts in Shanghai
10	Gov Co	Government administration and defense	Representative office	Provides Australian business with connections and contacts in Tianjin	1998	Tianjin
11	Agri Co	Agriculture, forestry, and fishing	Fly in fly out	Provides industry seminars, education, and information in China to government and consumers. Provides industry support to companies wishing to internationalize to China	1999	Beijing, Shanghai, Guangzhou, Hong Kong, and Taiwan
12	Uni Co 1	Education	Agents, representative office	Student recruitment, research, research collaboration, managing relationships, and developing a presence. Office in Beijing	2000	Beijing, Shanghai with agents that have a broad China reach
13	Pallet Co	Manufacturing	Supplier relationship	Sources supplies from China	2005	Shanghai

Case	Pseudonym	Industry type[28]	Entry mode(s)	Key activities in China	Year started in China	Location in China
14	Auto Interior Co	Manufacturing	Joint venture (70% Auto Interior Co, 20% Customer, and 10% Government)	Manufactures interior components for sale to automotive manufacturers located in China	2005	Wu Hu, Anhui Province, Changsha, Hunan Province
15	Flower Co	Agriculture, forestry, and fishing	Joint venture	Produces flowers in China for sale and exports to other international locations	2004	Kunming, Yunnan Province
16	Build Co	Building construction, and Engineering	WOFE	Designs, consults, and builds sterile pharmaceutical plants and others	1993	2 staffed offices in Shanghai and Beijing, 2 registered offices in Suzhou, and Harbin with projects around China
17	Law Co	Business and property services	Representative office	Advises corporate clients about legal issues when doing business in China	1997	Shanghai office
18	Auto Components Co	Manufacturing	WOFE	Manufactures products in China for sale to Tier 1 automotive manufacturers	2006	Changchun
19	Fibre Co	Agriculture, forestry, and fishing	Fly in fly out	Markets and educates consumers on industry products	1998	—
20	IT Co	Information technology	Fly in fly out	IT consulting in large banks	1999	Beijing and Shanghai

(Continued)

Table 1.1. Characteristics of the Organizations Involved in the Study (Continued)

Case	Pseudonym	Industry type[28]	Entry mode(s)	Key activities in China	Year started in China	Location in China
21	Import/Export Co	Business and property services	Exporting, fly in fly out	Imports and exports products including food, minerals, clothing, and also provides advice and consulting	1986	—
22	Wool Co	Manufacturing	Exporting	Exports niche, wool products to China, and attends trade shows	—	Shanghai
23	Book Co	Publishing	Licensing	Licenses a state-owned enterprise to produce their books, for sale in China. Written in Mandarin	2004	Shanghai
24	Engineering Co	Building construction, and engineering	WOFE	Provides design, planning, and building services in China	1990	Offices in Hong Kong, Beijing, Guangzhou, Shenzhen, and Macau
25	Uni Co 2	Education	Agents	Recruits Chinese students, builds international linkages, engages in academic and research exchanges, developed an alumni association, provides careers, and employment services	—	Nanjing and all over
26	Software Co	Information Technology	Joint venture (95% software co and 5% local Chinese partner)	Produces software in China, for the Chinese market in Chinese	2005	Chengdu (HQ), Beijing, Shanghai, Guangzhou, and Hong Kong

Case	Pseudonym	Industry type[28]	Entry mode(s)	Key activities in China	Year started in China	Location in China
27	Paint Co	Manufacturing	Exporting	Exports paint to business people wishing to migrate to Australia on the Australian Business Migration Scheme	2002	Shanghai, Shenzhen, Beijing, Guangzhou, Nanjing, and Wuhan
28	Brake Co	Manufacturing	WOFE	Manufactures products in China, for sale in China, and export worldwide	2005	North East China
29	Logistics Co	Transport and storage	Exporting	Provides freight services and customs documentation	2001	Shanghai
30	Machine Co	Agriculture, forestry, and fishing	Exporting	Exports machines to China and develops relationship with businesses to license the use of their machines	1999	Beijing
31	Medic Co	Health and community services	Fly in fly out	Develops relationships with clients, educates clients on their products	2003	Shanghai, Guangzhou, Nanjing, Beijing, Tianjin, Xian, and Zhōngguó
32	Chain Co	Manufacturing	WOFE (Greenfield and Acquisition)	Manufactures chains and heavy industry products in China, for the Chinese market and abroad	2007	Shanghai and Hangzhou
33	Responsibility Co	Business and property services	WOFE	Provides corporate social responsibility consulting and risk advice	2003	Shanghai and Hong Kong
34	Resources Co 2	Mining	WOFE, exporting	Exports resources to China, has offices in Beijing, Guangzhou, and Shanghai	1960s	Beijing, Guangzhou, and Shanghai

(Continued)

Table 1.1. *Characteristics of the Organizations Involved in the Study (Continued)*

Case	Pseudonym	Industry type[28]	Entry mode(s)	Key activities in China	Year started in China	Location in China
35	Gambling Co	Cultural and recreational services	WOFE	Operates gaming and lottery outlets throughout Shanghai	2005	Shanghai
36	Trade Finance Co	Finance and insurance	Exporting assistance and fly-in-fly-out mode	Provides export trade finance and payment methods. Interacts with Chinese business and suppliers.	2005	Shenzhen, Guangzhou, Dongguan, Shanghai, and Ningbo
37	Uni Co 3	Education	Agents	Partnership programs in various courses, articulation programs, recruitment, and pipelining of students. Offshore lecturing	2000	Beijing, Jinan, Kaifeng, Changsha, Liaoning, and Huang
38	Tafe Co	Education	Agents, joint venture	Pathways program for students coming to Australia to study. Offshore teaching	1990s	Chengdu, Hunan, Shenyang in Liaoning Province, Kaifeng, Zhengzhou, Jinan, Tianjin, and Lanzhou
39	Bank Co 3	Finance and insurance	WOFE	Branches in a number of locations, offers a number of banking services, and is waiting for extended banking approvals	1987	Beijing, Shanghai, and Hong Kong
40	Retail Co	Manufacturing/retail trade	Supplier relationships	Sources retail products from a small group of suppliers	2000	Guangzhou

Intended Audiences for This Book

This book presents the findings and analysis of a research study investigating the internationalization of Australian businesses into China. This book will be of considerable value to those researching Australia–China business relationships, as there has been little research conducted in this area, and little is known about the internationalization of Australian firms to China. This book thus makes a significant academic contribution to this important area of research. A better understanding of this phenomenon is especially important as the Australian government is currently attempting to develop its relationship with China, responding to the anticipated emergence of the Asian Century.[29] This research also has practical significance for businesses that are new to or are considering entry into the Chinese market and provides observations that would be of interest to practitioners. This research is also important for managers who are planning to have careers in China in the future. This book provides a thorough background of the Chinese business environment, based on a number of theoretical perspectives, and draws conclusions regarding the key issues identified in the research for organizations internationalizing into China.

Structure of This Book

This book first explores the trade and investment climate in China (Chapter 2), and analyzes the perceptions of the participants towards Australia's negotiations with China on a FTA, and China's accession to the World Trade Organization (WTO). Chapter 3 is devoted to understanding the deeper cultural values associated with "doing business in China," identified by the participants. This chapter examines the Chinese business culture and utilizes the research findings to identify a number of approaches, which could be used to address the cultural differences that foreign businesses will experience in China. Chapter 4 describes and analyzes the political system in China and specifically identifies how politics in China should be managed. This chapter utilizes the findings to identify a number of approaches for dealing with the political conditions in China. Chapters 5 and 6 provide an understanding of the legal and intellectual property (IP) regulatory framework in China. Chapter 5 focuses on the legal system, and the perceptions that managers had of the system, whilst Chapter 6 focuses on an analysis of the IP issues that the participants experienced. This chapter utilizes the findings to identify a range of approaches, which organizations could utilize to protect their IP-related assets in China. Chapters 5 and 6 also provide a critical assessment of the challenges associated with dealing with the Chinese legal system and IP laws. Chapter 7 focuses on the motivations, planning, and strategies that the participants used to enter China. Transaction cost, OLI (ownership, location, and internalization), internationalization, and the resource-based view theories were utilized in Chapter 8 to examine the entry modes that participants adopted when internationalizing to China and their locational choices. The international human resource management literature was utilized in Chapter 9 to evaluate the human resource management issues that the participants identified as relevant in the Chinese environment. This chapter focused on staffing preferences, dealing with skills shortages, and attracting and retaining staff. Chapter 10 concludes this book with a summary of the key findings and analysis of the data. Practitioners will find this chapter of interest as the findings offer suggestions for decision-making processes, which will increase the likelihood of success in establishing Chinese foreign business operations.

Conclusion

Deng Xiaoping, the mastermind behind the economic reforms in China, is famous in China for the saying "Search for stones to cross the river."[30] Deng Xiaoping used this statement to indicate that the people of China needed to search for stepping-stones to make the transition from a centrally planned economy to a modern day market economy, which is integrated with the world. Foreign businesses planning to enter the Chinese market, whether by exporting, FDI, or joint ventures, should also heed this advice and "search for stones to cross the river." This book presents and evaluates some of those "stones." It is hoped that this book will provide guidance for achieving success and prosperity in the Middle Kingdom, *Zhōngguó*.

CHAPTER 2

Exploring the Trade and Investment Environment in China

China's trade and investment framework has significantly, but gradually, changed since Deng Xiaoping's "Open Door Policy," in 1978. Developing from little or no trade and investment in the late 1970s to an economy, which is the largest exporter in the world,[1] is a remarkable achievement. China is now both a capital importer and exporter. Over the next two decades, it is expected that the world will continue to see many dragon multinational enterprises (MNEs), competing directly with the best of the best. Understanding the trade and investment framework is an important first stage in understanding the Chinese business environment. The aim of this chapter is to present the trade and investment environment of China and analyze what it means from the perspective of Australia–China relations. China is Australia's number one trading partner, and is extremely important to the Australian economy and its future prosperity.

China's Economic Miracle

It has been generally recognized that China's astonishing growth rates constitute an economic miracle. Since the year 2000, China's economic growth has averaged around 10.2% pa (see Figure 2.1).

This "miracle" is often attributed to the opening up of the Chinese economy to the West and the resultant increases in China's total productivity.[3] Other influences on growth have been foreign direct investment (FDI), technology transference, investment into education, and worker output (as a result of technology and education), among many other factors.

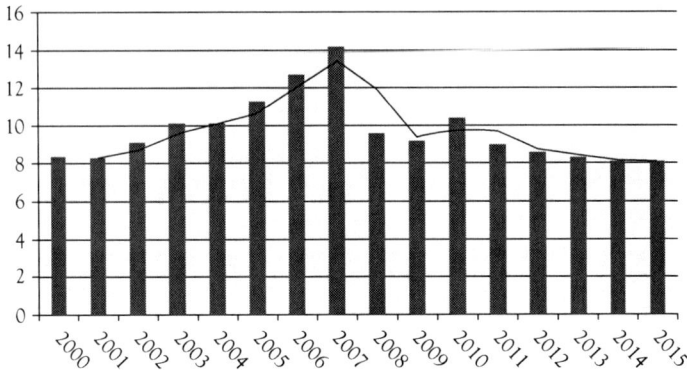

Figure 2.1. China's economic growth rate from 2000 to 2011, forecast to 2015.[2]

An interviewee (Case 1: Lab Co) from the study commented on his perceptions of China's growth, which he refers to as the 3S's of China:

> *There are 3S's that the world does not understand about China. The first S is the Speed of development; the world has no comprehension of this. The second S that they don't understand is Scale, they read a thousand times the population of China is 1.3 billion but they don't understand what that means; it's mind-boggling what that means, it's terrifying; and the third S is the one that's most surprising, the Sophistication of China. They're all aspiring to buy Hermes handbags ... the biggest market for Hermes is China.*

As this quote emphasizes, the speed of development in China has been phenomenal, considering that it has only been 34 years since China opened to the world. Evidence of this growth is apparent when one visits China and views the scale of development in terms of roads, infrastructure, apartment blocks, and shopping centers being built at a rapid pace. China has many signs of modernity and sophistication, for instance major cities, such as Shanghai, offer world-class restaurants, hotels, shopping, and transportation. Second-tier cities have also started to follow suit, and this will continue to occur throughout China, offering many opportunities for both domestic and foreign business.

Australia–China Trade

China's Exports

As a result of economic reforms, China's growth in exports has been impressive. In 1978, exports were valued at US$97.5 billion,[4] which then increased to US$326 billion in 2002 and then US$1,577.93 billion in 2010 (see Figure 2.2).[5]

China now ranks as the largest exporter in the world[7] and consistently retains a trade surplus, while other countries, such as the United States and Australia, have a trade deficit. China is often referred to as the "factory of the world" and, as a result of its competitive and comparative advantage, is a large net exporter. Price inflation, however, is a major problem that has affected China's growth recently. If this continues it will cause China's products to become expensive, and China will lose its competitiveness and its export trade levels will drop. Similarly, if the Chinese RMB increases in value (which it may), it may also have an effect on Chinese competitiveness.

Australia's Trade with China

It is often said that Australia punches above its weight in trade[8] and is a large exporter given its economic size and its population (22.6 million people).[9]

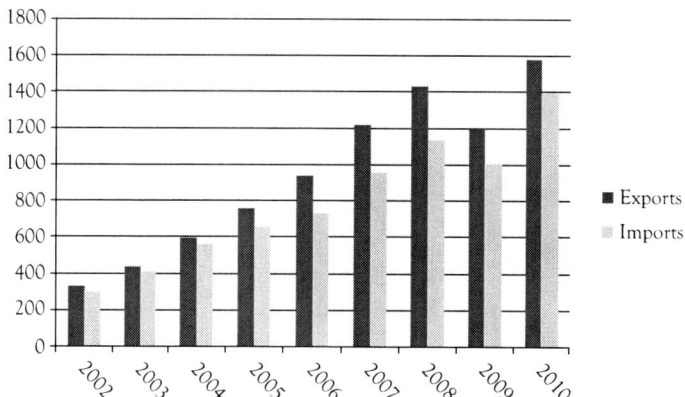

Figure 2.2. China's growth in exports and imports from 2002 to 2010.[6]

Along with China's growth, Australia's trade with China has increased in the last 10 years due to China's demand for Australian resources. A major consequence of China's economic rise is that Australia's economy is becoming increasingly dependent on China. China is now Australia's most important trading partner, representing 23.2% of total trade in 2010–2011, including exports and imports.[10] While merchandise trade has traditionally dominated Australia's economic relationship with China, service trade (such as travel and education) is also growing and assuming a greater importance.[11]

China's goods and services trade with Australia was valued at US$113.7 billion in 2010–2011.[12] Merchandise exports were valued at US$71.6 billion in 2010–2011, indicating an increase of 65.5% from the previous financial year, thus making China Australia's largest merchandise trading partner.[13] Total merchandise imports from China were valued at US$41.2 billion in 2010–2011.[14] In terms of trade, China is more important to Australia than Australia is to China. For instance, Australia exports 26.4% of its total exports to China, whereas China exports only 1.7% of its total exports to Australia.[15] This may be one of the reasons an FTA between Australia and China has not been finalized as of 2012, despite 7 years of negotiations.

In terms of Australia's exports to China, minerals and resources remain a significant component. For example, in 2010–2011, Australia exported iron ore to China to the value of $39.95 billion AUD,[16] or 57% of Australia's total exports to China (see Figure 2.3).[17]

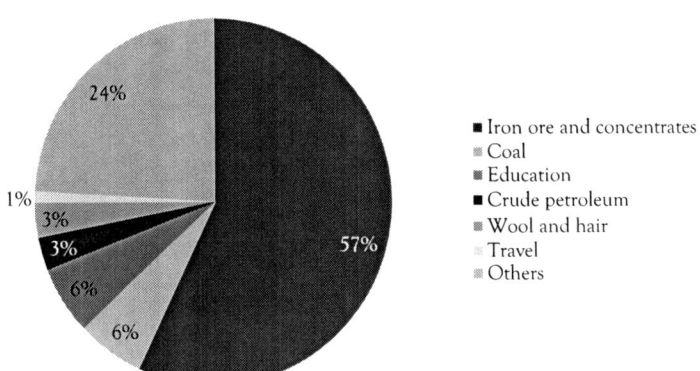

Figure 2.3. Breakdown of major exports from Australia to China—2011.[18]

Similarly, coal exports to China have become Australia's second largest export commodity (6%), after iron ore.[19] It is expected that, in the future, China's further economic growth and industrialization will continue to influence the Chinese demand for Australian resources.[20] Other key exports to China include education (6%), crude petroleum (3%), wool and hair (3%), travel (1%), and others (24%) (see Figure 2.3).[21] In 2009, a strong export performance in agricultural products included meat, wine, live animals, and fish.[22]

Education is another growing export sector from Australia to China, which, along with education-related and recreational travel, was worth $5.6 billion AUD in 2010–2011.[23] In 2009, China was Australia's largest source of international students, with approximately 155,000 enrolments in Australian educational institutions including secondary school and university.[24] Major Chinese imports into Australia included clothing, computers, telecom and equipment, prams, toys, games, and sporting equipment.[25]

China's Accession to the WTO in 2001

A discussion of China's trade and investment would not be complete without mentioning China's accession to the WTO. China's accession to the WTO in 2001 is regarded as a milestone in China's economic history. Membership of the WTO has meant that China must (a) engage in nondiscriminatory treatment of all WTO members in trade matters, (b) eliminate dual pricing as well as different treatment of goods produced for domestic sales versus those for export, (c) eliminate price controls that protect domestic companies, (d) revise existing laws to comply with the WTO agreement, and (e) remove export subsidies on agricultural products.[26] China's accession to the WTO has also meant that China is a signatory to the following agreements, which aim to promote free trade in both goods and services, develop an attractive environment for FDI, and finally, to protect intellectual property (IP) rights:

- General Agreement on Tariffs and Trade (GATT)
- General Agreement on Trade in Services (GATS)
- Trade-related Investment Measures (TRIMs)
- Trade-related Aspects of Intellectual Property Rights (TRIPS)[27]

Theoretically, being a signatory to these agreements has meant that all trade and FDI should be free, and that IP should be protected. However, this is not always the case in practice, and China has signed out of parts of the agreements to protect local industries (as do other members of the WTO). One example is China signing out of the "*National Treatment*" policy in the legal industry. For example, the "*National Treatment*" policy suggests that foreign-service providers should be treated in the same manner as local domestic providers.[28] Foreign legal firms in China, however, are prohibited from practicing with Chinese lawyers and from representing clients in a court of law, which means that they can only advise clients on legal matters, but not represent them. In this case, foreign-service providers are not treated in the same manner as local service providers. Despite these pitfalls and restrictions, WTO accession has been favorable for trade, FDI, and the development of the Chinese economy.

The research participants had an interesting range of viewpoints to offer regarding China's WTO accession. China's accession to the WTO was generally perceived by the participants to be a contributor to China's economic growth and supported companies importing and exporting from China:

> …*joining WTO is helping their economy and it's opening up a lot of potential opportunities there… .* (Case 25, Uni Co 2)

> …*it's just another tick in the box. I couldn't say how it has improved our business but it makes the climate better.* (Case 24, Engineering Co)

> …*the general things around transparency that come from China now being a member of the WTO, brings the economy along to something that all of us are more used to.* (Case 6, Resources Co 1)

One of the most attractive features of China's accession for companies importing into China was the removal of heavy import trade tariffs. It was believed that this will also drive Chinese industry to become more competitive:

> *WTO means that for them, they can't impose heavy trade tariffs on products imported into China, so they can't protect their own industry.* (Case 14, Auto Interior Co)

…the WTO agreement, now that has been signed and implemented, is the thing that is allowing foreign banks to compete head-to-head with local banks. The banking system is freeing up as part of the WTO. So retail banking is now starting to come into China. (Case 2, Bank Co 1)

One respondent observed that China's accession to the WTO accelerated the country's infrastructure development. Other respondents believed that the accession to international trade arrangements, coupled with increased regulatory certainty when dealing with China, would increase the level of FDI and, possibly, even national direct investment:

Now, if those sorts of developments help clarify and simplify and bring China into the normal international trade-type of arrangement, that's good. That would be the biggest hassle. And then policy certainty or regulatory certainty in China would be the next thing. (Case 38, Tafe Co)

…the better the market is for Australian industry, the more resources we will put to China. I think that was one of the catalysts for our timing to enter. (Case 39, Bank Co 2)

In addition, greater protection for IP under WTO accession conditions was considered to be a major advantage, as previously the risks to IP ownership in China were high.

China has not had a great reputation or respect for intellectual property and they now have to. (Case 14, Auto Interior Co)

I think China has now complied with all its WTO obligations. Now, it's still got a way to go in controlling piracy of intellectual property but… . (Case 17, Law Co)

We've got 2 granted patents in China already and we've got 3 pending ones as well. (Case 30, Machine Co)

Although China entered the WTO in 2001, some participants noted that some non-WTO compliant trade barrier mechanisms, such as export-driven tax reductions, were still in place many years later, although they were being reduced. Funds repatriation is one of the major concerns that have not improved since WTO accession and that the respondents hope would be resolved over time.

> …*the biggest issues are currency and repatriation of funds.* (Case 38, Tafe Co)

Another concern was the continuing misuse of trademarks and industry identifications in China, despite the government having signed WTO agreements to respect them.

> …*they don't police it in China so every little Tom, Dick and Harry is making woollen products, puts the wool mark on them and they've got synthetics in them, and… so it's very difficult* (Case 22, Wool Co).

Some participants observed that China's WTO accession had no visible impact upon their business either in or with China.

> *I'd say from a specific practical point of view, it hasn't yet particularly changed any of our activity. We are very conscious of it, but it hasn't led to any specific change to any of our offshore programs that I'm aware of as a result of that.* (Case 37, Uni Co 3)

> *It's not going to have any impact on us. If anything, it's going to accelerate the political system more than anything else. I think it's all pretty high macro level, rather than what we're dealing in. So, I don't think it's going to have any impact at all.* (Case 28, Brake Co)

A few participants felt that the economic power that China brings to the WTO may provide a valuable counterbalance to the other economically powerful member countries, such as the USA.

> *I think the WTO scenario is an interesting one because, at the moment, people will look at that from the perspective of the impositions that the WTO places on China. I think in the next period of time, we're going to see the impact that China has on the WTO itself.* (Case 33, Responsibility Co)

Overall, the participants indicated that the positive benefits of China's WTO accession outweighed the negatives. The reduction of previously significant trade barriers in some areas of trade, the increased transparency in regulations, and the reduction of difficulties with funds repatriation and increased IP protection were seen as advantageous features. The concerns focused primarily on how successful the WTO would be in ensuring that fund repatriation and IP rights, such as trademarks, would be respected at the level necessary to eliminate the current problems in these areas.

Average Tariff Rates Between Australia and China

The body that administers tariff rates on imports and exports in China is the General Administration of Customs.[29] In line with WTO commitments, China's average tariff rate is 10%, and countries (such as New Zealand) that have a FTA with China receive preferential treatment.[30] Australia has concluded 18 rounds of FTA negotiations with China, but does not yet have an FTA agreement.[31] China has 16 free trade zones, which are referred to as bonded zones, and around 60 export processing zones. Any goods that are imported into these zones will not face customs duties or import taxes.[32]

Free Trade Negotiations with Australia

Australia began negotiations with China for an FTA on April 18, 2005.[33] One of the key purposes of the FTA is to deepen and strengthen the relationship between Australia and China. An economic feasibility study was conducted, which indicated that there would be significant mutual economic benefits as a result of an FTA[34] and freer trade. Some of the key negotiations related to the following: (a) removal or reduction of tariff and non-barriers in relation to goods, (b) reduction or removal of regulatory barriers that restrict services, and (c) implementation of measures to encourage more foreign investment.[35] As of March 2012, the 18th round of negotiations was held in Canberra, in which negotiators discussed a range of outstanding issues.[36] As there has not been any time frame placed on the negotiations, and as the Australian and Chinese governments have been unable to come to an agreement, the talks are ongoing. As of 2012, there does not appear to be any resolution of an FTA in sight, and only time will tell as to whether an FTA will actually be signed between Australia and China.

A range of views on the FTA was provided by the research participants, who identified positive, negative, and neutral impacts of the FTA. Quite a few participants were fairly noncommittal about the FTA because, although they thought it would create opportunities for some companies, some participants operating in China and servicing the Chinese market found that it had no effect either way, as the following quotes demonstrate:

> …*we're making a product in China through a local partner, who is selling that product in China. So, we don't need to deal with any of those trade issues. So then, there haven't been impediments, from that perspective.* (Case 23, Book Co)

> …*they need us, so maybe the tariffs, at this point, are down fairly low [without the FTA].* (Case 34, Resources Co 2)

One participant noted that even if the FTA was signed, China would impose other forms of nontariff barriers that would continue to impede free trade with China:

> … *there is no such thing as a level playing field with China. If they remove duties they will impose domestic taxes on imported products.* (Case 22, Wool Co)

From the Chinese perspective, one participant suggested that the FTA would generally be in China's best interest because of the extra trade it would create and that it is a low threat to Chinese exports:

> *I think as China continues to enjoy economic and political success on a global scale, I think they'll gradually find it in their interests and not a threat to allow foreign interests to play a role. They shouldn't be worried about it because I think that any way you cut and slice*

it, foreign activity in China will always represent a minority of whatever goes on in China and I think, by and large, could play a valuable role and is part of the globalization of trade and economics. (Case 2, Bank Co 1)

Several participants suggested that the FTA should provide them with the same rights in China as a Chinese organization would experience entering Australia, such as the employment of locally registered professionals. This was noted by the legal firm, which also reported that foreign lawyers do not get the same treatment as domestic lawyers. Some participants had even based their Chinese subsidiary plans on the FTA, as the following quote explains:

I think that it's not going to have a massive influence on what we do, but I am very sure that the inception of this program that they are finalizing now in terms of tariff reduction etc. has been pretty fundamental to why we exist. (Case 36, Trade Finance Co)

According to one participant, price agreements for large volume exports to China, such as resources, are negotiated by the Chinese government separately to FTAs. Therefore, the FTA has no impact on them. Other participants commented that the FTA had little effect on them:

"…getting rid of tariffs on stuff, that's sort of very much at the margin" (Case 6, Resources Co 1), or *"Australia is almost free trade now. What difference is it really going to make?"* (Case 28, Brake Co)

Small company participants suggested that the FTA would have a binding effect on their prices.

…at the corporate level, you've got no decision to make because you're controlled and governed by the agreement between the two countries…. (Case 32, Chain Co)

Another participant pointed out that because China is currently acquiring large businesses in other countries the FTA may be renegotiated if Chinese FDI interest proves to be predominant in other countries. This could minimize any benefits from the FTA because, as some participants suggested, Australia's track record with achieving equity in FTA negotiations is poor.

One example of free trade agreement consequences with us was the FTA that went in with Thailand, within 2 weeks we had notification that we'd lost a fairly significant contract, which was now going to be made up in Thailand. (Case 18, Auto Components Co)

…we should have exactly the same rights, obligations, access as … would have if they came into Australia. We think FTAs are probably the only means that we will achieve that, and it's an admission that's never been delivered to date. (Case 2, Bank Co 1)

The most negative view offered was that opening up free trade between Australia and China is likely to encourage more businesses to shift their operations to China than at present.

If China and Australia had a free trade agreement it would place more of our business under threat here in Australia. But it may potentially enable us to export more out of China. (Case 14, Auto Interior Co)

So for us, the export is not sustainable long-term… that's why we were trying to find a manufacturing base in China. (Case 27, Paint Co)

Overall, the participants were generally relatively neutral about the benefits of the Australia–China FTA. A number of participants operating and selling in China indicated that the FTA would have no effect on them at all. Negative concerns were based around the fact that tariffs were relatively low in most areas and that it was not expected that an FTA that was equitable for Australia and China would be negotiated. The most negative observation was that more Australian operations would be likely to move to China and that some Australian business would be lost to Chinese organizations with the establishment of an FTA. The fact that other countries, such as New Zealand, have an FTA with China may put Australia at a relative trade disadvantage, because they receive preferential treatment.

Table 2.1. China's Free Trade Agreements[38]

Signed agreement	Under negotiation	Under consideration
• China–ASEAN FTA • China–Pakistan FTA • China–Chile FTA • China–New Zealand FTA • China–Singapore FTA • China–Peru FTA • Mainland and Hong Kong closer economic relations and partnership arrangement • Mainland and Macau closer economic relations and partnership arrangement • China–Costa Rica FTA	• China GCC (Gulf Cooperation Countries) • China–Australia FTA • China–Iceland FTA • China–Norway FTA • China–Southern African Customs Union (SACU)	• China–India regional trade agreement and joint feasibility study • China–Korea FTA joint feasibility study • China–Japan–Korea joint study • China–Switzerland FTA joint study

China's FTAs under Negotiation and Consideration

China has signed eight FTA agreements, is currently negotiating a further five, is considering entering negotiations for four more, and has one preferential agreement.[37] The above table lists the agreements that have been signed, are under negotiation, or are under consideration (Table 2.1).

Australia and China's FDI Relationship

FDI in China

China offers an attractive location for FDI, and the Chinese government has focused on reformation of this area while opening China up to the world economy.[39] Datamonitor suggests that there has been a high inflow of foreign investments into China, which has driven China's economic growth. China's original trade philosophy was "economic development through overseas participation."[40] This meant foreign investment was directed toward agriculture, science, and technology. It also required that FDI be conducted through joint ventures (JVs) where technology and knowledge transfer could occur. Successful FDI requires an understanding of the host country legislation, regional differences, culture, business practice, and history.[41] Originally, FDI into China came from Hong Kong and Macau, but with the progress and development of the Chinese economy, Hong Kong, Taiwan, Singapore, Japan, USA, Korea, the United Kingdom, and France are some of its significant investors.[42] FDI in China reached US$105.7 billion in 2011[43] and the total FDI stock as on December 31, 2010, was valued at US$578.8 billion.[44]

According to Gu,[45] China's FDI history can be divided into the following five stages:

- Stage 1, which occurred from 1979 to the mid-1980s, is described as the developmental phase, where China's economy first opened up, and preferential policies toward FDI were introduced.
- Stage 2, which occurred from 1985 to the early 1990s, involved the establishment of the "promotion and guidelines of foreign investment." This also included the creation of the Shanghai Development Plan in 1990.
- Stage 3, which occurred from the early to mid-1990s, emphasized investment management by regulation and the creation of tax- and duty-free zones as well as foreign trading companies, and permitted the entry of foreign financial institutions.
- Stage 4, which occurred from the mid-1990s until China's accession to the WTO in 2001, emphasized control over the types of industries permitted to enter China, based on the classification systems, "The Interim Rules on Foreign Investment Direction" and "The Guideline Category Industry for Foreign Investment Industries" (The Guidelines).[46] These guidelines included encouraged, discouraged, restricted, and prohibited industries.
- Stage 5, which occurred from 2001 till present, is the result of China's accession to the WTO. Foreign investors have become confident with the Chinese environment because of the structures that have been put in place as a result of WTO accession.

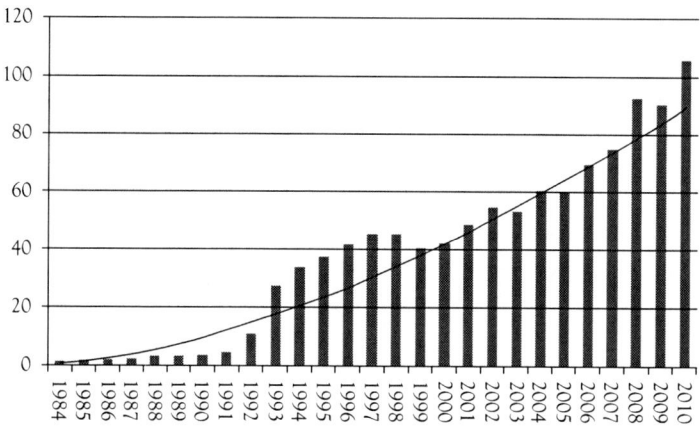

Figure 2.4. Utilized FDI into China (US$ billions) from 1984 to 2010.[47]

The increase in FDI in China over time can be seen in Figure 2.4. FDI was quite minimal in the developmental stages 1 and 2 described above (1979–1990). In stage 3, FDI started to increase as a result of China's development of tax- and duty-free zones. After 1992 (stage 4), FDI started to pour into the economy as an outcome of the implementation of "The Guidelines Policy." Further significant increases in FDI occurred in stage 5 after China's WTO accession.

FDI is encouraged in a number of industries, for instance, China now encourages FDI in advanced manufacturing, energy conservation, environmental protection, and modern services.[48] China's FDI policy has a focus on the "quality" of FDI and on the creation of new ways to utilize foreign funds.[49] China is now the number one destination in the world for FDI,[50] and although FDI numbers in China are expected to decrease in the future, the government would like to continue to attract investment.[51] Figure 2.5 shows the percentage breakdown of FDI per industry in China.

Australia's investment in China is relatively small in comparison to its investment in other countries.[53] For example, in 2009, only 0.7% of Australia's FDI stock ended up in China[54] because investors are motivated to invest in countries that share the same culture and legal and investment frameworks. Also, Australia's total FDI is around 2% of global FDI and is small in comparison to that of the USA, UK, and Europe. One reason for this is that Australia has traditionally been a capital importer and therefore is not a capital exporter.[55]

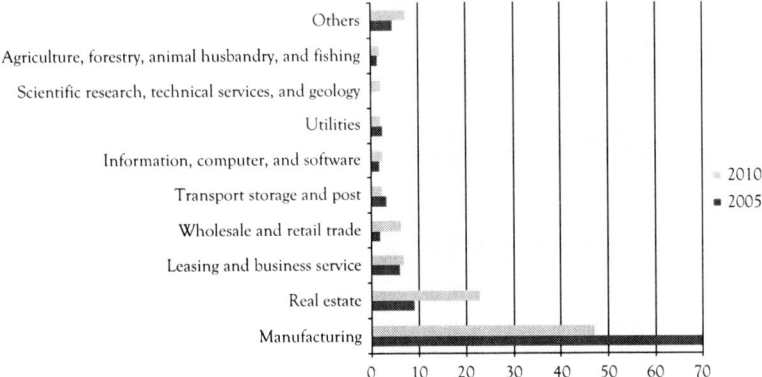

Figure 2.5. Industry breakdown of FDI in China from 2005 to 2010 (percentage %).[52]

Special Economic Zones in China

Another important aspect of FDI in China is the use of special economic zones (SEZs). Originally, 90% of FDI was in the eastern region of China, which may have resulted from the available infrastructure and proximity to seaports.[56] Originally, four SEZs were created, namely, three in Guangdong Province (Shenzhen, Zhuhai, and Shantou) and one in Fujian Province (Xiamen).[57] As of 2010, there are five SEZs, with the newest one in Hainan Province.[58] Similarly, a variety of other types of zones were created,[59] including 60 new and high technology zones, 16 free trade zones, and 60 export processing zones.[60] However, after criticism that there were too many zones, some have been closed down. In addition, the Chinese government has shifted its focus to the less developed western regions of China because FDI had primarily been directed to the east. Guiding the FDI to the West will enable those regions in China to benefit more easily from FDI inflows. One interesting example is from Bank Co 1, (Case 2): their strategy was to set up branches in eastern China, in locations such as Shanghai, where they were more profitable. In addition to these branches, they were also required by Chinese FDI regulations to set up another branch in the western region of China—for every branch they set up in the east. This is intended to "rebalance the economy" according to the directives of the 12th Five-Year Plan.[61] Only time will tell whether more SEZs will be created, and whether they will continue to attract FDI into China.

Australia's FDI in China

Australia's investment into China has gained relatively little attention, mainly because of the relatively small amount involved. Despite that, the investment relationship between Australia and China has been growing, although it has traditionally lagged behind the trade relationship. In 2011, China rose to become Australia's 11th largest investment destination, at around US$16.9 billion.[62] A major inhibitor to Australian investment in China has been the many different foreign investment barriers.[63] There are formal barriers to investment, but there are also many informal barriers, such as understanding the culture, language, and the way business is conducted. Foster's Group, a large Australian brewer and distributor of Foster's Lager, failed in its entry into China, as a result of not addressing the cultural differences.[64] In addition, some Australian investors want only to invest in countries that are culturally similar to Australia and that pose less perceived risk.[65]

On the other side of the coin, investment from Chinese firms in Australia has been increasing and, in 2011, it was valued at US$19.03 billion.[66] In particular, Chinese state-owned enterprises (SOEs) have invested in the mining sector in Australia in order to secure some much-needed resources for China's economic growth. This investment has faced considerable opposition in Australia[67] because of the desire to protect Australian resources. As a result, decisions made by the Australian Foreign Investment Review Board (FIRB) have been criticized for not being transparent, and have often appeared to be against the interests of the foreign investor.[68] The rate with which investment from China into Australia has been increasing in recent years is shown in Figure 2.6.

China's Current FDI Policies and to Set Up a Business

In 2010, China ranked 91st in the world out of 183 for ease of doing business.[70] Thus, while China is not the easiest place to do business, it is not the hardest. By comparison, Australia ranks 15th out of 183.[71] In China, investments may be approved at the central government level or by the provincial, regional, or municipal governments.[72] Usually, investments of more than US$300 million are approved at the central government level, and those below are approved at local levels. Tax rates for local and foreign businesses are the same.[73]

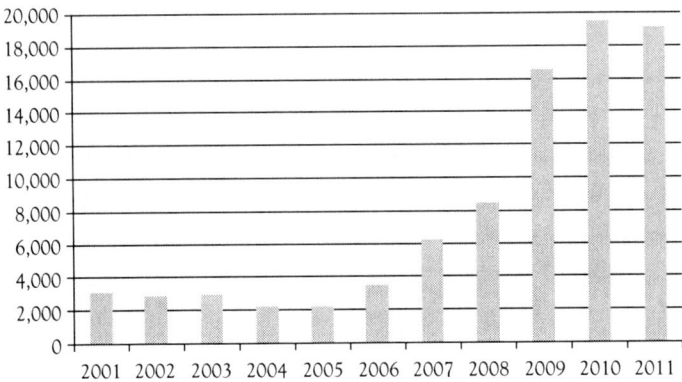

Figure 2.6. Inward investment into Australia from China (millions $A).[69]

Forms of FDI

China's Joint Venture Law governs FDI into China. It permits 100% ownership (wholly owned foreign enterprise) or joint ventures. Currently, the minimum ownership of foreign shares is 25%.[74] Joint ventures may be in the forms of Sino-Foreign Equity Joint Ventures or Sino-Foreign Cooperative Joint Ventures:[75]

- An Equity Joint Venture (EJVs) is a company that has joint local and foreign ownership with limited liability, and is set up to achieve a particular goal.[76] Both parties make an equity contribution, which determines the share of the profits. The law that governs EJVs was established in 1979, and later amended in 2001, and is called the Law of the People's Republic of China on JVs using Chinese and Foreign Investment.[77] The Ministry of Commerce (MOFCOM) has the overall responsibility for approving EJVs.[78] According to EJV law, the foreign partner has to contribute at least 25% of the total equity.
- Cooperative Joint Ventures (CJVs) are similar to EJVs; however, the obligations of each partner are detailed in a contract. The contract specifies items such as the minimum registered capital, capital contributions from each partner, and the share of profits. Given MOFCOM approval, the company may be structured

as a limited liability company or as an unincorporated JV.[79] CJVs are governed by the Law of the People's Republic of China on Chinese–Foreign CJVs, which was created in April 1988 and revised in 2000.[80]

- WOFEs are wholly owned by one or more foreign investor and are distinct legal entities. They are governed by the People's Republic of China on Enterprises Operating Exclusively with Foreign Capital Law, which came into effect in 1986, and was amended in 2000.[81] The benefit of this is that WOFEs entail full management autonomy, and can, therefore, better protect intangible assets.

- Holding companies may be established by foreign investors to hold equity interests in China.[82] Holding companies are not taxed as separate entities.

- Representative offices are another way by which foreign businesses can be set up in China. These offices are not a legal entity, and their scope of activities usually limits them from engaging in operations or invoicing customers.[83]

- Foreign companies in industries such as banking and insurance may set up branches. Similar to representative offices, branches are not a separate legal entity.[84]

China's Catalog Guiding Foreign Investments

In 1995, the state catalog from the state council gave clear guidelines for FDI.[85] This includes industries that are classified as "prohibited," "restricted," and "encouraged." Prohibited industries include those that are a threat to national security, the national economy, public interest, natural resources, and the environment. Restricted areas include those where domestic business is already prevalent, where monopolies exist, and where there is already over capacity, among others.[86] Encouraged industries include anything that is a new agricultural product, energy, power, raw materials, energy-saving, and high-value added products.[87] This Catalog Guiding Foreign Investments is important for foreign investment since a sector's classification influences the ease or difficulty of planned investment in China. This document also often aligns with the current five-year plan. The catalog for 2011 sets out the following changes according to the British Embassy in Beijing:[88]

- *Newly encouraged activities* include vocational training, venture capital enterprises, construction and operation of vehicle-charging stations and battery-changing stations, construction and operation of water treatment plants, new types of high-technology glass and optics products, and alternative energy sources.
- *Newly restricted activities* include heavy energy users, polluting activities, and resource-related projects.
- *Newly prohibited activities* include domestic express parcel services and construction.

China's 12th Five-Year Plan

Every 5 years, new plans are created by the central government, which set the direction of the country for the next 5 years. It is expected that the landscape for FDI in China will change as a result of the implementation of China's 12th Five-Year Plan.[89] Some key themes of the 12th Five-Year Plan is a focus on the environment, the development of an innovation-based economy, and, hence, a focus on research and development, boosting domestic demand or consumption and rebalancing the economy.[90] Thus, FDI policy is also likely to follow suit in this area and, for example, investment in environment-friendly businesses will be further encouraged.

Merger and Acquisition Law 2011

In March 2011, China instigated a new Merger and Acquisition (M&A) Review, which requires all foreign M&As to be reviewed. In particular areas, all M&As are to be reviewed on national security grounds, including national defense, agricultural products, energy, natural resources, infrastructure, transportation, equipment manufacturing, and technology.[91]

Conclusion

This chapter presented an overview of the trade and investment environment in China. Relationships with and between Australia and China were discussed. The trade relationship between Australia and China has been growing and is currently dominated by iron ore and concentrates exports, followed by coal exports and the education sector. China is now Australia's number one trading partner; however, Australia has still not signed an FTA with China, despite 18 rounds of negotiations over almost 7 years. Not having an FTA will continue to put Australia at a disadvantage in comparison to other countries, such as New Zealand, which signed an FTA with China in 2008. China's accession to the WTO in 2001 has reduced average tariff rates and, in general, has created a more favorable business environment. The FDI environment was also explored, and it was found that Australia's FDI in China is not as large or important as its trade with China. FDI into China has significantly increased since the opening up of its economy and, in particular, as a result of China's development of "The Guidelines Policy" and China's accession to the WTO. These two developments resulted in significant increases of FDI into China. Pre-2005, China's FDI was concentrated in manufacturing; however this is changing as the government has started focusing in on different industries, in line with China's current and 12th Five-Year Plan. Investment in environmental and sustainable business will become a feature leading into the future. The environment for FDI is reasonably attractive, although the "ease of doing business" in China remains relatively difficult. The different forms for FDI in China have been reviewed, with the most popular method being the WOFE. Thus, organizations considering investment in China need to investigate and carefully select the FDI framework before making their investment, to ensure they choose the best investment vehicle for them.

CHAPTER 3

Understanding the Cultural Gap Between Australia and China[1]

Doing business in a foreign country requires an understanding of that country's culture. Although host country nationals (HCNs) may excuse foreigners for making cross-cultural mistakes, it does not make good business sense to continue to make mistakes, as this may cause embarrassment, and at worst a loss of business opportunities and prospects. Accordingly, it is important to learn about the culture, and utilize local cultural idiosyncrasies when doing business in China. As respect and face are key Chinese cultural values, getting it right will increase the respect that a HCN may afford a foreigner. There are many cultural gaps that Australian businesses face when entering the Chinese market and, therefore developing strategies to bridge those gaps is critical. Previous research has determined that the cultural difference or gap is a key reason for business failure in China.[2] This chapter explores a number of strategies to deal with culture, including learning about the culture, relationship building, localizing the business, human resource (HR) strategies, and dealing with Chinese staff.

Culture: A Definition

Hofstede defines culture as "the collective programming of the mind which distinguishes the members of one human group from another."[3] Given this definition, the "programming of the mind," and hence attitudes, determines the differences of behaviors between two cultures. At a more developed level, culture can be defined as "the complex whole that includes knowledge, beliefs, arts, morals, laws, customs, and many other capabilities and habits acquired by man as a member of society."[4] At a practical level, Ferraro suggests that culture includes "everything that people have, think, and do as members of their society."[5] These factors are generally formulated over a long period of time. China is a country in which both past and present worlds coexist; for example, elements of Confucianism exist along with a mixture of modernism and Western values.

Examining the Cultural Distance Between Australia and China

Cultural distance refers to "the difference in social culture between the home and host countries."[6] The study of cultural distance, in general, has received wide-ranging interest from the international business research community.[7] Internationalization to China means that it is difficult for an organization to avoid interacting and engaging with the culture. Therefore, it is worth preparing oneself for the cultural differences.[8] Cultural distance often has an impact on how we perceive and interact with another culture.[9] Chung even suggests that Chinese culture is *alien*[10] to Australians and, therefore, they need to focus on understanding it.

Research has suggested that entering countries that are "culturally close" reduces the level of uncertainty an organization faces in the new market[11] as well as being easier to learn about.[12] For instance, Australia and New Zealand or USA and Canada have similar cultures. The closer the cultures, the less the (perceived) risk firms take when making an entry mode decision. However, the greater the "cultural distance," the more risk the firm perceives.[13] Compare, for instance, the cultural gap between Australia and China or Saudi Arabia. According to this logic, organizations should start their international experience in countries, which are culturally close, gain experience, and then venture into those which are more distant. In this way, organizations are able to develop experience from their previous market entries into culturally similar countries and apply this when entering culturally dissimilar countries.[14]

The implication of cultural distance is that it can make relationship building, negotiation, and entry costs expensive. It can also affect the efficiency of operations due to miscommunication and lost-in-translation experiences. It may also affect the ability of a firm to transfer its core competencies to their foreign business.[15] If an organization cannot transfer its core competencies, it will have difficulties in creating value in the host market, which will affect organization performance.[16] Previous research on cultural distance has found mixed results, with some research indicating that it does affect entry modes, and other research (including a recent meta-analysis of cultural distance and entry mode choice)[17] indicating that it does not.[18] Some of the key cultural differences between Australia and China will now be explored.

Hofstede's Cultural Dimensions of Australia and China

Hofstede's dimensions[19] are the most used constructs in cross-cultural studies, but the model is obviously not without its faults. Chinese culture is often characterized as having high power distance, resulting from Confucian doctrines and centralized political power.[20] This concept suggests that power is concentrated in the hands of a few people[21] and, in contrast, Australian culture tends to be on low power distance[22] and egalitarian. Uncertainty avoidance "is the degree to which people feel threatened by uncertain situations and have created beliefs and institutions that try to avoid these."[23] Hofstede defines uncertainty as "a situation in which anything can happen and one has no idea what might happen," and that uncertainty avoidance is not the same as risk avoidance, which can be a common misunderstanding."[24] China has a low score (30) on uncertainty avoidance,[25] meaning that individuals can manage a high level of uncertainty when required.[26] The implication of this is that Chinese staff are able to deal with instructions, which may be considered vague by Australians.[27] In contrast, Australian culture tends to be moderate (51) on uncertainty avoidance, which means that employees will be pragmatic, but may have difficulty in carrying out tasks when they are implicitly specified.[28] Instructions would need to be more clearly specified.

Chinese culture can also be categorized as a collective culture, because Chinese feel a sense of belonging and loyalty to a group, and the group's interests override individual interests. This characteristic stems from

Confucian values and political institutions.[29] Again, in contrast, Australian culture is categorized as individualistic.[30] Chinese culture has traditionally been categorized as feminine, which includes caring for others, and placing importance on the quality of life. However, the culture is becoming more masculine, with an increasing emphasis on success and money as the Chinese culture moves toward a market economy.[31] Australian cultural values tend to be masculine and goal-seeking.[32] So, given those differences, it would be expected that there is a culture gap between Australian business people and the Chinese business people, staff, consumers, and suppliers they deal with.

What Do Australian Organizations Perceive of the Culture in China?

In the study, the Australian managers were asked about the effect of culture on doing business in China, and they commented on the following issues.

Ill-prepared for the Chinese Culture Gap

This research found that organizations were often unprepared for the gap between the Australian and Chinese cultures. Some of the participant organizations found themselves surprised by this issue, which suggests that they were ill prepared to deal with cultural differences. In fact, the example from Machine Co (Case 30) indicates the managing director had done nothing to prepare culturally for China, although, ironically he did think this was the best strategy for him:

> To a certain extent it was good not knowing too much and just getting off the plane and going, "Who are all these people?" I am actually glad that I had been there twice before I started reading any books or doing study, because otherwise I might have got too nervous about what I should do or shouldn't do.

This suggests that his strategy for China was going in "blind," and not learning about it before he went. The representative from Fibre Co

(Case 19) indicated his views of other Australian organizations entering China:

> *So, cultural issues need to be understood but not overplayed, I think*
> *.... I don't think there is as much attention placed on those things as*
> *there should be. In an Australian business context, you will find a lot*
> *of Australian trading companies who might think they understand a*
> *bit of the language, but they don't really go out of their way to under-*
> *stand some of the deeper issues.*

The result of not addressing the cultural issues means some companies fail badly and others find it hard to make inroads into China. It is important, therefore, that organizations prepare themselves appropriately for dealing with the culture gap.

Learning about the Culture

Despite finding that some participants were completely unprepared for the culture gap, other participants had used a number of strategies to learn about the culture in China. Given that a core element of culture is learned behavior,[33] one way for the international business person to address the cultural gap is to learn about it. However, the success of this strategy depends on how open and ready an individual is to learn, which also depends on how ethnocentric an individual is. The more ethnocentric, the less ability the person has to learn about a foreign culture, as they will believe that their culture is better.[34] To learn about culture, a number of interview participants had attended one of the Australian Government's trade missions to China (organized by Austrade, the City of Melbourne or by local councils):

> *I actually went on a professional development program with the City*
> *of Melbourne. I spent some time there and what I was there for was to*
> *learn about the culture, some aspects of the people and the way China*
> *is ticking over at the moment. I was also trying to formulate how*
> *could I implement business development plans for Australian biotech-*
> *nology companies. (Case 1, Lab Co)*

Pallet Co was able to develop a business relationship as a result of attending a trade mission. Other organizations had provided cross-cultural training and field visits to their expatriates before their venture into China:

> "We had a half-day cultural briefing, my wife and I, before we went over to have a look at the place." (Case 2, Bank Co 2)

Other managers had learnt from their experience of setting up their venture:

> It has been a learning process for us, but it's not an impediment. It's like everything else: it's language, culture, finance systems, IT systems, people employment—you've just got to deal with each one and learn each one, and not consider any of them to be a major impediment. So, it just means going and asking lots and lots of questions and learning the hard way. (Case 14, Auto Interior Co)

Others also commented on the role of questioning. They also suggested that spending time learning about the culture first was important and to continue to learn about it as time goes on. As one participant suggested:

> "I always leave with questions ... each time I go I try to learn more about the local culture." (Case 24, Engineering Co)

And others had a fairly laid-back approach to learning:

> We went to Shanghai, and I guess, basically, we bumbled around and got a bit of a feel for the culture. But we didn't have any introductions and apart from getting a feel for China, we went into hospitals and just said we happened to be visiting and they gave us tours of their hospitals, which was great. (Case 31, Medic Co)

These quotes suggest that there was a variety of ways that organizations learned about the culture, and perhaps there is no right way to learn, but using a combination of methods is probably the best.

Communication, Language, and Literacy

Chinese culture is a high-context[35] culture therefore Chinese communicate in a high-context manner and diffused communication style[36] whereas, Australian culture is low-context and they communicate in a specific style. People from a high-context and diffused culture expect listeners to follow the train of thought of the speaker and understand the hidden agenda behind the words. That is, their language is not direct, and people need to be able to interpret the conversation. On the other hand, people from a low-context and specific culture will talk straight to the point and expect direct answers.[37] In low-context communication, meanings are delivered through words specifically used for their purposes.[38]

The official language of China is standard Chinese or Mandarin (Pŭtōnghuà), which comes from the Beijing dialect, whilst Yuè (Cantonese), originates from southern China including Hong Kong, and Wu (Shanghainese) originates from Shanghai.[39] There is also a multitude of minority dialects. Commonly, it is difficult for nonnative speakers to learn and pronounce standard Chinese, especially for adults who already have well-developed vocal cords. In addition, the Australian education system has been criticized as being poor in teaching Chinese, although in 2012 there has been a push to increase spending on Chinese language training from the Australian Government, as a result of their dissemination of the White Paper on Australia in the Asian Century.[40] The official language of Australia is English.[41] The likelihood that Chinese business people can speak English is dependent on whether they have had Western education.[42] It is becoming more common for Chinese to speak English, although this should not be counted on. Hence, the language gap is a key impediment to Australians conducting business with Chinese counterparts.[43] Organizations interviewed for this study were cognizant of this fact:

> *Language, we were very conscious of China being a country where language was going to be a much more significant issue.* (Case 12, Uni Co 1)

Learning Chinese is an excellent starting point to preparing for doing business in China. Organizations can also employ Chinese-speaking staff, or hire interpreters, especially in the first stages of internationalization. Once Chinese operations are established, local staff can provide translation.

> *We relied on translators. They were our lifeline when we first got there. We needed translators for everything. We still rely on them quite a bit. I can honestly say we wouldn't have a person employed as a translator anymore—that wouldn't be their only purpose. There are a lot more who speak English now, so we would employ someone who performs a task, has a responsibility, yet they speak English. Our accountant, when we have to discuss a tax issue with the Tax Authority, the accountant would do the translation. But for the other 4½ days of the week, he's doing the accounts.* (Case 16, Build Co)

When employing translators, it is important they are able to accurately convey the messages between foreign and Chinese nationals, as otherwise "lost-in-translation" situations may occur. In addition, when converting marketing messages from English to Chinese, it is important that the right meaning is obtained by the words chosen. For example, the direct translation of Kentucky Fried Chicken's "Finger Licking Good" message translates into "Eat your fingers off"[44] in Chinese, suggesting that it is important to use back translation to get the translation right and to use alternative words that have the right meaning.

Guānxi and Relationship Building

Guānxi is a key Chinese cultural value, which comprises ties between people, relationships, networks, and the development of trust within those relationships[45] and, accordingly, networks of associates, and friends are important. *Guānxi* as a concept has not been well understood by the majority of Western business people, and few have mastered it.[46] It allows for the side-stepping of formal regulatory or contractual obligations to seize opportunities,[47] and it is essential to do business in China. To develop *guānxi*, one needs to invest time, money, and friendship into a relationship, which results in trust and, once set up, will remain for the long term.[48] For example, *guānxi* with the government may assist with obtaining investment and planning permits in the future.

A company may need to develop *guānxi* with the businesses they plan to work with, local levels of government and members of the Chinese Communist Party (CCP).[49] The development of *guānxi* among individuals creates obligations for the continued exchange of favors. Similar to China, Australian business culture also relies on relationships and networks; however, outward displays of favors to connections or family members would be considered to be nepotism and inappropriate conduct in most cases. Although, it could be possible that Australian organizations would employ family members of current employees, as a recruitment strategy.

Relationship building was one strategy identified by participants in the study to bridge the cultural divide; however, participants acknowledged that it was a slow process. Respondents identified that business relationships in China were not as pragmatic or "to the point" as business relationships in Australia. However, failure to address the issue may seriously impact market entry and the ability to establish clients in China, as the following quote suggests:

> *It can affect the way you do business. Although you're selling the same product in the same industry, you might have to ... to do business with these people, it is first contingent on firstly establishing a rapport/relationship with them. No one walks in and says, "This is my product", and walks out with a purchase order. And, the cultural differences that exist in various parts of China can impact on how you go about establishing those relationships, or the sorts of things you would do to build relationships. Some things will work better in other areas than others.* (Case 8, Vat Co)

Developing relationships not only takes time but once established they also needs to be maintained. The costs of doing this, such as trip, gift, lunch, and dinner expenses over a long period of time need to be factored into a market entry budget. Lunches and dinners in China in business activities are not considered bribery.[50] Participants in the current study suggested that it would take a number of business trips before relationships were well established, and that those trips needed to be maintained:

> *I think you should develop relationships and maintain those relationships and recognize that there's a cost in maintaining the relationship*

and you need to factor that in. And if that cost is too high, then don't get into the relationship. But to think you can go once, build a relationship and not go back again for 3 years, it's not going to happen. (Case 12, Uni Co 1)

The following is an example of the extent of the relationship that Paint Co (Case 27) had developed, and the effect that his *guānxi* had on securing further business:

I don't know if it's my age or my personality or whatever, but I am part of several families now. They call me Grandpa. I have been to their weddings and we've got some christenings coming up. I haven't done anything special, just that I like them. When I go there they will take me to meet other people and say, "Look, Tony's in the paint business. Blah, blah, blah, blah." "Right, well I've got a project coming up in a year's time. It's yours." If they say that, that's it; it's locked in. That is worth huge amounts of money and you can't buy that.

Previous research has determined that Chinese business people will pass on buyer information to their *guānxi* and, therefore, developing good *guānxi* will assist in finding more clients.[51] Some organizations were not comfortable about the concept of *guānxi*, as the following points out:

Because a lot of people we deal with, like the shipping agents we have, may be the cousins of the buyer. He turns up as the agent and he is giving a kick-back to the buyer. We are funding it. We know it happens but there's nothing we can do about it really. But whose interests is the agent really looking after? We appoint them and pay them, but is he looking after us or is he looking after his cousin? Family means a lot more to the Chinese than a contract does. So, if family interests were better suited to them than the terms of the contract, they will just forget about the contract. (Case 32: Resources Co 2)

The majority of participants had positive comments associated with *guānxi*, with only a few negative comments, as demonstrated by the preceding Resources Co 2 quote.

Banquets, Eating, and Drinking

Attending banquets and dining and drinking together are special cultural features of Chinese business practices.[52] These occasions give business people an opportunity to socialize and get to know one another and work together. Important deals can be made and trust developed at a banquet; negotiations can be continued at lunch. Food to the Chinese is a business tool rather than a form of bribery. Food is the opportunity to be social. Food is eaten and shared to demonstrate personal quality and used as an effective tool in creating a business relationship, and drinking goes with it. Participants in the research commented on the usefulness of drinking sessions as relationship building exercises, as the following quote indicates:

> "Gan Bei. That's the biggest cultural factor for me, Gan Bei is to drink a whole glass and get drunk. It's horrible alcohol" (Case 11, Agri Co).

Drinking sessions and successfully "passing the bottoms up" (*Gan Bei*) test also develop "face" with Chinese counterparts.[53] Another Australian organization commented on their use of banquets as relationship builders:

> Are there any bribes or anything like that? Really, it's never as open as that. In 95% of the cases, it will be just maintaining a relationship and it will be the dinners and the banquets and showing them that you are ... . Our longevity in China sort of benefits us a lot. They can see that we're not a fly-in, fly-out company. We're there; and we plan to be there for a long time. (Case 16, Build Co)

Reciprocity (Rénqing)

Participants also pointed out it is not only appropriate to accept the hospitality that the Chinese offer, it is also appropriate to reciprocate in kind, which should be seen as an investment in business relationships with the Chinese:

> And that's how I guess we work, is the level of reciprocity. Whatever we get we reciprocate. And sometimes we push the envelope and then they'll follow up. And particularly Chinese government departments are incredibly hospitable. They have huge budgets, compared to ours,

for official entertaining and things like that. And so they do offer things, and I think people forget that sometimes. They think, "Oh well, that's just the Chinese. I'll take it." But when they come out here they give them a plate of sandwiches. It's just ridiculous. So, we focus on that, and I think because we focus on that, it certainly gives us a bit more leverage. (Case 10, Gov Co)

Presents and gift-giving are very much a key component of doing business in China; therefore, it is important for those visiting China to take small gifts as an acknowledgment of their appreciation and to help develop the relationship.[54] On occasions, it may be suitable to take a larger gift for host organizations that are visited, such as a memento of the visitor's country, or bottles of wine, that highlight the importance of the relationship. Chinese anti-bribery laws states that giving gifts is tolerated to a certain extent, because it is part of Chinese culture, but giving an expensive gift such as a family holiday would not be acceptable.[55]

Bribery

It is commonly known that bribery is an issue in China and is often intertwined with the Chinese culture of *guānxi*, relationships, and reciprocity:

What we call payments for speeding matters up, the unwritten rule. We don't call that bribery, and it is a cultural difference between Australia and China. In the Chinese culture it's part of doing business. There is a reward for effort. So we have some flexibility on how that's done. But obviously, bribery, incentives, payment before decisions is not permissible. However, I think you have to accept the fact that if I want something done in 2 weeks when it normally takes 3 months, you should be paying for a service, as long as the service is speeding the process up.

The research participants indicated that these payments needed to be upfront and transparent, and, if not made, a project could be cancelled. This practice is seen as a key cultural difference between Australia and China but, when doing business in China, organizations need to adapt to it. It should not be viewed as an absolute rule, however. It is important to make a very careful assessment and interpretation of the need for such payments, in comparison to Australian cultural values and actual law. In Australia, it is illegal for an Australian national to engage in bribery in a foreign country,[56] and the Chinese, too, have anticorruption laws.[57]

Face (Miànzi)

Face (*miànzi*) "concerns one's status and respect received."[58] Different ranks, levels, wealth, and professionalism, among other factors, influence the amount of face that should be accorded an individual. Individuals should be given respect, where respect is due, and people should be addressed and treated according to their rank.[59] Therefore, it is important to know who the people are that you are meeting, their rank, their job title, and where they stand in the pecking order of an organization to give them appropriate "face." People's words, manners, and etiquette also give them face. So, if a person were to go back on their word or break a promise, they would lose face and the confidence of others.[60] Other face-losing activities can include showing anger, frustration, disrespect, being dismissive, mocking, or disgracing another individual publicly.[61] For example, putting a work colleague down in front of other colleagues, or saying, "I do not like certain elements of a business proposal" in negotiations could cause "a loss of face."

Face is an important element in doing business with the Chinese,[62] because it can result in an organization losing business opportunities, or cause failure in business. The concept can be difficult for Western business people to understand. However, "mutual respect" is an appropriate alternative because, in practice, not only does one try to maintain his or her own face, but one also tries to preserve the other party's face through self-respect and respect for others.[63] Respect is not about giving in, but it is about parties not losing face during negotiations. Organizations must understand appropriate negotiation strategies, to assist with the formulation of successful business strategies:

> Face is one major issue for us ... . The Australian attitude is you be blunt, to the point, upfront and you don't hide anything. Perhaps in China, that is actually not seen as appropriate. That makes conducting

projects quite challenging. You might come up with a design; the client won't like it; they won't say that because it's an issue of face. So, they will then spend the next month or two kind of working around you, and then slowly, bit by bit, telling you everything you need to know, which in Australia they would say that on day one. They would say, "We don't like it because of x, y and z". The Chinese will say, "We love it. It's fantastic. We'll give you some feedback in a few days." And then, the feedback will be a couple of minor things and a couple more a few days later, and a little bit more. And certainly, that makes projects a bit challenging at times because you're not fully aware of why or what's coming next. You're not really getting a sense of their honest opinion at times, which we're used to. (Case 3, Architect Co)

Foreign organizations need to understand this aspect of negotiating with the Chinese and try to adapt to the process. An alternative explanation for the situation described above could be that the person that Architect Co were negotiating with may not have had the appropriate rank or authority to make decisions, and therefore needed superior approval. Therefore, hierarchy and power distance could have also been influential.

Hierarchy (li): A Key Confucian Value

Confucianism is a complex value system, which covers a series of moral conventions in Chinese culture.[64] A key Confucian value is that of hierarchy, or *li*. Chinese culture is based on a family state, where social structure and organization is autocratic, hierarchical, and not at all democratic.[65] Confucianism was developed as a series of values that allows a ruler to govern the country.[66] Within these values, individuals at lower levels of the hierarchy need to give obedience to those at a higher level. This means that there are distinct relationships between those at different levels of the hierarchy, based on familial relationships. The term *li* is used to represent a range of relationships and obligations between different parties.[67] These relationships include those between ruler and subject, father and son, husband and wife, older brother and younger brother, and friends.[68] Under Confucianism, the ruler needs to show the subject kindness and, in exchange, the subject will display loyalty.[69] The father needs to show his son protection and consideration and, in return, the son will display respect and obedience to his father.[70] A husband needs to show obligation to his wife and, in return, the wife will need to submit to his demands.[71] An older brother needs to show care for his younger brother and, in return, the younger brother will model the older brother's behavior.[72] This hierarchy is mirrored in the workforce, for example, between superiors and employees:

> *The other part in their natural hierarchy is that they are always told what to do. Their father tells them what to do, or government tells them what to do. So, lateral thinking is not there. The account plan example, "Can you develop an account plan?" "No problems." And so in a couple of days' time you will go in and say, "Have you been out visiting your resellers?" "No, you told me to develop an account plan." "Well, I actually meant that could happen at the same time." "Well, you didn't tell me that." Again, that has now delayed you another week while you figure out how to manage that. (Case 26, Software Co)*

In this example, hierarchy issue caused a problem for Software Co, which meant the employee did not take the initiative the company was looking for. Therefore, Western organizations wanting staff to complete all tasks need to carefully explain the entire set of tasks, and back it up with further reinforcement. In addition, it must be remembered that Australia is an egalitarian society, where power is diffused, people of high and low status have informal relationships, people in higher positions can be questioned, and people in power can delegate authority,[73] which is distinct from Chinese culture.

Localizing Your Business in China

Participants also commented on setting up a Chinese-style business, rather than using Australian models of business operation, as a way to deal with the cultural divide:

> *It depends on the nature of the business you want to set up, but for us, we set out with the intent of creating a Chinese business, bringing the best of what we have from Australia into that business. We never*

set out to create a foreign business in China. There is a big difference between how you approach the two. A lot of foreign businesses will have a foreign general manager, a foreign CFO, will have a Chinese team that all speak English. We actually have a Chinese General Manager and a Chinese CFO. (Case 14, Auto Interior Co)

This suggests that transplanting business models from one country to another can be problematic, and, instead, organizations should seek to share practices between the two countries.[74] Previous research has found that large organizations, especially the well-established ones, tend to take an ethnocentric approach to their own organizational culture, which is often forced onto joint venture partners, Chinese staff, managers, and customers when they enter the Chinese market.[75] However, a majority of the organizations investigated for this study wanted to focus on using as many Chinese staff as possible in their Chinese operations:

Well, I think that's one of our strengths, is we have all local people in our offices. We don't send Australian staff along—apart from having a few Australians in Hong Kong. We tend to have internationally-educated people running the offices and most time they're locally born, educated overseas and come back. (Case 24, Engineering Co)

Other organizations felt they had benefited from the fact that some of their existing employees had a Chinese background:

So, we had the good fortune of actually having a member of our staff who actually did come from China and is well-regarded obviously, as I have discovered since. She comes on all of our trips with us. We also have in the organization a number of Mandarin-speaking people. So, we'd use those as an interface to the China business. (Case 31, Medic Co)

Localization has been an important strategy as local managers are more familiar with the local environment and can manage employees more appropriately.[76]

The Use of *Hǎiguī* (Returned Overseas Chinese)

Hǎiguī refers to a Chinese national who has either been educated or has worked abroad and has returned to China.[77] It is critical to distinguish between overseas Chinese with a mainland background and those with other country backgrounds. One interviewee believed that *hǎiguī's* added a positive element to organizations recruiting them:

> *The sea turtles, the people coming back from overseas education are starting to be felt now in business. I think we are moving to that new generation of business people: young, entrepreneurial, know about Western business, still with some of the characteristics of the past.* (Case 19, Fibre Co)

Some firms did err on the cautious side of using *hǎiguī*:

> *So, a Western education is a good thing if it enables a Chinese person to understand how a Western company needs to be managed and controlled, but it can go too far. They can lose too much of that cultural connection. This guy is not well-liked at all by the workforce; he just doesn't do things in a Chinese way. He's much more American than Chinese.* (Case 8, Vat Co)

In the past, companies recruited overseas Chinese and believed they were familiar with the mainland Chinese and market. This strategy has sometimes proven to be ineffective, because these employees will not have a purely Chinese background.[78] Individuals' minds are programmed by the surrounding culture, so overseas Chinese, such as the American-Chinese mentioned above, have different perspectives to mainland Chinese. The recruitment of *Hǎiguī* is problematic because they lack cultural credibility amongst Chinese nationals, and often have a different value set to the HCNs.[79]

Guoqing

Guoqing is a Chinese concept that suggests that Chinese behavior can be explained and justified because of where the Chinese have come from, their "national situation," and the level of economic development.[80] A manager from Architect Co (Case 3) suggested that the Chinese were different exactly because of this reason.

*It's just the fact that they haven't got that 40 years of experience build-
ing urban infrastructure and, therefore, it's a new ball game for them,
and it's not as if they've done this 20 times before. It's a bit different. And I think our expectations before we went in there were that
they had 40–100 years of experience doing things like they have in
Australia, and perhaps that's very naive to take that approach.*

A number of other participants in the study were mindful of this. Therefore, understanding that Chinese suppliers, consumers, and clients are on
a different level to those in the West is important when doing business
in China, and needs to be factored in when developing plans or projects,
and creating products and designs.

Acceptance and Adapting to the Culture

The participants suggested that once they had learned about the culture,
they believed that they needed to adapt to Chinese culture and interact
with it, and view the Chinese through their eyes. They suggested that
people should not be ethnocentric about the views they held of Chinese
culture and individuals. It was also suggested that they should behave like
Chinese when working with them:

*We have just found it interesting and we have got to enjoy the differ-
ent culture. It does mean that there is a thought process that we can't
understand at times. We just have to accept that. Just maintain the
Aussie humor and just accept that that's a thought process that we can't
follow, but that's the way it is.* (Case 16, Build Co)

*I think there has been some compromise on the other side, that
they don't expect so strongly that everything will be perfect and that
everyone will understand every last detail of, say, Chinese cultural
issues and ways of doing business.* (Case 17, Law Co)

Others thought of the culture differences in a positive way:

*But I don't think anything really prepared us for actually arriving
and finding what the culture was like, which was not a problem.
Not to say that we were thinking, "Shock, horror! Here we are. My*

God, what have I done?" It was more, "Wow! Isn't this interesting!"
And we'll have a lot of fun in the next 3 years trying to get our heads
around some of this. So, I think they were keen to make sure they had
people who thought that way. (Case 39, Bank Co 2)

This quote suggests that this participant would have found it relatively
easy to adjust to the culture, because they were quite open.

Use of a Bicultural Consultant

Apart from the other suggested strategies, another solution to cultural
difficulties suggested by one of the participants was to employ a bicultural
consultant to bridge the culture gap, as the following quote suggests:

My first two trips were not nearly as productive due to cultural and
communication difficulties. XXX set a busy schedule and demon-
strated excellent communication, organizational and cultural skills
with top results. We are now moving ahead fast in China. Without
XXX, the project would have been abandoned by now. (Case 12,
Uni Co 1)

A bicultural consultant has a sound understanding of both Chinese and
Australian business cultures and can bridge the cultural gap.

China Is Becoming More Western and Cultures Are Merging

Apart from the many differences between Chinese and the Western cultures, another important finding was that Chinese culture is becoming
increasingly Westernized in certain areas. This means that organizations
should not assume that the Chinese are entirely different:

I started going there about 5 or 6 years ago and the change that I have
seen occur, particularly in Shanghai and the surrounding areas, was
enormous and I could see … how it's becoming more Westernized.
(Case 29, Logistics Co)

Therefore, the merging of cultures is a strategy that organizations could focus on in the future. A bridging cultural course may be one way to do this. The following is an example of integration:

> *I think it was evolutionary, that part of the reason that we're so Chinese in our orientation is in fact the fact that she's leading it, and that her cultural way in Asia is to integrate into Asia rather than to impose on Asia.* (Case 33, Responsibility Co)

The key differences between Australian and Chinese cultures identified in this chapter are presented in Table 3.1.

Table 3.1. Cultural Differences Between Australia and China

Australia ←——————— The gap ——————→ China		
Low	Power distance	High
Individualistic, immediate family.	Social orientation	Collective, extended family is important.
Moderate	Uncertainty avoidance	Low
Masculine	Goal behavior	Feminine moving to masculine
Low context	Communication	High context
English	Language	Mandarin, Cantonese, and other dialects
Predominantly Christian	Religion	Atheist, Muslim, Buddhist, Daoism, Taoism, Christian, Confucianism
99%	Literacy levels	95.9%
Relationships are more business-like and pragmatic.	Relationships	Relationships are important, and need to be developed over time to establish trust and rapport.
Respect is moderately important; Westerners will face conflict straight away.	Face/Respect/Conflict	Face is important, respect should be given and conflict avoided.
Reciprocity is important, but not to a large degree.	Reciprocity	Rénqing feelings of reciprocity, those who do not return a favor will lose face.
Egalitarian, tend to minimize power, and status differences.	Equality/Hierarchy	Hierarchical, people expect that status and power are maintained.

Strategies to Reduce the Culture Gap

Based on the research conducted for this study, a number of strategies were developed to assist businesses in overcoming the obstacles associated with different cultures working together and are summarized in Table 3.2.

In order to reduce the impact of the culture gap, it is important to learn about the culture through a number of activities. This can include pre-visits organized by government-sponsored trade missions, which

Table 3.2. Strategies to Deal with the Culture Gap

Strategies to reduce the cultural gap
Learn about the culture • Pre-visits • Assignment cultural training • Read books • Use staff with Chinese background for initial entry translation and interpretation • Employ a bicultural consultant • Learn the language/employ translators • Ask questions about why people do certain things • Learn from your experiences with the Chinese culture
Relationship building • Make relationship building a slow process • Engage in face-to-face interaction with Chinese • Make time and resource commitments to build the relationship • Realize the importance of food, banquets, and drinking as relationship-building tools • Reciprocate hospitality
Localize the business • Set up a business that is Chinese in its orientation as opposed to Western in orientation • Do things in the Chinese way • Adapt strategies and products to China • Adapt to Chinese values • Combine and merge cultures
HR strategies • Recruit bilingual Chinese nationals in the business • Use Western-educated Chinese (*Hǎiguī*) staff with a Chinese mainland background • Use Western managers with experience in China
Dealing with Chinese staff • Show and demonstrate to Chinese staff how to do things • Back up with further reinforcement of the message • Engage in cooperative strategies to gain consensus from Chinese workers • Develop team-building exercises • Find flexible staff who will listen to you

allows one to develop a personal understanding of the country and its culture, and to also develop contacts. Cross-cultural training, reading books or courses on the subject will also increase understanding. The participants suggested that allocating staff with a Chinese background to assist with initial translation and interpretation was an effective strategy. When suitable staff members are not available, a bicultural consultant should be employed to provide a comparative understanding of both their home country and China. Other obvious strategies include learning the language or employing translators in China.

These different strategies have different costs associated with them, so balancing up the cost and benefit of each is important. The participants also noted that they learned about the Chinese culture over time; as they interacted and experienced it and as a result of asking questions about why people do what they do.

Guānxi is an important element of Chinese culture and suggests that some strategies should relate to relationship building. The participants believed that developing the relationship was a worthwhile strategy, but they also emphasized that it was a slow process. Creating relationships through direct face-to-face interaction was preferred over emails or telephone, as the latter methods would not build the necessary trust. Without establishing trust, business is unlikely to proceed.[81] Relationship building requires time and a resource commitment by the organization. This included spending time attending banquets, giving gifts, and engaging in social activities to build the relationship. In addition, it is important that foreigners reciprocate any hospitality provided for them. The "three most important factors in doing business with the Chinese are relationships, relationships and relationships."[82]

To help bridge the cultural gap, foreign organizations can establish a local business, which will then be seen as a Chinese organization, rather than being seen as a Western organization doing business in China. This means doing things the Chinese way, recruiting Chinese staff (including staff for key positions), adapting strategies and products to China, and adapting to Chinese values in general. Some participants reported on an attempt to merge the Chinese and Australian culture in their Chinese locations. They recruited mostly Chinese staff, but implemented an Australian work ethic, which they felt was less rigid than the Chinese work values. The Australian work ethic included flexibility and humor in the workplace, and knowing when to enjoy oneself, and when to work hard.

To achieve a localized business, some participants employed bilingual Chinese staff (*Hǎiguī*) in their China operations. Some participants believed the strategy of recruiting such staff was beneficial because of their Western orientation and because they were seen as the new generation of workers. Others were not so confident about the use of *Hǎiguī*, as they believed it could backfire on them. A number of participants suggested using Western managers with extensive Chinese experience, which was important, given the maturity of the Chinese market.

To deal with Chinese staff, the participants suggested demonstrating to staff how to do things rather than just telling them. This can be a more effective method of learning, especially where language is a barrier. Demonstration and the full explanation of tasks is important, as Chinese staff are reluctant to take the initiative because of their hierarchical culture,[83] or they may be frightened to ask questions, which may result in a "loss of face." Backing messages up with further reinforcement is also important to make sure that the message has been completely conveyed. Engaging Chinese staff with cooperative strategies will result in trust and commitment, which will assist foreign and local staff to work together.[84] This result may be achieved by developing team-building exercises. The final strategy is to recruit flexible, new generation staff, who are open to new ideas and thoughts, and can listen to what managers have to say.

Conclusion

Chinese culture is significantly different from the Australian/Western culture. This cultural gap causes impediments to Australians doing business with China. These differences were highlighted in the literature and also in responses from the research conducted for this book. The feedback from the respondents provided the basis for developing a number of strategies, which will reduce the impact of the cultural gap. The strategies are summarized in Table 3.2 and include learning about the culture, relationship building, localizing the business, HR strategies, and dealing with Chinese staff.

CHAPTER 4

Using the Political Structure in China

Can We Ever Make Sense of It?[1]

The political environment in China differs greatly to political environments in Western countries, and as a result it is imperative that foreign businesses understand this environment and develop a range of strategies to deal with it. Although China has made dramatic changes to its economic, legal, and trade and investment frameworks over the decades, little changes have been made to the country's political structure. The country is still a "one party socialist state," and there is no significant opposition from any other party. This government plays a greater role in business than what is expected in the West, and as a result it is important that foreign organizations understand this difference. For instance, government-developed rules and regulations may impact on the entry mode an organization can choose, and also their future operations. As a result it is essential that organizations engage in corporate political behaviors, with a focus on developing relationships with government officials who may have a say in whether an investment proposal goes ahead or not. Accordingly, getting the support and introductions through the Australian government's trade office, Austrade, is also highly beneficial in managing the political factor. This chapter focuses on how political negotiations can best be approached when internationalizing to China.

The Context

The Political Structure

The political environment in China is that of a socialist state without substantial political opposition groups.[2] Therefore, China's system of government can be defined as a "single party socialist republic."[3] This would normally be considered a negative feature of the business environment as the lack of a democratically functioning government could mean that unexpected and disruptive policies are introduced, which could potentially threaten the viability of an international business. However, as China is a single-party state, it has provided stability for the past 64 years.

In November 2012, the head of state, President Hu Jintao was replaced with Xi Jinping, who was the former Vice President of China. Xi Jinping was elected General Secretary of the CPC Central Committee, in the 18th Congress of the Communist Party of China.[4]

The governing party is the CPC, and beneath the CPC is the Chinese Government whose primary function is to implement CPC policies.[5] The government (state) consists of the National People's Congress (NPC) and the State Council.[6] The NPC holds the highest level of power underneath the leadership of the CPC.[7] Every 5 years, the NPC selects the Central Committee at the National Congress of the Party. The Central Committee appoints the Politburo Standing Committee (PBSC), which is the main decision-making body.[8] There are three branches, including (a) the *Executive*, which includes the President and Vice President elected by the NPC for a five-year term, the Premier nominated by the President and confirmed by the NPC; (b) the *Legislative*, which includes the unicameral NPC (with 2,987 seats; members elected by municipal, regional, and provincial people's congresses, and the People's Liberation Army, who all serve five-year terms), and (c) the *Judicial branch*, which includes the Supreme People's Court, Local People's Court, and Special People's Court.[9] There are 23 provinces in China (China considers Taiwan to be its 23rd province); five autonomous regions, including Tibet; and five municipalities directly under the State Council, which form its administrative divisions.[10]

China operates with a socialist market economy in which capitalism is encouraged, although the Chinese government oversees and influences the economic development at the macro level, where capital is allocated in major areas of importance, through the implementation of its five-year plans.[11] The current five-year plan is the 12th and will last until 2015. The political system has been described by some as authoritarian,[12] as the Chinese government exercises great power in every aspect of the country's activities, including business policy formulation.[13] Political reforms have been occurring gradually but less dramatically than China's economic reforms, which are still considered to be in the transitional stage.[14]

Political Risk and Stability in China

With China being a single-party state, the risk of party change is negligible. However, there are other risks in the Chinese political environment that may influence the stability of the country. These risks include the levels of corruption in China, the increasing levels of inequality, which may lead to social unrest, and the volatility as a result of disputed territories such as Tibet and Taiwan.[15] Recently inflation has also been a significant issue in the Chinese economy, and the government is trying to ease the problems of rising food prices and unaffordable housing by increasing interest rates.[16] Increased inflation rates are likely to affect those at the bottom of the economic pyramid, those already affected by poverty and inequality, more than those in the middle or upper socio-economic levels. This could lead to social unrest. Participants in the study did not indicate that they believed there were significant political risks in China, as the following quote indicates:

> We would always advise clients about sovereign risk in any country, but it's not a major issue with China. The risk there is no more than many, many, many other countries so that's not a major issue. It's certainly not a reason to dissuade people from investing in China. (Case 17, Law Co)

Using the Political Structure in Home and Host Country when Internationalizing to China

The model shown in Figure 4.1 indicates how political structures in home and foreign countries can be managed. For example, a business beginning the internationalization process should first understand the political environment, then consult with their home country government trade office (in Australia this would be Austrade) about the services that they provide. This may include general information or attending

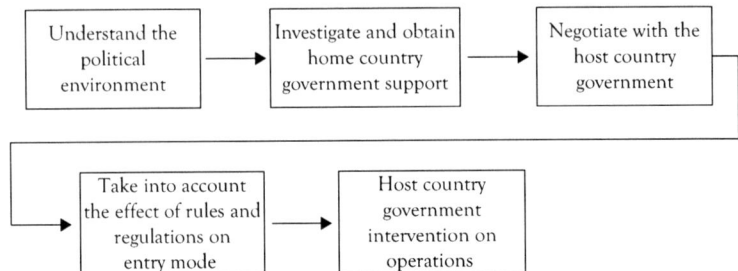

Figure 4.1. Process for using the political structure in home and host country when internationalizing to China.

seminars on specific topics and the trade office may also provide introductions to contacts and networks in China. In addition, organizations may wish to interact with business councils and Chambers of Commerce to reach a greater understanding of the environment. Depending on the entry mode choice, the organization may need to negotiate and interact with the Chinese government to set up their business or make an investment, especially for Wholly-owned Foreign Entities (WOFEs), but less so for exporting modes. This negotiation may be influenced by the rules and regulations of business set-up in China. The Chinese government will have an influence on the day-to-day operations of business, and the business may need to gain support from the home country government, and trade associations to assist them with operational issues in this environment. The steps of this model will now be explained in greater detail.

Understanding the Political Environment in China

Understanding the political environment is a critical factor in the selection of an entry mode when internationalizing to a foreign country, and also for overall business operation.[17] Government policies and regulations create opportunities as well as barriers for companies doing business in China. The Chinese political environment is transitional, but has not been as rapid or has had as fundamental changes as the economic system. Understanding the political environment is important as the Chinese government has the capacity to only encourage foreign investment on the basis of the fit of the proposed investment with the government's economic goals[18] and its desire to protect certain industries, through "The Guidelines Policies." The following organization laments on some of the issues:

> *Because of the way in which China is structured, and the politics and the culture, those sorts of things made it quite unpredictable, which added to the complexity and increased the challenge of actually being able to try to be successful there.* (Case 29, Logistics Co)

Participants in the study were asked about whether they had collected information on the Chinese political environment. Six participants had actively sought to gain information about the Chinese political environment before making a decision as to their best approach for entering China. For example, a services participant said, "*We would negotiate and find out information and then try and get a favorable interpretation of regulations. So that's a major part of the job which we do through the Shanghai office*" (Case 17, Law Co).

The process of collecting information from government sources, however, was not always successful; for example, one participant stated that when dealing with the Australian government advisory service, Austrade, "*I was trying to find out some information about wage rates and all those sort of things. And luckily I had one of my friends there, but they weren't sort of telling me. They certainly weren't forthcoming with the information that I needed. Maybe it's just a commercial thing and they would like me to pay them something*" (Case 30, Machine Co).

Government sources were quite frequently used as a starting point to gain more information before selecting an entry mode, followed by organizing meetings to provide more detailed information. For example, one participant stated:

> *I used Austrade because it's a good starting point and then you talk to Chinese people that you know and you look up the internet. I mean, you ask around, it's the same thing as you do here. So, if you're starting up and you're green and you say, oh gee, I'd be interested in getting the source ... or doing a joint venture, then you can ring up VECCI, Austrade, you can ring up the Australia China Business Council, a number of the universities have short courses. There are lots of places you can tap into, apart from consultants.* (Case 15, Flower Co)

Another participant identified how important it was to learn about the political environment:

> *I think it's just as you're going through this, you're learning what the differences are in the way you think, in the way you operate and in the way the country operates. Things that you have to, from our perspective, learn about, because you just really don't have that background or back drop.* (Case 4, Parcel Co)

Therefore, as can be seen from these quotes, managers collected information from a variety of sources, including approaching the trade office in the home country, using the Internet, and asking around.

Home Country Government Support

The actual support that multinational enterprises (MNEs) receive from their home country government when internationalizing is becoming better understood. Assistance from the home country government typically comprises export service programs (such as seminars for potential exporters, export counseling, how-to-export handbooks, export development grants, and export financing) as well as market development programs (helping to generate sales leads, participation in trade shows, market analysis, and export newsletters).[19] Providing assistance, and allowing for free trade agreement (FTAs) and trade bloc memberships of rapidly developing countries such as China, creates particular challenges for home country governments. As noted in Chapter 2, the Australian government has increased its emphasis on assisting two-way trade and investment with China[20] by continuing negotiations for an FTA with China.[21] These negotiations are a direct response to pressure from Australian MNEs on the Australian government to provide more political support and assistance when conducting business in China. This FTA is still under negotiation.

From an institutional perspective, home country governments establish structures designed to provide political support for their international businesses. In Australia, various federal bodies, such as the Department of Foreign Affairs and Trade (DFAT) and Austrade, promote Australian businesses in host countries.[22] For example, Austrade have offices throughout

Australia that may assist with trade and investment planning, information, and contacts. As of December 2011, Austrade had 14 offices with 100s staffs in China.[23] Austrade claims that they can assist in navigating Chinese business practice, identifying new business partners, customers and opportunities, accessing urban and regional areas, and separating myths from reality.[24]

In the study, 15 participant organizations had used the services of Austrade in one form or another. For instance, some organizations had attended information seminars or launches run by Austrade, or had used them to check the [credit] worthiness of Chinese organizations they were planning to become involved with, or received assistance and feedback in general through consultation sessions. Others received export market development grants to pay for their marketing expenses in China, while others had a partnership model where they would work in unison, sometimes using them as their representatives in China (e.g., Case 11, Agri Co). Two cases (Case 8, Vat Co and Case 15, Flower Co) had used Austrade for their main introductions and contacts in China, as the following example specifies:

> Through Austrade, we had that connection with one particular guy who was able to give us the introductions that we needed and he facilitated a lot of the meetings. This fellow was ... I'm not sure how he went about doing it, it was over a long period of time but it was obvious to us in that early phase that he was well regarded by these people. Not only is he a Chinese national but he's also a native of Changzhou City so, you know, he's a card-carrying man ... he knows how the party machine works and how things have to be done, who you have to talk to, how to grease the machine. (Case 8, Vat Co)

In this instance, Austrade had assisted with introducing the right person with the right Chinese governmental contacts. Furthermore, Austrade was perceived to be very helpful. On the other hand, some participants had perceived Austrade to be inappropriate for a company of their size. For example, some of the large participants such as banks and mining companies felt they did not need their services, while other participants perceived their services to be expensive (which is an interesting comment from an organization with sufficient financial resources to consider internationalization):

Austrade are really great, but very, very expensive—ridiculously expensive. I think the last time they wanted $1900 a day, Aussie. Now, I've got a bloke I've been using for 5 years for $100 a day and he's brilliant. He's my advisor, my translator, my everything. But Austrade, it's just completely over the top in my view. (Case 17, Paint Co)

Local state-level institutional structures may also support small businesses internationalizing from specific regions of the home country. For example, the Australian state-level investment support agency, Invest Victoria, operates an office in Shanghai and provides Victoria-based international businesses with free office facilities and services in China.[25] Institutional arrangements may even exist at the municipal government level. For example, the Australian City of Melbourne has a sister city relationship with the Chinese city of Tianjin and a representative office there. These grassroots institutional bodies are particularly effective in providing contacts and introductions specifically for businesses internationalizing to China.[26] Previous research has confirmed that sister city relationships are important for developing economic relationships between Chinese and foreign cities.[27]

Other home country bodies may also assist with internationalization, and although they are technically not government bodies, industry associations such as the Australia China Business Council (ACBC),[28] and AustCham, with offices in Shanghai, Beijing, Southern China, and Hong Kong,[29] are helpful and offer support to businesses doing business in China. These associations offer support from other like-minded company members, and provide membership lists, networking opportunities, seminars on doing business in China, organization of trade missions, as well as the opportunity to interact with home government and host country government members, often those at the forefront of FTA negotiations, and are able to make submissions on important issues affecting business in China. Therefore, these bodies are an important link in assisting businesses internationalizing to China.

Corporate Political Strategies, Behaviors, and the Cooperative View of Organization and Government Relations

A popular approach MNEs take to create an attractive environment in a host country is to politically influence that country's government to create favorable conditions.[30] The types of political approaches used to influence the local government vary between countries.[31] The principal factors behind these variations are the nature of the government (e.g., democratic, authoritarian, or dictatorship) and the differences between the home country and host country government. Approaches to influencing the host-country government can include: policy formation (i.e., policy development, and lobbying), relationship management, management of organization, and government interactions,[32] communication techniques, knowledge of issues management, and the establishment of organization–government and organization–employee relationships.[33]

In a similar vein, the cooperative view of MNE and government relations suggests that businesses develop relationships with host country governments to; (a) gain support and approval for entry arrangements, (b) gain special monetary and anticompetitive favors from government, and (c) manage the environmental turbulence created by governmental threats to organizational goals such as changes in foreign direct investment (FDI) rules.[34]

A home country government may assist an organization with its internationalization by providing support (including diplomatic services), information (such as political risk assessments and advice), introductions and contacts, and may negotiate on behalf of organizations and industries (e.g., free trade negotiations to provide better access to markets in the host country). International businesses usually seek to influence the local government at the initial point of their entry into a country.[35] The most common mechanism involves negotiations and relies on the bargaining power of each party.[36] This suggests that a cooperative view of political behavior is important in establishing entry mode conditions.

Although the approach is well identified, little is known about how the cooperative behavior of MNEs operates in the political arena. Networking with local officials has been shown to be valuable.[37] Personal relationships between MNE staff and government officials have been shown to be valuable in boosting trust and suppressing opportunism, where there is a risk of the host country government taking advantage of the MNE's commitment to that country by introducing regulations and costs.[38] In addition, MNEs frequently engage in cooperative political behavior to maximize economic returns from their international expansion, and to mitigate the liabilities of foreignness and minimize transaction costs.

Personal relationships or *guānxi* are particularly effective in the Chinese political arena because of their priority over contractual relationships, as discussed in Chapter 3. *Guānxi* reflects the Confucian values of social relations and dealing with personal behaviors.[39] *Guānxi* is more complex than the Western concepts of networking and business favoritism and provides an alternative path to formal, regulatory, or contractual processes to enable organizations to identify and take up opportunities.[40] For example, Foster's Brewing Company's joint venture in the Chinese city of Tianjin had a much better relationship with the local government than the joint venture in Shanghai and was more successful than the venture in Shanghai.[41]

It has been argued that the initial role of *guānxi* in Chinese businesses resulted from the need for mechanisms to establish trust in an environment in the absence of market institutions developed for this purpose.[42] *Guānxi* is less valuable now because market institutions also affect the political environment.[43] The success of Chinese business is still, however, directly linked to the ability to manage relationships, and to use information provided from the relationships for effective decision-making.[44] Because *guānxi* shapes the establishment of systems of trust in the Chinese political environment as they relate to international business, *guānxi* has been incorporated into this research by considering relationships with key political actors.

MNEs frequently employ staff whose role is to span the organization and the host country government to assist with establishing cooperative political relationships. Over time, the managerial ties that form between these staff can evolve into interorganizational relations.[45] In emerging markets such as China, personal level trust is frequently institutionalized. This creates an opportunity to establish interorganizational relational capital between the MNE and host country government, which cannot be achieved through market or hierarchical mechanisms. As a result, the focus of political relationship management is to reduce the uncertainty associated with dependence on the host country government, rather than to reduce dependence on the host country government. Therefore, it is important for organizations entering China, with available financial resources, to have staff focused on developing governmental relations. For example, Resource Co 1 (Case 6), had staff, including a senior manager, devoted to developing governmental relations. Organizations should also take a cooperative view in managing the MNE government relationship. In addition, MNEs that align their strategies and interests along the lines of the Chinese five-year plans, will more likely have their business plans approved. The following example from Case 33, Responsibility Co, is indicative:

> So we were actually invited to go into China through academics in Shanghai, who were members of the CPC, and obviously in a position where they had some clout. And they saw an opportunity for Shanghai to position itself leading this area of sustainability and carbon and governance. We then held a summit, which was of really major key thinkers on governance in China. And they were top people (Chinese people), and that really gave us the traction then to sort of build the business. Our business was then, we were encouraged … . Our business registration is a wholly-owned foreign enterprise, not a joint venture, was fast-tracked, and so we had a very quick pathway towards the registration of our business: literally 6–8 weeks it took us for the registration of the company, so that tells you we had people who wanted us to be there on our side.

The cooperative view of political relations with the host country government explains the importance of the provision of Chinese government assistance for internationalizing into China. It reduces the perceived level of risk and affects the entry mode decisions as well as the overall value of the investment. The participants formed relationships with the Chinese government as part of their internationalization. Furthermore, they found that doing so provided significant benefits when establishing foreign businesses in China, as the example above suggests. A total

Table 4.1.   *Relationship Behaviors as Part of the Entry Mode*

Industry	Relationship behaviors	Entry mode(s)
Banking and finance	Negotiated with the mayor of Tianjin to determine the equity level of their investment.	Acquisition
Building, construction, and engineering	Needed to obtain permits/know the right people in government to get the business running. Needed to maintain relationships with local/provincial governments.	WOFE
Resources	Influenced the government in pricing negotiations. Needed relationships and interaction at a senior level with the Chinese government.	JV, WOFE
Manufacturing	Needed relationships at local/provincial levels to get approvals, and get their business running. Needed to be perceived as long-term by the government.	Representative office, EJV, WOFE
Services	Required close relationships with government to access local organizations.	EJV, WOFE

of 22 participants claimed that relationships with local government facilitated the establishment of their businesses. Table 4.1 demonstrates the different relationship behaviors and entry modes the participants adopted.

Different political channels will offer different levels of effectiveness in assisting an organization to establish itself and operate. Knowing which is the right channel and organizing access to it will make the local environment more hospitable for doing business. For example, one participant in the architectural industry noted: "*In terms of politically being a bit more aware of relationships that exist … it would certainly help*" (Case 3, Architect Co).

In a similar vein, a manufacturing participant noted:

I have guys whose companies have been up there for 4 years prior to us and we have some of them coming and asking us how did we get this done quickly. Again, I get back to government relationships, the confidence you have in the people you're dealing with and, in the end, it is personal. For us to go up there, we had to have US$29 million— not greater than $30 million because then it has to go back to Central

Government. So we had $29.5 million. You have to be above $25 million investment to get a reasonable position in the pecking order in the government structure. There's no point trying to see the mayor if you're only putting $5 million in. (Case 28, Brake Co)

Accessing the most effective political channels can also result in the host country government providing direct assistance for an organization's entry into China. Of all the participants, 27 claimed they were assisted by the Chinese government to enter. One participant noted that, *"The Tianjin municipal government was quite helpful, from my understanding, with our investment there. The people running ABC Industrial Park ... have been very, very helpful"* (Case 7, Metal Co). This organization was encouraged into these areas as both of the municipal governments wanted FDI.

The assistance provided by the Chinese government to organizations entering China often followed mutually complementary paths. For example, a participant from the agricultural industry observed that:

[t]he Chinese government has realized the importance of dairy in people's diet. A long time ago, like 10 years ago, back in '95, they realized it's a real issue. And, of course, the farming side, it's very important to the rural population. So, the government did a lot of work to push the industry to go ahead. And the company did a lot of advertising to educate the consumers to eat more dairy. (Case 11, Agri Co)

Impact of Host Country's Trade and Investment Policies and Regulations

There is considerable variation between countries in the regulations they apply to FDI and trade. The regulations can function either as obstacles or incentives to FDI and trade. This situation reflects a hierarchical authority view of business–government relations, emphasizing the formal source of governmental power as inherent in official positions.[46] The government possesses legitimate power, whilst foreign MNEs in that country possess only delegated power resulting from their political negotiations and home country government support in the host country.[47]

One of the most important areas of host country regulations is trade barriers, which reduce the activities of MNEs in host countries and have a significant effect on the entry mode chosen.[48] International trade agreements, on the other hand, support the activities of MNEs in host countries,[49] and also significantly influence the entry modes chosen. The main impact of trade barriers is to limit the entry mode options of foreign MNEs, especially those of manufacturers.[50] For example, high tariff barriers will make imported goods and services more expensive than local goods, and under those conditions, manufacturers will favor local production. Non-tariff barriers may force foreign MNEs to enter partnerships with local providers, thus favoring contractual agreements as a mode of entry.[51] The following quote demonstrates some of the issues associated with regulation by the Chinese government:

> *I guess it's more so the regulatory authority is in relation to that if you're trying to import something here into Australia, it's fairly cut and dry and there's also an appeal process in place. ... I know China's made headway in that area over time but I think there's a lot more work that needs to be done there. Which I think, adds risk to when you're looking at wanting to go into a particular market in China.* (Case 29, Logistics Co)

It was found that policies for FDI directly influenced the China entry modes adopted by the participants. Of the participants, 22 claimed that their organizations were not affected by any Chinese policies or regulations, leaving them open to adopt any entry mode and scale of entry that they chose. The remaining 18 participants, however, experienced some impact from policies and regulations on their entry mode choice and approach. Ten participants found that their entry modes were significantly influenced by Chinese government policies and regulations.

The impact of Chinese policies and regulations on the entry modes of the 18 participants who were affected is summarized, by industry, in Table 4.2.

Table 4.2. Barriers/Restrictions and Influences on Entry Modes

Industry	Barrier/restrictions	Entry mode adopted	Level of impact
Finance and insurance	Restrictions on ownership levels of local banks.	Limited equity ownership in acquisition	High
Transport and logistics	Restricted to joint ventures.	EJV	High
Mining	Restrictions on mineral exploration, owning of utilities and mines. Tariffs on imports.	JV, WOFE	Medium
Government, administration and defense	Home country government regulation that only embassies can set up offices in foreign countries.	Representative office	Low
Education	Restricted to local agency and partnerships.	Agents and partnerships	High

The restrictions which did not influence the entry mode of the participants included:

- Australian government restrictions on Chinese tourists to Australia (accommodation, hotels, and café industry).
- Regulations at provincial level in China (manufacturing industry).
- Building design regulatory approval requirement that building designs are locally designed (construction, building, and engineering industry).
- Content limitations (publishing industry).

Even when the policies and regulations did not affect entry modes, some impact on business operations was identified by most of the participants. A participant from the education industry noted that:

If not for all of the universities in China and mainly because of all the regulatory restrictions, there is only so much that foreigners can do on their own. So, in that regard, we are restricted to using representatives over there who have got licenses issued by the Chinese government. (Case 25, Uni Co 2)

A few participants found that fundamental product characteristics were also influenced by local regulation, which had a secondary impact on choice of entry mode. For example, a participant from the publishing industry experienced government policy impacts on the content of the books they published. They had initially established licensing as an entry mode; however, the government policy impact that they experienced caused them to consider moving to a WOFE in the future:

> *The key thing is our editorial independence and line in our books, which is often contrary to what the Chinese government prefers to have us say. I have been pulled into a session with the organization, which owns our partner. It's owned by the Ministry of Propaganda, as all state publishers are, and asked to explain our position on China, and why we see Taiwan as independent and that's no good. It's all issues around Taiwan, Tibet, Tiananmen Square, which we are obviously very open in our books about ... so they asked if we could change our views because they were perceived to be incorrect. And they were also putting pressure on us, saying, "You're dealing with one of the key publishing brands in China."* (Case 23, Book Co)

A respondent from Case 17, Law Co, which provides legal services in Shanghai, also found government policy restricted the range of services they could provide. They were only allowed to provide legal advice and not representation services. In addition, they were not allowed to employ Chinese lawyers. This form of service control did not directly influence the entry mode selected; however, it did significantly influence the size and scope of the business activities and future development opportunities. The participant from this organization suggested that Chinese regulations and policies were still strongly protectionist:

> *[I]t's natural, they are looking for investment in newer fields. But they don't want foreigners just to come in and replicate what Chinese institutions are already doing and taking business away from Chinese institutions. So, there is a bit of protection going on there.* (Case 17, Law Co)

Chinese Government Intervention

The authoritarian nature of the Chinese government means that it is likely to intervene in the operations of foreign MNEs. Such government behavior may be a legacy of China moving from a centrally planned economy where SOEs were 100% government controlled. The Chinese government's political bias still leans strongly towards maintaining control over businesses, especially foreign organizations, through both policy and direct influences on company processes.[52] Although, a large number of Chinese SOEs have now been privatized and other private enterprises established,[53] institutional controls and structures are still in place that influence the entry behaviors and operations of foreign MNEs. Foreign MNEs considering joint ventures (JVs) as an entry mode find that the only partners they are allowed to access are SOEs or government bodies.[54] A valuable side-effect of this government control is that JV agreements in China frequently lead to direct relationships with the Chinese government.[55]

The participants did experience intervention from the Chinese government in their operations, and the impact was mostly negative. Thirty-three participants claimed that the political system influenced the operations of their business in China. Seven participants identified no influence. Most of the participants who were affected characterized the influence as reflecting the differences between operating in a communist/socialistic system with market characteristics, and operating in a democratic market economy. For example, one participant noted that China's *"legacy from the past"* was still apparent today and impacted on their operations:

> *I think it's just a function of where they've come from and their sort of political landscape. And ours—we're coming from quite different models in terms of communism and democracy.* (Case 4, Parcel Co)

In addition to influencing the type of operations that could be established in China, Chinese government's intervention also influenced the profitability that could be achieved. A participant from the mining industry observed that Chinese government's intervention affected both operations and profitability in that industry:

> *There are issues in China, but what do they look like? One is about the desire of the Chinese government to insert itself into the marketplace ... the general point is the role of government in markets and pricing in iron-ore negotiations.* (Case 6, Resources Co 1)

Often the intervention was not focused on one specific organization, but on whole industries or even groups of industries. This created complex and systemic influences with which organizations entering the market had to deal with, in addition to the issues endemic to the industry. For example, a manufacturing industry participant noted that the main characteristic of the intervention was a high level of control in all aspects of business operations in China:

> *So much of China's infrastructure and industry is state owned. ... So for us, ABC Automobile, our main customer, is state owned—mainly by the Province, but also by the local government, but ultimately they are answerable through to the state. And in the hierarchy, in the Western world, the guy who is the CEO of General Motors is king. But when you go to Wu Hu, the guy who is the CEO and chairman of ABC Automobile is actually the number 2 or 3 or 4 in the hierarchy. The local mayor is actually his boss. Then the local Communist Party Chairman is actually his boss ... and the role of government is far greater there than it is here...* (Case 14, Auto Interior Co)

Summary: A Political Negotiation Structure for MNEs Internationalizing to China

The political issues identified above and the findings from the research participants can be represented as a typology. Typologies for international strategic political activities can be constructed around the organizational objectives and interventions that can be expected.[56] A typology has been developed based on the above information and incorporates the input available from the Australian government and from the Chinese

Table 4.3. A Typology of Political Activities

Organizational objectives	Australian government input	Chinese government input
Understand Political/ regulatory environment	Gain advice on political system, regulations and contacts. Use trade offices—(commonwealth and state). Use Sister City Relationships. Use business councils and chamber of Commerce.	Gain information from Chinese government websites.
Identify and develop entry mode access markets, suppliers	Facilitate and support contact with relevant Chinese government officials	Develop relationships with relevant government officials. Negotiate with Chinese government. Get approvals from Chinese government.
Develop/maintain successful business	Obtain ongoing advice from trade offices, business Councils, and chamber of commerce.	Maintain relationships with Chinese government for an ongoing successful business.

government that would assist with achieving the organization's objectives. This typology is shown in Table 4.3.

The typology incorporates three organizational objectives—understanding the political and institutional environment in the host country, negotiating political opportunities that create and define the entry mode, and undertaking the political negotiations that are needed to create long-term conditions that will support the success of the local business. The two principal inputs (home and host country governments) that affect the main political objectives were both composed of two types of support—providing information and facilitating the development of local relationships. This is consistent with the identified importance of relationships in managing the political environment in China.

Each of the organizational objectives in this typology requires the international business to understand and establish relationships with the host country government. In this research, the home and host countries possessed a significant psychic distance between their government structures.[57] The psychic distance between the Australian and Chinese governments required them to collect information before identifying the correct entry mode; it also affected the entry mode approach adopted for Australian companies entering China, and the manner in which they maintained their business operations.

Conclusion

The political environment in China is particularly difficult to manage due to the fact that China has a "single-party state," government led by the CPC, which is more authoritarian than most Western political parties. International businesses in China can improve their ability to manage the political environment by developing their negotiation skills. They can also reduce the impact of the gap between their home country government and the host country government policy through the use of Chinese culture training and appointing Chinese staff to introduce this knowledge into the organization. These actions will reduce the organization's dependence on external sources of information regarding political conditions and develop its ability to negotiate in the Chinese political context.

International businesses operating in China must also be able to manage the impact of the high levels of control and intervention from local government and political representatives that is prevalent throughout China. This narrow institutional environment requires complementary management techniques that facilitate the outcomes listed in Table 4.3. Although the adoption of these approaches represents an extra transaction cost associated with operating in international business in China, adopting these practices can result in improved circumstances, which compensate for the increased transaction costs.

CHAPTER 5

The Legal System

How Can You Use It to Your Benefit?

The legal system in China is often described as complicated, non-transparent, hard to understand, heavily influenced by the government, and unenforceable. China uses a bureaucratic law system, which is distinct from common law used in Australia, and is derived from Soviet and European civil code principles.[1] The case involving the Chinese-born Australian national and Rio Tinto Manager, Stern Hu, who was arrested in 2009, demonstrates the ambiguity in the Chinese legal system.[2] At the time, analysts questioned whether Stern Hu's arrest was a result of allegedly "stealing state secrets" or was it a political reaction to Rio Tinto's withdrawal from a deal proposed by the Chinese company Chinalco.[3] Chinalco, an SOE, attempted to purchase 30% of Rio Tinto's iron ore mines in the Pilbara, Western Australia. Rio Tinto did not proceed with the proposal in response to pressure from its shareholders and the Australian community.[4] There was some speculation that Stern Hu's arrest reflected the Chinese government's dissatisfaction with the outcome. Nonetheless, Hu and three of his colleagues pleaded guilty soon after the start of the trial. Collectively the four of them had accepted $7–8 million in bribery.[5]

How Is the Legal System in China Described?

To make China an even more attractive destination for FDI, trade, and doing business, China needs a legal system that is transparent, upholds the rights of both the local citizens and foreign investors, has due process,[6] and has reliable procedures to review and make decisions.[7] On the surface, China appears to have created many laws that create a favorable business environment; however, an underlying problem is the unenforceability of the law and the fact that corruption or bribery influences decisions in the favor of companies willing to pay or those who have good relationships or *guānxi*.[8] It is well known, that the CPC will interfere with court decisions,[9] senior officials can overturn decisions and substitute alternative outcomes.[10] There are also regular un-foreshadowed changes to laws, and these are often introduced without the consultation of business.

China's legal system reflects its communist history, and the fact that the economy is still "state-controlled." The economy and business environment in China is developing faster than the evolution of the Chinese legal system to accommodate industry needs.[11] To promote both local and foreign business it is important that a country such as China has a clearly specified set of rules for the conduct of business. For example, Datamonitor[12] suggested that although the support for FDI from the Chinese legal system has been improving, Chinese investment is risky because of weak corporate laws, a lack of resources at the judicial level, political interference and corruption in legal matters. In addition, there is a notable lack of safeguards in the system, which prevents the total independence of the judicial system.[13]

It is also important for businesses operating in a foreign culture to be able to understand the legal system. As China is socialist and authoritarian,[14] the government has total authority for making and enforcing laws. The Organization for Economic Co-operation and Development (OECD) reports that China needs a legal system that is transparent, stable, and internally consistent and is easily understood by foreign investors.[15] The Economic Analytical Unit[16] reported that China's legal system is "puzzling", suggesting that improvements still need to be made in regards to the system.[17]

How Is Law Created in China?

As discussed in Chapter 4, the highest organ of state power in China is the NPC.[18] The Politburo Standing Committee, which forms part of the CPC, has the authority to establish the laws in China.[19] Laws are also created at a local level, including the People's Congress in provinces, municipalities, autonomous areas, and cities.[20] The laws and regulations passed at a local level must conform with those passed by the NPC and the People's Congress, to which the NPC reports.[21]

Where Is Chinese Law Published?

China's State Council Legislative Affairs Office[22] (SCLAO) publishes many laws, rules, regulations, or policy measures on international trade and investment regarding China, to provide a transparent and accessible system. The SCLAO also offers to help any individual, organizations, and other WTO members to understand the rules and regulations in China. As a result, China has become more effective and faster in making new and revised regulations available on the internet and in official journals.[23] In addition, all legislation is published in the gazette of the body that issued the legislation and in the national daily newspaper.[24] For example, Ministry of Foreign Trade and Economic Cooperation has been publishing foreign investment and trade-related regulations in an official gazette since 1993.[25] The English translation of the laws tends to lag, however, is eventually produced.[26]

The Court System and Where to Get Your Court Case Heard?

Unlike Anglo-Saxon common law, Chinese courts do not have a tradition of following precedents or past decisions and requiring the publication of cases.[27] Therefore, this is very foreign to those who are from a common law system. Civil law systems such as China's use a system where laws are codified and interpreted.[28] In the Chinese legal system, the responsible Ministries determine, interpret, and supervise the relevant regulations.[29]

In the Chinese legal system there are four levels of people's courts:[30] (1) the Supreme People's Court has jurisdiction over appeals or protests from the Higher People's Court and Special People's Court; (2) the Higher People's Court deals with major criminal cases impacting an entire province, and hears cases of appeals or protests against judgments and orders of the lower courts; (3) the Intermediate People's Court can impose life sentences or capital punishment and deals with cases involving foreign parties and cases transferred from lower the courts, and (4) the Basic People's Court is not able to rule on death sentence or life imprisonment cases, or on certain foreign civil cases, but it can request to transfer cases to the higher courts. The arrangement of these courts is shown in Figure 5.1.

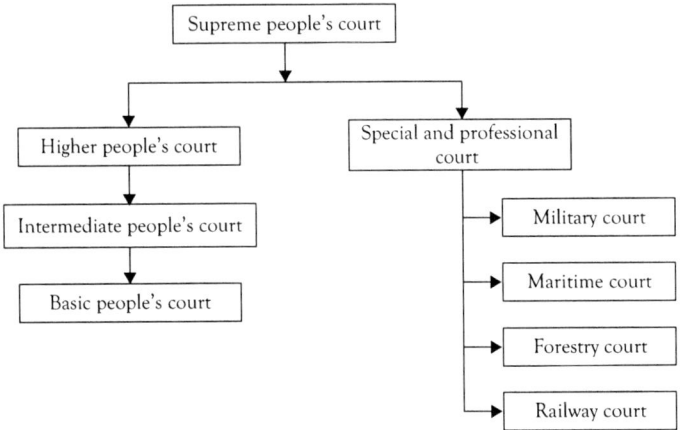

Figure 5.1. Court structure in China.[31]

Foreign investors have the option to use arbitration if they prefer not to use the court system. The Australian Economic Analytical Unit has found that foreign organizations actually favor using arbitration in China to resolve commercial disputes rather than the court system.[32] The China International Economic Trade Arbitration Commission (CIETAC), which is also known as the Arbitration Court of the China Chamber of International Commerce (CCOIC), is the primary body used for Sino-foreign arbitrations in China.[33] CIETAC has headquarters in Beijing and sub-commissions in Shanghai, Shenzhen, and Tianjin as well as a multitude of liaison offices across China.[34] To be able to use arbitration at CIETAC, contracting parties need to insert a model arbitration clause, which explicitly states that arbitration shall be conducted where there is a dispute, into their contracts.[35] CIETAC has proved to be an effective arbitration commission, with 1,097 cases solved out of the 1,230 cases submitted in 2008.[36] Apart from CIETAC, there are approximately 140 local arbitration commissions, which exist across China.[37] These can hear disputes involving both domestic and foreign businesses. The Beijing Arbitration Commission is the most active of these commissions.[38]

Foreign investors may also use mediation in China to resolve disputes. There are around 800,000 mediation committees in rural and urban areas. These committees resolve most of (90%) China's civil disputes, without any cost to the parties involved.[39] These mediation committees may be a suitable mechanism to resolve international business disputes, considering that most foreign businesses cannot rely on other courts to provide a fast or reliable resolution to disputes or for the enforcement of contracts.[40]

Despite all the different mechanisms available, such as the courts, arbitration, or mediation for the resolution of disputes, the actual enforcement of outcomes remains difficult. Court judgments are difficult to enforce in China, because there is a lack of any effective enforcement mechanisms.[41] China has made efforts in recent years to improve the enforcement of laws and legal contracts, but their enforcement is strongly affected by local protectionism and the lack of experience of local courts in foreign business matters.[42] To help deal with the lack of enforcement, China allows for international arbitration under either Chinese or foreign law.[43] In the past, more enforcement of international arbitration has been achieved than enforcement of a domestic arbitration decisions[44]. Previous research has found that during the 1990s, organizations from the USA in China managed legal issues by inserting clauses into their contracts to hear international business disputes at the International Court of Arbitration.[45]

A Legal System in Transition

Developing a new legal system, which encourages market activity and protects the legal and property rights of individuals, is a formidable task. China's legal system had to be rebuilt from scratch after 1978 as a result of China's reforms and opening up to the world economy.[46] The progress that has been made in developing China's legal system to make it more suitable for a market economy over the last 30 years has been noteworthy. Prior to 1978, there were no lawyers in China—Communist Party bureaucrats set the laws, local judges interpreted them, and the army and police enforced them.[47] As a result of Deng Xiaoping's reforms in 1978, the legal system and a judiciary was re-established. During the 1980s, most Chinese lawyers were seconded from their posts in the CPC, or the military, and did not have a university education or legal training, and judges were often the local Communist Party Secretary.[48] As a result, this suggests that neither the lawyers nor the judges had the same level of legal training, experience, and background common in countries, such as

Australia. This situation persists and continues to influence the operations of the Chinese legal system. It is exacerbated by the shortage of judges, particularly in rural areas.[49]

In regards to business, changes to the Chinese legal system were made in the areas of individual property rights, contract law, forms of foreign entities, and employment laws.[50] As a result, businesses need to keep themselves updated with the changes in the law, which can increase costs and potentially cause confusion, especially where laws are vague.

The legal reforms in China have resulted in the practice of "rule by law" rather than "rule by the people." The reforms have been made in four key areas.[51] First, reforms were needed for the transition from a socialist public ownership system to the protection of private property rights. Second, changes to the education and training of lawyers were required, including the process by which they become lawyers. The Chinese government has also focused on improving the quality and quantity of lawyers.[52] Third, more business laws have been passed to create a better business environment and to protect business practices, in line with WTO regulations. Examples of recently changed business laws include the Company Law, the Banking Law, the Foreign Enterprises law, and the Law of Consumption.[53] The final change has been to improve legal procedures and due process, in contrast to the previous system of operating courts without formal procedures. These transitions mean that, in theory, foreign investors and business people can now have their cases heard and their disputes resolved. But the reality of is questionable because of the need for more improvement in the Chinese legal system.

Some Important Chinese Laws for Foreign Investors

Government Rules and Regulations for Establishing a Foreign Business

Foreign enterprises engaged in business in China must obey Chinese laws and regulations, which include not harming social and public interests. To establish a foreign business, its directors need to register their business.[54] To establish a foreign enterprise, investors submit a proposal prior

to application. The proposal includes the following: the purpose of setting up the enterprise; the business' scope, the type of products produced,
the technical equipment used; and the land area and requirements.[55] The
"Opinions" issued by the State Council of China on April 6, 2010, made
the approval process for foreign investment more efficient by reallocating
approval authority to local government levels.[56] For example, a local government may approve any foreign investment project under US$300 mil-
lion, unless it is classified as "restricted."[57] However, problems may arise as
local authorities often apply different interpretations to national regulations.[58] This has included decisions to block the merger of foreign firms
in China, if the merger is likely to affect the operations of local companies
in China.[59] Foreign ownership of businesses was dealt with in Chapter 2.

Labor Contract Law

In 2008, a new Labor Contract Law was introduced into China.[60] The
purpose of the law is to "govern the employment relationship, including
employee performance, amendment and termination of employment."[61]
Key differences in this new law are the encouragement of long-term or
non-fixed term contracts, the setting of more stringent regulations for the
termination of employment, and the enforcement of those conditions.[62]

The aims of the law are to protect the legitimate rights and interests
of workers, to establish the worker/enterprise labor relationship, to establish and maintain the socialist market economy and labor system, and
to promote economic development and social progress.[63] The rights of
workers include equal rights of employment and choice of occupation
[for men and women]; the entitlement to payment for labor and to take
rest breaks; to work in safe conditions with their health protected; to have
vocational skills training; to be given social insurance and welfare rights;
to have labor disputes settled, as well as other rights and labor rights laws;
and participation in trade unions.[64]

Contract Law

In 1999, contract law, which also covers foreign contracts, was established
by the Chinese government.[65] As suggested above in The Court System

and Where to Get Your Court Case Heard? on p. 83, foreign business people should include an arbitration clause when drafting a contract. This enables arbitration to occur if there is a dispute. Although it is often suggested that one should not rely on a contract when doing business in China, it still makes sense to create a contract, in case of a dispute. Contracts in China should focus on specifying key details and be flexible with minor details. They should be negotiated with tact, patience, and politeness.[66] Relationship building, such as dinners, banquets, and getting to know business partners, also form a key part developing a contract.

Perceptions of the Legal System in China by Australian Businesses

Some Characteristics of the Chinese Legal System

The study participants learnt about the Chinese legal system over time. Also, using the Chinese legal system requires not only understanding the regulations, but also building relationships. For example, a representative from an automotive supplier company stated:

> *If you want to work with your Western lawyers in China, that doesn't work. If you want to work with a Shanghai lawyer setting up a business in the provinces, that sort of works, but rules are different wherever you go. So, you have to find the balance of understanding the local rules and regulations and building the right relationships with the people that control those, versus the Western rule of law that we're used to.* (Case 14, Auto Interior Co)

The participants commented on the transitional nature of the Chinese legal system and how the rules were constantly changing, which required them to update themselves with the current rules, and respond (Case 32, Chain Co). Another key issue mentioned was the lack of a legal structure in place. A banking and finance participant, stated that there was a lack of developed laws, rules, and regulations for Western financial services, such as personal and home mortgages, which affected the types of financial products they could offer in the Chinese market (Case 2, Bank Co 1). A manufacturing industry participant suggested that it was good to have a Chinese lawyer who is bicultural, can explain the problem and find a solution. He suggested:

> *The Chinese legal system is completely different to ours. They don't run a common law system. If you're a lawyer I guess you could spend a lot of time coming to terms with what it all means, but I'm not ... I don't have the time or the information to start burrowing into the Chinese legal system. What you really need is the same as it is here, you need to have a good lawyer that you can utilize but you have to have someone who can speak in his language and explain the problem, explain what you want to get out of it, how you want to get out of it, and what you want to get out of it.* (Case 8, Vat Co)

A university participant commented that the legal system in China was ambiguous and believed that it was created to confuse foreign investors. They suggested that every law was open to interpretation by any person (including the CPC), which resulted in inequality and injustice for foreign investors. They also suggested that they would not want to end up in a court of law, because they did not trust the outcomes of a court hearing. They preferred to sort out their issues based on relationships:

> *The legal system just isn't as strong. We're struggling with this a little, but in a country like Australia, you look at the laws and the regulations and there are usually good administrative explanations of those. And you can create a contract based on those and you know that contract can protect you. That doesn't seem to be the case in China. Number 1, the laws are ambiguous—deliberately, I suspect, so that they're open to interpretation. Number 2, it depends on who interprets them, and that's not a written interpretation—it's on an individual basis. So, if you're trying to do something like create a joint university, it will depend very much on who looks at those laws and who interprets them and who advises them.* (Case 12, Uni Co 1)

Other participants suggested that the legal system in China was a minefield, full of red tape and bureaucracy:

> *The business red tape is pretty horrific but it's being reduced. The legal stuff is still a minefield.* (Case 18, Auto Components Co)

This last quote suggests that foreign businesses wishing to do business in China should take a "caveat emptor" (the buyer is responsible) approach to using the legal system.

Weakness, Distrust, and Unenforceability of Contracts in the Legal System

China's weak legal system and infrastructure allows individuals to play a more significant role than the laws in shaping commercial activities.[67] One of the greatest weaknesses of the system is that it can be "a tool of state administration"[68] and subject to interpretation. The following example describes the complexity of the Chinese environment:

> *But there isn't this well-defined set of laws like we have in Australia, where you can look up to the last dot what you're allowed to do and what you can't do, like the ESOS Act which absolutely lays out everything. ... I imagine that sort of thing just wouldn't be laid out in China's law. There would be something about foreign students being looked after or something, but it would be vague and then the local area would interpret and define a set of guidelines. There are advantages to this system, for instance, it is much more flexible, but of course, it's open easily to corruption as well, and that's the risk.* (Case 5, Uni Co 1)

The IT Co participant commented that they "distrusted" the legal system, which put them off pursuing any type of legal issue through the courts:

> *The laws in China are written very different to here. ... The real difference is that any decision of any court, within any jurisdiction in China, can be reinterpreted by the executive, the top standing committee, the very top level of the Communist Party. A court in Guangdong somewhere can make a decision and then it can just be overturned by Beijing.* (Case 20, IT Co)

The lack of enforceability and the uncertainty in the legal system creates more risk for a foreign investor and would discourage some from doing business in China.

Research suggests that legal action in China provides limited returns.[69] The inadequate enforcement mechanisms and the government's influence on commercial litigation means that, even though a foreign firm may have won their case, they will find it difficult to recover damages or to have authorities enforce the judicial orders.[70] An export participant commented on the unenforceability of the legal system in China:

> [B]ut the point is in China it's unenforceable, so you're wasting your time. At the end of the day, if the relationship goes wrong, I question whether a legal document prepared by a Collins Street lawyer in Chinese, is going to rectify the problem. So, is it not better to, shall we say, back-off the legal side and prepare a gentleman's response? (Case 22, Wool Co)

This quote suggests that foreign organizations in China should rely on good relationships more than the legal system. To deal with these legal problems, foreign firms should conduct a careful risk assessment of partners, seek to develop *guānxi* connections, build penalties into their contracts, and regularly renegotiate contracts.[71]

Firms Prefer to Rely on Relationships, Not Contracts

It is often said, "Don't rely on a contract in China, rely on your relationship."[72] The Chinese government can interpret laws the way it wants to, or it can withdraw licenses if it wishes.[73] The government's attempt to evict McDonald's from a store in Beijing in 1994 to build the Oriental Plaza is a case in point.[74] McDonald's had a 20-year lease with the Beijing City government for their store on the corner of Wangfujing and Chang'an Avenue.[75] The government ordered the eviction of McDonald's, causing uproar in the international business community. The Beijing City government's wanted a Hong Kong property developer, who had developed significant *guānxi*, to build a world-class mega complex in that location.[76] McDonald's refused to leave for 2 years, before reaching an agreement with the city in 1996 to finally leave. This example demonstrates how the authoritarian nature of the Chinese government, motivated by individuals with strong connections, will attempt to override legal convention.

A manufacturing industry participant said that they tried not to rely too much on contracts, because of the inability to pursue legal matters satisfactorily through the court or arbitration systems, but relied more on the relationships that underpinned those contracts (Case 30, Machine Co). Another manufacturer suggested that for minor things, such as purchase orders, they would use local lawyers who had good connections to sort matters out:

> For local contracts such as purchase orders, employment agreements, equipment purchases and so on, land purchases, we will use a local lawyer in Wu Hu that knows the local areas and is well connected. (Case 14, Auto Interior Co)

However, for more important legal processes, such as setting up a company in China, this organization would use representatives of their Australian legal team in China to do the work. The representative from Auto Interior Co stated that for M&A processes, their organization would use their Australian legal team, rather than the one based in China. They also suggested that it was very difficult to do due diligence in China, because:

> (1) Financial information is not available; (2) if it is, it's all in Chinese and probably in line with different laws that you are not familiar with; (3) things change so quickly, whatever financial data you're looking at is quite considerably out of date; and (4) you can try and protect yourselves as much as possible by writing up lots and lots of detailed contracts, but ultimately you've got to have a relationship. (Case 14, Auto Interior Co)

In common law countries, laws are used as a set of "rules of conduct" governing society, and is the primary form of redress when things go wrong.[77] In a Confucian society, ethics and standards of behavior form the "rules of conduct." The organization Retail Co (Case 40), who outsourced their production to suppliers in China, commented on how they preferred not to use legal contracts with suppliers, but used an order system based on supplier partnerships in which relationships were developed. They believed that using contracts would *scare the living daylights*" out of their suppliers. In China, decisions are made according to personal relationships.[78] This puts foreign investors who lack personal relationships at a disadvantage, thereby favoring the local competitors who do.

Corruption and Bribery

A discussion of the legal system in China would not be complete without a discussion of corruption, paying bribes, and "who you know." Prior research has identified widespread corruption in the legal system.[79] Transparency International ranks corruption in China as high, with a transparency score of 3.6 out of 10 in 2011, which places it as the 75th most transparent country out of 182 countries.[80] Australia's transparency score in 2011 was 8.8 out of 10, placing it as 8th out of 182 countries.

To obtain appropriate legal outcomes in China, companies often find it necessary to bribe officials. Bribes and *guānxi* can influence the approval of a new business or a court decision.[81] Previous research has identified more than 1,200 laws, rules, and directives relating to corruption, which indicates that the government is paying more attention to dealing with corruption; however, commentators have suggested that the majority of these laws are not enforced.[82] The probability that an official accused of corruption will face punishment is about 3%, suggesting there is very little enforcement.[83] Corruption also creates disadvantages for Western organizations facing local rivals who engage in illegal practices to win business in China.[84] The influence of corruption is exacerbated by the insufficiency of safeguards in place to counter the influence of bureaucrats and senior officials, which makes the legal system ineffective and unfair.[85] Some of the participants commented on corruption and said that it was an issue that had affected them:

> *There's a lot of corruption, which I can understand, but it also makes it very difficult when you're actually trying to get into a market. And because of our small size, it usually depended on who was there at the time, when we were trying to get the product into the country. So, for instance, if that person was sick or wasn't at work or was moved, and there was someone new, there tended to be a different set of regulations pushed forward, which I think is a China problem that China needs to look at and address. (Case 29, Logistics Co)*

Is the Legal System in China Getting Better?

China has committed itself to reforms in the areas of legal transparency, the consistent application of laws, and judicial review.[86] These reforms are needed to ensure that China meets its liberalization goals and its WTO commitments. Foreign investors view the inconsistent application of law and lack of transparency as major risks when conducting business in China.[87] China has established an internal review mechanism to monitor non-uniform application of law; however, as the example above points out, the problems persist.[88] Despite this, there are some positive stories as an automotive industry participant explains:

> But, in saying that, you hear good news too. You hear the system now is catching up. A citizen now does have a say. Smaller companies do have a say. The government is definitely clamping down on corrupt businesses, and companies now have had their businesses shut down and, in some cases, repossessed by the government. I think they're making a genuine attempt to do that. But, again, you hear stories the other way. But, generally speaking, I think they are trying to clean it up. But it is very political on a broad scale; I think they're making good progress. (Case 28, Brake Co)

There is also evidence that an increasing number of local and foreign nationals are now using the Chinese legal system. China's entry into the WTO means that China has to meet international legal standards, which will result in a better business environment as the Chinese legal system should continue to improve into the future, which will further promote and encourage foreign business in China.

Approaches for Dealing with the Legal System in China

Building relationships is only one way of ensuring that other organizations meet their obligations. Marketing Co (Case 9), believed that they would not be able to use the legal system to deal with non-payment for services and, instead, required clients to make 50% of the payment before the project commenced, ensuring that they at least cover their costs.

Using a local legal service was another important strategy used by the study participants. Responsibility Co (Case 33) preferred to have a local law firm in China to represent their interests, as they believed they had a better knowledge of Chinese law than the foreign legal firms did. They also found this to be cheaper. Logistics Co (Case 29) also preferred to use local lawyers, as they perceived that their Australian lawyers, whether they were located in Australia or China, could not give them proper advice on legal matters, and they were not as well connected. A bank industry participant, had a different perspective:

> *I think the secret is probably going to be to use legal and account-ancy firms who operate in both jurisdictions, because there will always be an Australian leg to what we do in some shape or form. So it makes sense that we can do things in China that would come back out in Australia using the same firm. It seems to be a sensible way to approach it.* (Case 39, Bank Co 2)

The consensus would appear to be that companies should have legal representatives in China who know the law, will act in their interests, and have some connections.

Conclusion

There are a number of important conclusions to draw from the findings presented in this chapter. The most important is that the participants found that the Chinese legal system was inconsistent, vague, difficult to understand, in a period of transition, and affected by corruption. They also found it to be relationship-based rather than rule-based and currently largely unenforced. From a practical perspective, the participants noted that the legal system was incomplete, open to interpretation, transitory, and very different from common law systems such as Australia's legal system. They preferred to rely on relationships when doing business in China. Some participants also found that the level of corruption was an inhibitor to successful business in China. Despite these negative perceptions, both the participants and the literature confirmed that there has been immense progress with the legal system since China's "Open Door

Policy" was introduced in 1978. This has been particularly apparent in the creation and enactment of relevant business laws, establishment of functioning court, arbitration and mediation systems, better training and development of lawyers and judges, and the adoption of due process. In the future, foreign organizations operating in China will be able to rely more heavily on the legal system to support their rights. Contracts, however, are unlikely to ever provide a complete substitute for relationships in China.

CHAPTER 6

Intellectual Property in China

Are the Issues All They Are Cracked Up to Be?

Intellectual Property Issues in China

China is well known as the country of the fake Gucci™ handbag, pirated DVD, and fake pharmaceuticals.[1] But, how would you feel if you just had open-heart surgery and found out you had received a counterfeit copy pacemaker?[2] Or would you know, after all, you could be dead? Like the ladies in the knock-off handbag shop, will the doctor ask you, "Would you prefer good quality, bad quality, or in-between, or would you like to come and see my 'special pacemaker,' behind the secret door?" The story continues; statistics reveal that more than half of the pharmaceuticals sold in China are counterfeit, and some of the drugs can be ordered online, which means that ultimately counterfeit drugs are also ending up in the West.[3] Have you recently ordered drugs off the internet? How can you be sure that they are real, safe, and will have the intended effects that the label on the pack says they will? Counterfeit drugs can fail to treat a patient, injure them, or even cause death.[4] The story goes on. There are reports of counterfeit Starbucks outlets, HMV stores, and even counterfeit business schools in China. Where does it stop? Recently, there have been reports of five fake Apple stores in Kunming,[5] and the authorities could only close down two of them because the other three were selling real Apple products. As the following article in *The Age* demonstrates:[6]

> *The proliferation of the fake stores underlines the slow progress that China's government is making in countering a culture of rampant piracy and widespread production of bogus goods that is a major irritant in relations with trading partners.*

China amended its Intellectual Property (IP) laws and strengthened its legal system to align with the agreement on Trade-related Aspects of Intellectual Property Rights (TRIPS) as a result of joining the WTO in 2001.[7] Despite having changed these laws, China's WTO membership has been criticized because it was not contingent on those laws being enforced. According to the World Intellectual Property Organization (WIPO), China's laws on IP are the most developed in the world;[8] they look great on paper to investors, but on a practical level, the laws are not being properly enforced. Given the authoritarian nature of the Chinese government, if it were serious about wiping out the "counterfeit culture" of China it would do something about it. However, the economic turnover, jobs created and whatever tax revenue is generated from this black market may make the counterfeit industry in China attractive to the government at this stage.

The former Australian Prime Minister, and Minister for Foreign Affairs, the Honorable Kevin Rudd, recently commented that: *"with China starting to develop their own products and IP, the importance they place on IP will increase, as a result of their need to protect their own IP."*[9] This developing need should create an impetus for China to also move to protect international businesses' IP in China. In a similar vein to Kevin Rudd's comment, *The Economist* reports that as China becomes innovative, it will take IP more seriously. Better IP protection will lead to the production of more IP-related products in China. If ideas are protected, the Chinese people will produce more products containing them.[10]

Piracy Rates and Losses in China

The Organization for Economic Co-operation and Development (OECD) estimates that international trade in counterfeit and pirated goods from China was approximately $250 billion in the 2007.[11] Business Software Alliance (BSA)[12] reported that 78% of software users in China

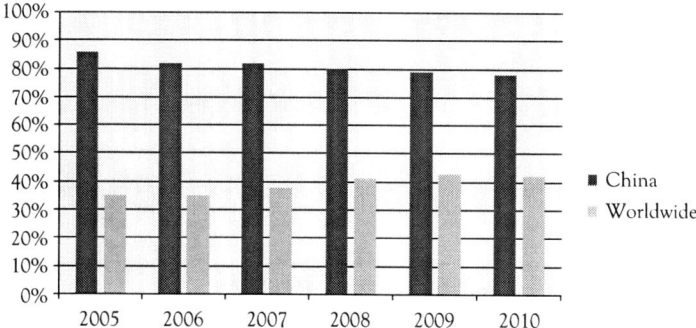

Figure 6.1. Software piracy rates in China and the World.[15]

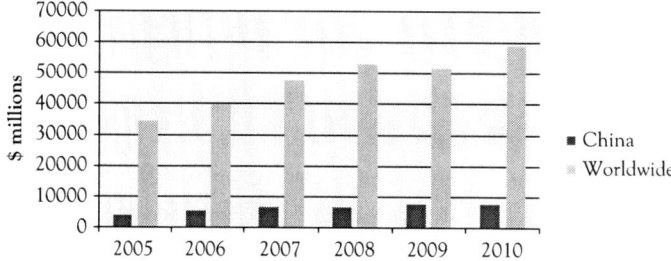

Figure 6.2. Software piracy losses in China and the World.[17]

utilized pirated software in 2010, down from 86% in 2005, as shown in Figure 6.1.[13] Whilst this downward trend is encouraging, it is important to note that global piracy rates are significantly lower than the rates within China. For example, in 2010 the global pirated software usage rate was 42%.[14] Contrary to the trend in China, however, the trend for the global pirated software usage rate has been increasing, and the two may be much more comparable by 2020.

In addition to the percentage of customers utilizing pirated products, the financial losses to international businesses from piracy are quite significant. In addition, although the pirated software utilization rates are declining in China, the losses from pirated software in China have been increasing (see Figure 6.2).[16]

What Are the Laws for IP Protection in China?

According to the Chinese government, IP rights have been protected in China since the introduction of Deng Xiaoping's Open Door Policy in

Table 6.1. IP Agreements that China Has Ascended to

Year	Agreement
1980	WIPO
	TRIPS
	Berne Convention for the Protection of Literary and Artistic Works
1984	Paris Convention for the Protection of Industrial Property
1989	Madrid Agreement for the International Registration of Trademarks
1996	Sino-US Agreement on IP Rights

1978.[18] At least at the political level, the commitment that China has shown to developing IP rights has been quite significant.[19] In fact, the WIPO identified China's patent office is one of the best in the world and China operates the world's largest trademark office.[20] Table 6.1 lists the various intellectual property rights agreements that China has adopted since the introduction of the Open Door Policy.

These international agreements are usually directly adopted as Chinese regulation. For example, court hearings in relation to IP, may quote one of these agreements directly. In China, IP has been protected through legislation and government regulations for patents, copyright, and trademarks. There are three key national laws that have been passed by the NPC, in regards to patents, copyright, and trademark. These actions were a central part of the Chinese government's plan to create an innovative and knowledge-based economy, culminating in the release of a national IP strategy in 2008.[21]

Patent Law and Process

Economic theory suggests that investment in education, research, and development will influence economic development.[22] The Patent Law of the People's Republic of China (PRC) was established to encourage science and technology, and also to stimulate new inventions. This legislation is considered by IP Australia to be valuable for the protection of IP and comprises 96 provisions.[23] The legislation allows for patents to be registered by an authorized patent agency, approved by the State Intellectual Property Office (SIPO).[24] SIPO is responsible for administering patents, registered through the Chinese Patent Office.[25]

The registration of a trademark, patent, or design in China requires that the applicant have either a residential or business address in China. The applications are filed through Chinese agents or attorneys.[26] Documents filed with the patent or trademark office must be translated into Chinese.[27] China has two forms of patents: invention patents and utility patents. Invention patents are similar to standard patents in most countries and are valid for 20 years. Utility patents, which are for lower level inventions, are only valid for 10 years.[28] An inventor can apply for both an invention and a utility patent for the same invention. Designs (e.g., fashion, interior, building, architecture, engineering) can also be patented for up to 10 years.[29]

China is a member of the Patent Cooperation Treaty (PCT).[30] This means that if an organization from another member country, such as Australia, develops an invention, they can apply for an "international" patent through the PCT process, and then seek to apply this patent in China, as long as a similar patent does not already exist.[31]

Copyright Law and Process

Copyright refers to the rights possessed by an individual or organization that creates either literature, artistic, or scientific works. The creator is termed the lawful owner of those works as a result of their intellectual creation. An individual who holds the copyright has the sole right to halt others from copying, reproducing, publishing, or broadcasting their work without authorization.[32] Copyright in China is mainly governed by the Copyright Law of the PRC, which was introduced in 1990. The Implementing Rules for the Copyright Law of the PRC were created in 1991 and revised in October 2001 and January 2010.[33] The Chinese laws for copyright are similar to the copyright laws in many countries. For example, the duration of copyright lasts for the life of the author, plus 50 years. Copyright lasts for 50 years for movies and photographic material created by organizations.[34]

China is a member of the Berne Convention for the Protection of Literary and Artistic Works and the Universal Copyright Convention. As a requirement of this membership, the Chinese government introduced the *Regulations on Implementation of International Copyright Treaties* in 1992.[35] Copyright developed in any other country, which is also a member of the Berne Convention, such as Australia, can enjoy protection in both jurisdictions and it does not matter whether the works were first published in Australia or China, or any other member country. These regulations provide international holders of copyright, protection for their IP in China. The State Council in China passed the *Computer Software Protection Rules* in 1991.[36] As a result, software is treated as a form of literary work, and the rules around the registration, examination, and approval of computer software programmes in China are specified in that legislation.[37]

Copyright registration in China is voluntary.[38] Under Chinese law, a certificate of copyright registration only serves as prima facie evidence of rights. Despite this, it is still normally recommended to register copyright in China. Without registration of copyright, proving eligibility for the rights of copyright later on can be difficult. In addition, if there is an infringement, lodgment of a complaint with the Copyright Bureau is much easier when the copyright is already registered. Where there is a copyright infringement dispute, and this is taken to a court, the disputer will usually be required to provide other evidence, which proves that the registered owner owns the copyright. The court or authority handling the dispute may conduct a assessment of whether the copyright is actually owned by the registered owner.[39]

Trademark Law and Process

The Trademark Law of the PRC applies to trademark protection in China. It was first enacted in 1982 and was amended in 1993 and 2001.[40] The law was created to improve the administration of trademarks, specify the protection of trademark owners' exclusive rights, ensure and encourage producers to maintain the quality of their products or services (in order to preserve their trademark registration), and assist with protecting consumer interests.[41] China is also a member of the Paris Convention, which provides priority in trademark applications for applications submitted in China, by nationals of countries that are also Paris Convention members. To put this into effect, the government passed the *Provisional Regulations Governing Application for Priority Registration of Trademarks in China.*[42]

The State Administration of Industry and Commerce is responsible for administering trademarks in China. Approved trademark registrations are subsequently listed with the China Trademark Office.[43] IP Australia describes that as a "first-to-file" rule for obtaining trademark rights,[44] which means that the first person to file a trademark application will generally have priority over the trademark in China.[45] Therefore, organizations internationalizing to China are advised to file trademark applications at the outset. Enforcement of a trademark can occur without registration, although the process is less predictable, and tends to be more expensive.[46] Enforcing the trademark without registration will require the organization to prove that they were the creator of the trademark.

The IP Issues for Australian Businesses in China

The conditions described above suggest that most organizations internationalizing to China would be apprehensive about the protection of their IP and would be likely to react by focusing on the protection of their designs, products, or IP. The study participants were less anxious about these conditions than expected.

Architect Co (Case 3) expressed the view that, "*if someone ripped us off with a design, we probably would not pursue it through the legal system because of our perceived lack of trust in it.*" They did have an instance where a Chinese partner stole one of their architectural designs, and instead of pursuing the case through the legal system they chose not to work with them again. Evidently, the value of the copyright infringement was not sufficiently great to require disputation. The alternative market opportunities and costs, and time involved encouraged the organization not to pursue action.

Some organizations internationalizing to China may not consider IP to be very significant. For example, a mining and resources industry participant noted, "*we have nothing to copy, as we are just supplying resources to China*" (Case 6, Resources Co 1). Similarly, Agri Co (Case 11) said that IP was not a problem for the educational programs they ran in China for the agricultural industry because there was no motivation for other organizations to steal the IP that was at risk in this environment. Despite that, they were careful about what the information they provided when running their programs. This evidence indicates that it is possible to offer competitive products and services in the Chinese market that have low direct IP value.

Vat Co (Case 8) had a similar attitude, noting that it would be easy for competitors to steal the designs of their metal vats, but that: *"part of our competitive advantage is our quality, and the way we manufacture these; this is something that would be difficult for (Chinese) competitors to replicate, and therefore, at the present time, we are not so worried about our IP being stolen."* Retaining the IP, which results in product features such as quality in the home country is a good way of protecting IP in China.

Organizations should not be too confident, however, that they can fully protect their IP in foreign markets. For example Marketing Co (Case 9) felt that there was potential for the software they used as part of the business consultancy services to be copied. Rather than trying to control this, they minimized the consequences of IP theft by ensuring that their fees were sufficient to recoup their costs if their IP was stolen:

> *We have a number of software products we've developed that measure channel performance and market performance and, I guess, if we sold those in China anything could be copied, I guess. But how we go about stopping that I wouldn't have a clue. I guess we would just have to charge enough for it so that if they did do that it, then it doesn't really make any different to us. But we haven't gotten to that stage yet.*

A manufacturing industry participant was of the view that, as a result of China's accession to the WTO, it had enacted international standard IP laws and enforces them. On the other hand, they also noted that they did not want to reproduce one of their patented products in China because they were concerned about having their IP stolen:

> *In effect, part of our joint venture arrangement is that all information is available to ABC automotive. For IP here in Australia, we will protect and restrict the use of that and we put filters in place in our business so they won't be exposed to China. We also have a couple of our own patented technologies that we are selling in North America, and we've taken the decision not to take those to China yet because we're not comfortable that the protection is sufficient yet. (Case 14, Auto Interior Co)*

An IT industry participant responded to IP risks by building software-copying protection into their product, which protected their IP from being stolen. They also had mixed views about the impact of IP theft, believing that it was inevitable but, ultimately, also good marketing:

> *I think there might be some pirated versions out there. In some ways pirated versions is getting your brand out and about. Ultimately, you'll get them back. In accounting software, our research would suggest that the piracy is quite low because if you are running your business do you want your data files on something that is going to get corrupted? Probably not ... You are prepared to buy a video or a game or whatever. If it crashes, fine, but if you started to put a year's worth of accounting data in, you don't want it to crash.* (Case 26, Software Co)

Some companies did display a proactive approach to registering their trademarks, for example:

> *We only registered our logo and name as a trademark in China about 2 or 3 weeks ago. So we haven't used that in any way as yet. We haven't tested whether or not we have any grounds to use that. We've put it in place anyway.* (Case 3, Architect Co)

This organization also had put plans in place for dealing with trademark theft:

> *And I think it's good to be proactive about those things. You might not follow up on them but at least you can say, here's a nasty letter to them saying, "Don't use it again. If not, we'll take you to court," and most people at that point would probably not use your logo or something again. So, I totally agree. We have been registered now for a while, but we may never take anyone to court on it because we won't waste the money.* (Case 3, Architect Co)

The comments above suggest that many of the participants would not take legal action for IP or trademark theft because of the time and expense involved. Some participants had experienced problems as a result of reverse engineering of their products:

I have had problems with reverse engineering...so I warn clients to be very, very careful about handing over information unless they need to, unless they absolutely have to. They shouldn't hand it over and they shouldn't leave equipment there on site unless absolutely necessary, because it's too tempting for someone to try and take it apart. (Case 17, Law Co)

A participant from the book manufacturing industry utilized pricing differentials to reduce the risk of pirating, as part of their agreement with an SOE:

To some extent, because our product, which is locally produced, is low price, it's Chinese Yuan price—there is less incentive for pirates to pirate this because it's relatively cheap for people to buy. (Case 23, Book Co)

As the price of products and services increases in China—in accordance with inflation, increased quality expectations and disposable income of the Chinese—reducing the incentive to pirate by providing competitive pricing options will become increasingly attractive.

IP Protection in China for Australian Business

Analyzing the risks associated with IP and trademark theft is an important component of preparing for entry into China. For example, Vat Co (Case 8) had a competitive advantage in the Chinese market and a product design that could be stolen, however, they were protected, in part, by the difficulty of Chinese competitors matching their quality control processes, which were hard to imitate. Whilst businesses with an inherently low level of exposure to the risks associated with IP and trademark theft can internationalize with minimal protection, it is likely that, as the industry in China develops, the exposure to companies from these risks will increase. It is important for organizations operating in China relying on the difficulty of stealing the most valuable parts of the intellectual property and trademarks for their products or services in China to keep abreast of changes in the industry in China and reevaluate their level of risk exposure.

At this stage, because of the costs and trouble associated with pursuing infringements, the participants generally chose to either accept the risk or find other strategies to protect them. A novel approach adopted by an Australian surfboard lock manufacturer involved dividing the manufacturing process up into three separate activities and sourcing each of the three components from a different manufacturer to make it difficult to steal the entire product design.[47]

Strategies to Protect IP in China

The intellectual property literature and findings from the interview participants have been utilized to identify a list of strategies for protecting IP in China. These strategies will not completely prevent IP theft;[48] however, they will reduce the level of risk. It is expected that the environment for IP protection in China will improve, however, as China is focused on becoming an innovation-based economy and it can be expected to increase the protection of all IP rights. The strategies developed for protecting IP will now be discussed.

Strategy 1: Work Out What Your Intellectual Property Is?

The first step is to identify the relevant IP. IP is usually defined as "intangible property or intangible assets. This includes everything about the business that has value that cannot be reduced to a physical asset or to a monetary cash flow."[49] It can include "music, film, books and magazines, designs (clothing, products, architecture), software, games, and phone 'apps', or even management processes."[50] For industrial organizations, IP can include inventions, industrial processes, and management know-how, and for other businesses, it can include brand and image, business planning, and corporate strategy.[51] This analysis can lead to the conclusion that the organization does not have any IP at risk, as Resources Co 1 (Case 6) found when they examined the IP at risk in China.

Strategy 2: Work Out the Risk That Your IP Could Be Stolen?

Many kinds of intangible assets can be subject to IP theft; ranging from trademarks to logos, to books, designs, music, medicines, and movies.[52] Some IP will be unlikely to leave the organization because of the nature of the operations or the nature of the IP. An evaluation of the risk of IP theft should consider the likelihood of it occurring and the impact upon competitive advantage. For IP theft to be significant, it must both be likely and the impact substantial. Management know-how and processes, for example, is relatively easy to lose (i.e., by headhunting staff) and can have a significant impact on competitiveness.

Strategy 3: Act Local and Obtain the Traditional Legal Protection For IP in China

It is important to adopt locally relevant approaches to protecting IP in China. For example, it is important to stake a claim to the legal rights of IP immediately in China, if not before, and enforce them wherever and whenever possible. Obtaining the relevant protection for IP, including patents, trademarks, and copyrights is particularly important for organizations with IP-related assets. Applying for a patent to ensure that the organization has the right to use and produce the technology when introducing a new technology or product to China is important.[53] It is not uncommon for foreign organizations to introduce a technology to China and find that a Chinese organization has patented the technology first. If this goes unnoticed, the foreign organization could be sued in a Chinese court by the Chinese competitor, for using their own technology.[54] Therefore, organizations should seek to apply for a patent as per the processes described above.

Strategy 4: Go Beyond Traditional Protection Measures

A range of other approaches also exist for protecting IP in China. These include: secrecy and disclosure agreements; licensing and trade secrecy agreements, trade secrecy agreements with employees and joint venture partners, as well as encryption and other forms of data protection.[55] Manufacturing and licensing contracts that articulate the scope of their IP, as well as the financial penalties if that IP is stolen can be helpful also. The Chinese version of the contract should be vetted by a Western lawyer fluent in Chinese.

Strategy 5: Choose Your Entry Mode for China Taking into Account Internalized Production Modes

It is better for organizations faced with a high IP theft risk to produce those products themselves than to contract manufacture or to license their production to local Chinese organizations. This can be considered to be internalization of production. According to Dunning's eclectic model,[56] where the transaction costs of creating, monitoring, and enforcing contracts in regard to property rights in a country are high, firms should internalize their production rather than license or contract manufacture it to other producers. A relevant example involves a producer of large earthmoving equipment, which licensed the production of motors for a particular model of earthmoving equipment to a Chinese organization.[57] The producer of the equipment made their IP available to the Chinese company who began parallel production and are expected to ultimately overtake the original producer and become the number one manufacturer in the world.[58] Had the original company internalized the production of these motors in the first place, this situation may not have arisen. Therefore, it is vital that organizations choose entry modes that protect their IP.

Strategy 6: Design Products and Price with IP Theft in Mind

Organizations can reduce IP theft by competing only in value segments, and not premium segments.[59] For instance, in China, per capita income is low at around US$8,394 purchasing power parity (PPP) in 2011.[60] Therefore, if an organization offers expensive products there will be a desire and, hence, a market for Chinese organizations to copy it. However, if organizations designed products, which were priced at levels the average Chinese consumer could afford, there will be less likelihood of the product being copied. Book Co (Case 23) found that keeping the price of their products down resulted in a reduction in the incentive for piracy.

Strategy 7: Develop Harmonious Relationships with Staff and Employees

IP leakage can result from disgruntled staff,[61] or from staff moving between organizations. Organizations should try to develop harmonious relationships with staff and encourage their loyalty to the organization to reduce this risk.

Strategy 8: If You Are Renting Your Office Facilities, Check Them to Ensure That They Are Not Bugged or Monitored

IP theft can take many forms in China. In one interesting case, the offices of a foreign organization were bugged with recording devices by the local Chinese government, who subsequently shared the knowledge with SOEs.[62] To prevent this situation from happening, organizations should be careful about the ways in which their IP can be exposed. This may include inspecting premises to make sure that bugging has not occurred.

Strategy 9: Wall Off Core Manufacturing Processes to Trusted Employees

One of the ways in which the IP can be better protected is to partition their core manufacturing processes off to their most trusted employees.[63] This ensures that only trusted employees have access to important information.

Strategy 10: Manage Passwords, Codes, and Access to Data

Theft of proprietary and code data is especially likely for software and services businesses. Organizations who wish to protect this type of information should prevent employees from taking files or memory devices from demarcated zones. In addition, organizations should prevent the transfer of files outside of the organization's server.

Strategy 11: Develop Relationships with the Government and a Locally Based Law Firm

Developing relationships with government bodies in China may assist in protecting the technology of foreign organizations. For example, if a foreign organization has a good relationship with the Chinese government, the government can assist with the protection of their IP. Through these relationships, foreign organizations can also lobby the government and communicate the message that protecting IP rights is integral to the development of an innovation-based economy. In addition to developing a relationship with political bodies, organizations should also seek to develop relationships with a local law firm that is either Chinese or international. This law firm can more appropriately advise on IP issues, better understand the organization's situation, and can pursue legal issues if they arise. This also signals to other firms that the organization is serious about pursuing legal issues if their IP is stolen.

Strategy 12: Break Up Research and Development Cells Across Multiple Locations

Organizations based in developed countries have traditionally located their research and development (R&D) in developed countries, which have an R&D culture, good education levels, and infrastructure. However, this trend is now changing, with organizations starting to locate their R&D operations in China.[64] To deal with this issue, foreign organizations should locate their R&D in small cells across multiple locations, to ensure that entire R&D efforts cannot be copied. Potential IP thieves would then only have the access to a segment of the IP, which may not be useful on its own.

Strategy 13: Split Up Parts of the Production Across Multiple Locations

Apart from splitting up key R&D cells, organizations can spread their production across various locations to ensure that a competitor cannot copy the whole product or production process. This approach was adopted by an Australian producer of surfboard straps, as mentioned earlier.[65] In addition, having the most crucial element of the product produced outside of China would further reduce the risk. Products for which the IP has already been utilized can be assembled in China, which reduces the ability of other organizations to copy the process for producing the product, although, this can be an expensive option. Alternatively, product components could be produced through various suppliers in China, and other countries, and sent to another country, such as Thailand, for final assembly.

Strategy 14: Incorporate a Mandatory Service Element into the Product

Products accompanied by and requiring after-sales consulting services, product support, and ongoing maintenance are least attractive to property theft. Similarly, requiring customers to put in software codes annually to maintain the functionality of the product can reduce piracy.

Strategy 15: Make Your Invention Difficult to Copy, and Do Not Train Your Chinese Partner on Your Designs

If intangible assets cannot easily be copied, IP thieves in China will usually wait to be trained by the foreign business.[66] They will rarely appropriate foreign technology on their own initiative.[67] Chinese companies are frequently motivated to work with foreign businesses by the desire to acquire technology, trade secrets, and know-how via training from the owner of the IP. This training can occur when Chinese companies work with foreign businesses in technology licensing projects, joint ventures, original equipment manufacturing, and product design and development agreements.

Strategy 16: Keep on Innovating!

The final strategy is to "keep on innovating" as fast as possible.[68] Copycat competitors will not be able to keep up with innovative organizations and the technology they develop. Once an organization has introduced a new technology, the next innovation should already be on the drawing board and have an anticipated release date.

Organizations should always keep on paying attention to IP protection when operating in China and should implement as many protection strategies as practical and possible. By implementing these strategies, organizations will develop an overall preemptive and proactive strategy, which will go some way in managing the IP risks in China.

Conclusion

There is a general consensus that organizations should be concerned that their IP will be stolen if they internationalize to China. It is important for organizations to be careful not to hand over their IP to partnering organizations or competitors; however, the fears about loss of IP are overstated. An Australian legal industry participant offered this opinion:

> It's an overreaction to say you can't do business with China because they don't enforce intellectual property. And we actually recovered a debt in China through the court system for a client recently, so that was quite an interesting step forward. I must check up whether we've actually collected the money, but the main thing is, at least the court gave an order that the Chinese party had to pay over money to the foreign party. (Case 17, Law Co)

There is no question that management of IP is a critical issue for foreign businesses internationalizing into China. Without an understanding and knowledge of the IP landscape, foreign business managers will be unable to correctly identify the risk or develop techniques for addressing it. The research conducted for this book has determined that the IP issues in China cannot be ignored, and there are many cases where foreign organizations have had their IP stolen. However, as the interview participant from Law Co stated, it is an overreaction not to refrain from business in China because of potential IP issues. The IP protection laws in China should enable foreign organizations to be more confident about taking their IP to China. Organizations operating in China should utilize the approaches mentioned in this chapter to protect themselves against IP threats. To help stimulate enforcement of these laws, foreign organizations operating in China should take all opportunities to promote their legal rights when liaising with government officials and the organizations they deal with. It is very likely that, as China continues to develop its economic policies in line with global approaches, the effectiveness of its IP rights laws for both foreign and Chinese organizations will also develop.

CHAPTER 7

Motivations, Planning, and Strategies for China

Internationalization of organizations has been the subject of considerable investigation. As this book has demonstrated, internationalizing to China requires different processes and results in experiences different to the internationalization experience associated with other countries. The differences are due to the rate of economic, social and political developments in China, as well as some of the unique characteristics of each of these influences.

The process of internationalizing to China requires answers to a number of questions, which include, "Why internationalize to China?" "Should the organization plan for internationalization?" and "What is the best strategy for the internationalization?" The preceding chapters have demonstrated that China is an attractive location for many industries; however, internationalizing there involved significant challenges and risk. For this reason, the decision to internationalize must be based on clearly identifiable benefits. The motivation to internationalize can reflect proactive or reactive anticipated benefits. Both types of benefits will be explored in this chapter.

This chapter will consider how much planning the research participants invested in their decision to internationalize to China and how frequently decisions were reactive, rather than proactive. The participant's most popular strategies for internationalizing will then be discussed and the chapter will conclude with a consideration of the level of customer focus integrated into their strategies.

Motivations for Internationalization to China

Motivations influence the way a firm configures and selects the scale and scope of its operations, and assembles and allocates its tangible and intangible resources to international markets.[1] Organizations will usually increase their level of internationalization over time; born global organizations are still a rarity. In addition, the decision to internationalize is usually the result of several different motivations. These motivations will result from a variety of causes. For example, lower production costs may motivate an organization to move their production to another country, as would the ability to leverage the organization's strategic assets in China, or a desire to pursue the growth opportunities in the Chinese market.[2] How an organization internationalizes will also vary between organizations, depending upon the industry, circumstances, and internal resources. Despite this, it is usually possible to identify common patterns of internationalization.[3] Organizations located in a small home country market may start exporting because the domestic market is too small for them to achieve economies of scale that make their products competitive. This situation is typical for many industries in Australia, due to the size of the domestic population (22.6 million people).[4] In order to build and grow the domestic economy, the Australian government has encouraged organizations to internationalize and, in 2011, goods and services exports constituted 21.1% of Australia's total gross domestic product (GDP).[5] Other reasons for internationalization are often based on the strategic thinking of management. Irrespective of the source of the motivation, determination, international orientation, commitment to succeed in international markets and tolerance and learning through failure are essential ingredients.

Sources of competitive advantage that will support internationalization can include financial resources, unique products, technological advantages, or exclusive information that can be exploited in international markets,[6] tax benefits, and economies of scale.[7] These competitive organizations will often create a stimulus for internationalization, as the organization attempts to make better use of the underlying capabilities.[8]

Similarly, there are a range of reactive motivations that will encourage an organization to internationalize. These motivations include the competitive pressures in the global industry, chasing suppliers and technology, saturated domestic markets, declining domestic sales, and excess production capacity.[9] Organizations internationalizing as a result of a reactive motivation may effectively be forced to internationalize. Needing to internationalize, however, will not automatically create the capacity to be successful in internationalization.

The key proactive motivations for the participants in the study to internationalize included the perceived size of the Chinese market, China's need for Western technologies, the benefit of international scale marketing, the opportunities offered by the Chinese market, especially the growing middle-class segment, and the opportunities to increase economies of scale. Twenty-five firms in the study had proactive motivations to internationalize.

The study participant's reactive motivations included a diminishing Australian market and the reduction in protection provided by the Australian government. Other motivations included encouragement or demand to enter the market from customers or clients already operating in China, invitations from potential customers to provide services in China, chasing suppliers who had moved to China, or an inability to compete in Australia with globally produced products and services. Government departments and government-funded bodies in the study experienced reactive motivations resulting from China's increasingly important economic influence, and its market growth and future market potential. A total of 15 organizations in the study utilized a reactive motivation. These motivations will now be considered in greater detail.

Growth Opportunities

Growth opportunities were a major driver for the study participant's decisions to enter China (Cases 2, 7–11, 14, 18, 26, 29, 30, 38–40). These decisions were mostly influenced by proactive motivations; however, some participants made the decision in response to the reactive motivation that their market in Australia was diminishing. The participants also noted that China had demonstrated its stability and suitability as an investment destination to the international community, having maintained its "Open Door Policy" for over 30 years. Vat Co (Case 8) commented that they did not want to invest in China until they knew that China's economy was stable, and growing:

> *Yes, that took a while to filter through. What drove it was when they finally started managing their economy sensibly and growth started to happen in China … until the economy actually developed to have steam, no one was interested in investing there. But by the time we got to the early 90s, it was evident that that was genuinely happening. The only question was, was it sustainable? No idea of the answer to that.*

Other participants considered China's market to represent a huge potential, but that it was not fully mature or developed yet. Agri Co (Case 11) believed that China's market for their products was still in a developmental stage, and represented very attractive first mover opportunities for Australian organizations. The Chinese consumption of their agricultural products was approximately 23 kg per person per year; whilst, at in Australia it was 100 kg, and the world average consumption was 90 kg per person. Other participants identified the growth in areas including building and construction, books, food, tourism, education, transportation, and manufacturing. These were considered to be a result of Chinese consumers' increased wealth, the increases in size of the middle-class, and an increase in demand for Western products. Hotel Co (Case 5) focused on attracting Chinese tourists to their Australian hotel, as Chinese consumers had developed an appreciation for overseas travel.

The reactive motivations resulting from the limited size of the Australian market also included a proactive motivation based on the size of the Chinese market, which was over 50 times the size of the Australian market.[10] "… *the two primary drivers: our customer base and growth opportunities*" (Case 28, Brake Co). Bank Co 2 (Case 39) considered the Chinese market to be large and had large-scale plans for China. China's restrictions on foreign banks, which required them to meet profitability standards and operate in China for 3 years before they could apply for licenses to provide more business services in China, were a significant restriction. Foreign banks commenced operations in China providing services in their home country currency, and then become licensed later to provide services in local Chinese currency. The initial operations can be fairly modest—even only a representative office. As one of the banking company participants: "*I think there was always a view that China was somewhere that was obviously big, obviously growing, and we would keep a rep office in place … just to be there*" (Case 39, Bank Co 2). This indicates that, in addition to meeting the profitability and time in market requirements, the knowledge and understanding of the market gained was a valuable contribution to the establishment of the more developed operations that would follow.

Customer Base and Markets

The participants expressed interest in the various types of customer segments in the Chinese market, as well as its overall size. The attractive segments included both business-to-business customers, such as auto components manufacturers selling to other manufacturers, and business to customer consumers. These markets offer different characteristics to those available in other countries, such as the rate of increase in wealth, and "*new tastes*" of Chinese consumers. One participant focused on China because it was the 5th largest market in their industry, and was to become the largest by 2020 (Case 1, Lab Co). A number of participants already identified China as their largest market, accounting for 19% of Resources Co 1 (Case 6)'s total revenue and 40% of Build Co (Case 16)'s total revenue. University Co 1 (Case 12) and 2 (Case 25), and TAFE Co (Case 38) experienced a huge demand from Chinese students for Australian education. These students were attracted to Australian education because it was cheaper than the equivalent education in the UK or US and was believed to be of a good standard and contribute to good job prospects.[11] Wool Co (Case 22), a producer of niche woollen blankets, decided to export to China because Chinese consumers were increasingly able to afford their product and "*like the product, probably more so than Australian consumers*". Wool Co (Case 22) even concluded that they would charge Chinese consumers more for their products in China than they did in Australia, as the increasing wealth of Chinese consumers meant that they would not flinch at paying a high price for a quality product.

Strategic Motivations

A number of the study participants also had strategic motivations for being in China. Some had an *"Asia Pacific"* focus and strategy, and it made sense for them to internationalize there, if not a necessity,[12] as China was the largest market in the region (Case 2, Bank Co 1; Case 11, Agri Co; Case 24, Engineering Co; and Case 35, Gambling Co). Book Co (Case 23) took a global approach, and wanted to publish their books in the key languages of the world, which naturally included China. Bank Co 2 (Case 39) internationalized to China as part of a strategy to be *"Australia's largest world bank."* This did not prove to be sufficient to achieve this strategy, and another Australian bank is much more international and global than them. Agri Co (Case 11) internationalized to China to remain competitive because its industry had positioned itself to be in China. The two principal objectives for its Chinese activities was to demonstrate that they were globally competitive by operating in China and to be ready to take full advantage of the perceived future potential of the Chinese market. This organization had developed the view that China is an emerging primary product producer, and Australia's primary producers needed to develop Chinese operations:

> *It's the whole industry's position. We are definitely only following the exporters, but we are also doing our own research and we know that it's a huge market potential there—a lot of opportunities there. So the whole industry agrees that China has got great potential. And now, Chinese are actually the third-largest producers, but in the past few years Australian exporters have realized that, and they have actually moved to high-end products, the more value-added products which China cannot produce themselves.* (Case 11, Agri Co)

Some participants reacted to the economic conditions in Australia by entering China, especially the high cost of manufacturing and the reduction in government protectionist policies. Some participants identified this as a proactive response to developing trends. Auto Interior Co (Case 14) stated that locating their WOFE in China was part of an *"offensive, defensive strategy"* which may prove to be important because car manufacturing in Australia may cease in the future as a result of decreased tariff protection. Auto Interior Co viewed China as the next big location for car manufacturing in the world:

> *In our industry, in the automotive industry, where we looked at where the global growth was going to take place, it's nearly all in the Asia Pacific Region, and of that, in the next few years it's nearly all in China. That, coupled with the fact that we are under extreme pressure in this market with reducing volumes of cars being built, significant pressure on costs and the threat from the Asia Pacific competitors to our business, we felt that a defensive strategy, or an offensive-defence strategy, if you like, was best to get up to China, get our own position in the market there, and if we then need to bring product out from China we are actually bringing it from our organization in China and not outsourcing business to another supplier. So, for us it was taking advantage of the growth, but also protecting our business here in Australia.*

Exploitation/Transference of Technology in China

A number of the participants were primarily motivated by the opportunity to transfer their technology to China. Machine Co developed a technology (which has been patented in Australia, China, and other countries in the world) to cut wood in a more efficient manner, and was motivated to internationalize to China because no other competitor was providing that technology in the Chinese market. Their secondary motivation was the large customer base in China:

> *I thought China was a good place because I think there is a great need for our technology there and I think they'll like it and understand it, and of course it's a big market, so that has appealed to me.* (Case 30, Machine Co)

Lower Production Costs

The majority of the manufacturing organizations involved in the survey were motivated to internationalize to China by the "*lower production costs*" (Case 7, Metal Co; Case 8, Vat Co; Case 14, Auto Interior Co; Case 28, Brake Co; Case 32, Chain Co). A number of the other organizations were also motivated by the access to cheaper suppliers in China (Case 13, Pallet Co and Case 40, Retail Co). Retail Co was "*forced*" to move their manufacturing base from Europe to China, because of China's lower labor costs and a labor-intensive nature of their industry. They found that their Chinese operations produced products at a much lower cost than in Europe or Australia. An automotive manufacturing participant experienced a similar motivation:

Wages, they play an important role, but I don't know to what great percentage it plays an important role. Like, if we take an average hourly rate for an operator in Australia, it's something like about $15–$18. An average employee in China would be paid 8–10 RMB, which is $1.50. So, it makes a big difference. It's a big difference in the cost. (Case 28, Brake Co)

To Provide Services to Australian Businesses Internationalizing to China

The motivations of the public sector organizations in the study tended to be more relationship-based. Local government departments were also seeking links and relationships, to share information and also to assist businesses in their jurisdiction. Gov Co (Case 10) was motivated to set up an office in China, because the state level government had pursued sister city relationships with Tianjin in China:

Both NSW and Victoria had established sister state relationships. Back in 1980, the then Lord Mayor, I think, had visited China and felt that we needed to do something and connect with them. There was a relationship between the Port of Tianjin and the Port of Melbourne through some collaboration or cooperation. And it was on the basis of that that the Foreign Affairs Ministry of China suggested that Tianjin would be an appropriate city. (Case 10, Gov Co)

Other participants such as Lab Co (Case 1), Law Co (Case 17), Trade Finance Co (Case 36), Fibre Co (Case 19), and Agri Co (Case 11) were motivated to internationalize to China to provide services to Australian businesses operating there. Law Co provided both legal and investment advice in China, and Trade Finance Co provided short-term finance, and payment options such as letters of credit. Lab Co, Fibre Co, and Agri Co were more focused on providing industry-based assistance, information and seminars, as the following example from Agri Co (Case 11) explains:

> *But in China we take the Australian specialists, and sometimes company representatives, to do seminars, to give technical presentations—sometimes industry-wide presentations—to get to know more people and to kind of promote these Australian products to a more wider audience.*

Led by Clients or Encouraged by Contacts

The participants that were motivated to enter China by external agents were most frequently encouraged by their clients, asking them to provide services in China, although some were also encouraged by their contacts to take advantage of the Chinese market. The clients of these organizations were either Australian or international organizations. Organizations motivated by clients included Architect Co (Case 3), Build Co (Case 16), Engineering Co (Case 24), IT Co (Case 20), Responsibility Co (Case 33), Medic Co (Case 31), Trade Finance Co (Case 36), and Law Co (Case 17). All were service businesses. Responsibility Co was even encouraged by senior academics and Communist Party of China (CPC) members to establish operations in China. Architect Co's internationalization to China was a result of their relationships with clients in Australia, who invited them to work with them in China. This organization then took on other types of work and developed new networks in China. Medic Co was not invited by their clients; however, one of their industry colleagues encouraged them to investigate the opportunities in China, which led them there. Therefore, it appears that relationships and connections were an important source of reactive motivation for the participants to internationalize. The following example from Engineering Co (Case 24) is illustrative:

> *That started for us in the 90s and it was really driven by working with Singapore developers who were investing in China, and they would*

ask us to work on projects with them. So, instead of trying to find clients on the ground in China, this was a big opportunity for us, but a minefield as well, but we'd go with some comfort and to minimize our risk as well, by going with clients we'd already worked with before.

In summary, a range of motivations for internationalization to China were apparent, both proactive and reactive, and the type of industry was sometimes an indicator of the type of motivation used. The key reasons for the participant's internationalization to China were opportunities for business growth, the stability of the economy, opportunities for market development or potential to sell products, the limitations of the Australian market (due to size), and the customer base and markets in China. Strategic issues and the overall strategy of the organization were also major motivators for some organizations. Most motivations were proactive, except for those organizations that were reacting to competitive situations. Exploitation and transference of technology, and lower production costs were the motivators affecting the manufacturing participants or those looking for cheaper suppliers. Finally, being led by clients or encouraged by contacts were major motivators for business-to-business service organizations (the building and construction industry participants were predominantly motivated in this way). Some participants were also invited by their local government.

Planning Processes Used to Enter China

The literature and practitioner experience strongly supports a formal, rational planning process for entry into international markets. Despite this, the participants frequently did not utilize a formal market entry planning process, although some did. The following discussion considers the levels of planning adopted by the participants.

No Plans

Thirteen of the organizations investigated used an "ad hoc" approach to enter the Chinese market, or what was referred to as "no plans." The participants indicated that this approach was taken in response to opportunities presented by clients, colleagues, or associates that had business and contacts in China. These clients and contacts tended to drive the internationalization plan. This process has been described in the previous section; *motivations to internationalize*. This "no plans" internationalization process was characterized by limited control (relying heavily on emergent opportunities) and a lack of proactive thought. The following example from Architect Co (Case 3) provides an example of this process:

> *We had some good relationships with some architects in Australia at the time and they were starting to work in China. ... So we kind of just hopped along via some Australian colleagues, and that kind of got us involved. From that we did a couple of projects, met some people over there, started to get a better feel for it. Chris started to go over there a couple of times and that was really how it started. A bit of luck really.*

Build Co (Case 16) took a similar approach to Architect Co. They did not plan and were motivated to internationalize as a reactive approach to unsolicited orders from clients they served in Australia:

> *It came about with one of our clients that we worked for in Australia. One of our international clients had a project in China that they asked us if we could help them with. So, that was in the mid-90s. So in '93 we did some design work for them on their new investment, a new facility that they were setting up.* (Case 16, Build Co)

Some participants preferred not to plan because of the uncertainty and changes occurring in the Chinese market. The dynamic and continuing changes in the Chinese market do provide an argument for taking a flexible, emergent approach[13] when entering China. Architect Co (Case 3) did not have a formal business plan, and relied on emergent opportunities to deliver on a set of basic objectives in China:

> *I wouldn't say we have a business plan—but we have like a series of maybe half a dozen dot points that are our mission in China, or what we're trying to do. That's been a good approach for us in the last 12–18*

months, because every 3 months something changes and the dot points kind of become a bit irrelevant after a while. I think that's probably why we haven't gone and prepared a 30-page business plan about everything we need to do, when something will happen in 3 months and you have to change your whole direction.

Certainly there was no shortage of organizations that identified themselves as having "no strategies." The tactical approach that many of them adopted was based on trial and error and a steep learning curve:

I think it's fair to say we didn't have a strategy we went in tactically, we basically ... were invited in by a business partner on the basis that they were looking for experts in large systems for banks. For several years we worked via that particular partner in China. (Case 20, IT Co)

It is interesting to note that, apart from the work that IT Co did for major banks in China, they did not do any other work for other clients there. This may reflect the lack of planning for their internationalization. Other participants had existing relationships in China, which provided advice and compensated for the lack of planning and allowed them to develop their business in China at a good rate:

So, I guess that's how it evolved. But it really came out of the relationship that existed between what the company wanted ... and then the ambitions of our companies. Our business had already moved down the logistics space, and a similar business in China wanted to go there, albeit it quite a few years behind in pursuing that. (Case 4, Parcel Co)

Relationships or *guānxi* was important in internationalizing this logistics business to China, which confirms it is important to have the right contacts when internationalizing. Prior research suggests it is common for business service providers (i.e., taxation advisory, accounting and management consulting) to follow their clients to foreign locations,[14] usually providing the same services they did in their home country. This may provide both an immediate market and the foundation for internationalization plans; reducing the uncertainty associated with internationalization and providing a focus for the development of expertise, skills, and reputation in China.

It is surprising that most (11 out of 13) of the organizations with "no plans" were successful in China. The main reason for their success may be they already had a client in the Chinese market, and therefore were guaranteed some support and revenue generation at the outset. This would have been a distinct advantage over organizations entering the market without prearranged customers. Of the two participants that were not successful, Architect Co described their entry without a plan as having mixed success and Lab Co (Case 1) were unable to attract customers and referred to itself as a "*mini-China-tragic.*" Some of the participants which did not plan and successfully entered China, also conducted little or no market research, as the following quote describes:

> *No we didn't have a formal rational plan. It was pretty much; we talked amongst ourselves here and said that this could be an opportunity; we didn't try and research it like that. We knew that they'd be needing a lot of oxygen and nitrogen and those sorts of things if their industries were growing the way they were reported to be growing, we didn't have to research that. Given that is the case they should require storing of gas and they're going to have transport from one place to another from where it's produced to where it needs to be stored so it can be used in an industrial process. That didn't need to be researched. We didn't know the magnitude of the competition that might be on the ground in China, we just guessed that. I don't know that it could have been researched. I suppose you could have researched these things possibly in China at the time but that looked a far more complicated exercise to us than just jumping in and having a go at it.* (Case 6, Vat Co)

Formal Planning

In contrast to the 11 participants who successfully entered China without a business plan, 27 of the participants had some form of a strategic plan for entering China. These organizations utilized formal market entry plans to generate internal support and secure capital either internally or in external capital markets. Law Co recommended that their clients have a business plan with an explanation of time frames when entering China:

I think a very clear strategic plan, a business plan that they stick to, rather than just going up there and talking to everybody in an optimistic way and everything they hear is optimistic and they come back and they put a good spin on everything for a board of directors. It probably needs to be a bit more realistic about what's achievable. And the timeframe often, I think, boards of directors don't understand or are not properly briefed to understand that really, there might not be a return on investment for 5 years and that's quite a long time in Australian business. (Case 17, Law Co)

These findings demonstrate that market entry planning for entry into China needs to be aligned to the specific conditions there. Most of the participants with a business plan incorporated elements specifically reflecting the conditions in China, as the following quote demonstrates:

So, obviously you need a strategy. You've got to have a strategy, you've got to have a plan, you've got to have milestones. I want to know the market that we're going to be working in by this date. I want to know who will potentially be our customers by that date. I want to know who will be our suppliers to help us make our product by that date. I want to know who we're going to buy our raw materials from by that date. I want to know what the government due diligence is or the legal, the set up, the registration, insurance—all those things by that date. So, have a corporate business plan, supported by a corporate marketing plan, to support a corporate manufacturing plan. If you don't do it in that order…then I believe you will fail. (Case 32, Chain Co)

Interestingly, Chain Co's approach also contains the requirement for customers, which appeared to be the principal ingredient for success amongst the participants such as Build Co, who successfully entered China without a plan. In contrast, Chain Co formally identified the development of customers, along with the other milestones for a planned

Table 7.1. Success of Organizations That Planned

Successful		Mixed success
Bank Co1	Brake Co	Parcel Co
Hotel Co	Logistics Co	Metal Co
Resources Co 1	Machine Co	Fibre Co
Marketing Co	Chain Co	Software Co*
Gov Co	Resources Co 2	
Uni Co 1	Gambling Co	
Auto Interior Co	Trade Finance Co	
Flower Co	Uni Co 3	
Auto Components Co	TAFE Co	
Wool Co	Bank Co 2	
Book Co	Retail Co	
Uni Co 2		

*Failed and withdrew from the market in 2010.

project, whilst Build Co did not plan either. This clearly indicates that success in China can be achieved with either a formal or an emergent business plan,[15] although having identified customers seems to be a critical success factor. Furthermore, Build Co's timing was a major contributor to its success, whilst Chain Co was less reliant on the specific advantages available at that particular point in time.

Twenty-three of the twenty-seven organizations that had a market entry plan for China were successful, and achieved their objectives, as demonstrated in Table 7.1. The other four organizations had mixed success (Parcel Co, Metal Co, and Fibre Co), or their venture was on track, but had not delivered a profit (Software Co). Software Co's China operations continued to be unsuccessful and, in 2010, they shut down their Chinese operations.

Customer Focus of Strategies for China

This section presents the customer focus strategies that the participants used when entering China. Generally, these strategies strongly reflected the motivations to internationalize. The strategies can be categorized into: organizations servicing the Chinese market, organizations servicing international businesses (including Australian) in China, and organizations using China as a manufacturing or supply base to service Australia, international markets or China.

Table 7.2. Organizations Servicing Chinese Consumers or Business-to-Business Customers in China

Organizations servicing consumers in China	Organizations servicing business-to-business customers in China
Bank Co 1	Resources Co
Flower Co	Metal Co
Wool Co	Vat Co
Book Co	Marketing Co
Software Co	Agri Co
Gambling Co	Auto Interior Co
Bank Co 2	Auto Components Co
Hotel Co	Fiber Co
Uni Co 1	Paint Co
Uni Co 2	IT Co
Uni Co 3	Medic Co
TAFE Co	Machine Co
	Responsibility Co
	Resources Co 2

Organizations Servicing the Chinese Consumers or Business-to-Business Customers in China

The participants in this category were market-seekers and focused on obtaining consumers, customers, or clients in the Chinese market. They came from a variety of industries, as shown in Table 7.2. As the table indicates, some organizations focused on servicing Chinese consumers and had adapted their products to the Chinese market. This approach is consistent with one of the central tenets of international strategy—the localization and adaptation of strategy and products to local conditions.[16] Where the cultural and legal requirements of a country are influential, the local dimensions of strategy must be adapted to those conditions. For example, Book Co and Software Co produced books and software in the Chinese language for this market, even though they could have saved costs by focusing on the English-speaking segment of the market, to ensure that they were valued by all segments of the market. Flower Co (Case 15) took a similar approach and produced flowers in China that appealed to that market:

> *We realized that it would be many years before the Chinese got to take Australian flowers on board in a big way because they're used to chrysanthemums and roses and carnations, the more traditional flowers,*

and this is a different look, different smells and so there wasn't going to be a cut flower business for a long time. However, what is also saleable in China is pot plant business because that's very much a Chinese culture of giving a gift of a pot plant.

Bank Co 1 and 2 did not adjust strategies or products, only adapting signage and marketing to local conditions and continuing to offer the same services as in Australia, where local regulations allowed them. Similarly, Hotel Co, Uni Co 1, 2, 3, and TAFE Co's did not adapt to the local market but instead, attempted to attract Chinese consumers/students into the Australian environment and their generic services were suited to the Chinese market. This approach is a reflection of global level strategy, in which a standard product is designed to provide sufficient appeal to a global marketplace (in the case of Uni Co 1, 2 and 3 and TAFE Co).[17] The economy of scale resulting from servicing several markets with the same product improves the ability to compete on the basis of price.

Some of the participants focused on selling their products and services to other international businesses located in China and, therefore, did not need to adapt their product. These organizations produced internationally standardized products such as steel, paint, auto interiors, and components.

Organizations Servicing International Businesses (including Australian) in China

Organizations servicing international businesses in China (foreign businesses operating in China) may also adopt market-seeking behavior. One such participant preferred not to service Chinese clients to avoid competing on the basis of price with low-cost local organizations offering discounted *"Asian prices"* (Build Co, Case 16) because international prices were much higher. They also found it difficult to deal with Chinese clients as the following quotation indicates:

We have dabbled in local clients. I think local industry using foreign-service providers in our line of business isn't quite matured enough yet that they really value it. Whereas other companies are there because of the huge China market, we are there because of the foreign companies that are there. It is a good, safe model. Certainly one of the main difficulties you have with local companies is getting paid. So, that's the problem. We tested that. We re-tested it a few years later, and we will keep re-testing it. But it is still a problem. They have a problem for valuing and paying for services you might provide, for example, in Building we charge a management service fee, on top of the price of the building, and some local clients don't understand that.

The organizations servicing international businesses in China are listed in Table 7.3.

Organizations Using China as a Manufacturing or Supply Base to Service Australian and International Markets or China

Several participants utilized China as a manufacturing or supply base to take advantage of cheaper factor endowments and centralizing all production in China to supply multiple markets and to achieve high economies of scale.[18] Some of these organizations used their Chinese operations to supply the Chinese market as well, including Vat Co, Auto Interior Co, Auto Components Co, Flower Co, and Chain Co. These organizations were motivated to enter China to gain advantage of lower cost operations and because it was a good location from which to export to international markets. For example, not only does China have several airfreight hubs, the Shanghai port is one of the largest in the world.

Table 7.3. Organizations Servicing International Businesses in China

Lab Co	Import/export Co
Bank Co 1	Engineering Co
Architect Co	Brake Co
Parcel Co Vat Co	Logistics Co
Build Co	Chain Co
Gov Co	Trade and Finance Co
Flower Co	Bank Co 2
Law Co	

Other participants chose to use China as a supply base. For example, Pallet Co manufactured their pallets in China because of the access to cheaper nails there, and Retail Co purchased their products at a lower cost in China for sale in Australia. Apart from Flower Co, all of these participants used standardized strategies and products in their Chinese operations.

In summary, it can be concluded that a clear identification of the customer in China to be serviced and their needs is central to a successful Chinese market entry.

Conclusion

The participants demonstrated both proactive and reactive motivations for entering China. The key motivations included growth opportunities, accessing a much larger market, response to industry trends, exploitation and transference of technology, reduction in production costs, taking up the opportunity to provide services to other businesses internationalizing to China, and responding to the requests of customers already in China. The majority (27) of the participants had planned their internationalization to China. The others indicated that they had no formal planning process or a strategic objective to internationalize to China. Most of the participants were successful in entering China, even those participants, which did not formally plan their entry.

The participants that did plan appeared to be slightly more successful. Of the 27 organizations that had used strategic planning, three of them achieved mixed success, and one failed. These outcomes suggest that planning is not sufficient for success in China; a deep understanding of the market is also required. In addition, it was found that the participants that utilized a reactive strategy were also successful, possibly because they already had a client base, which supported their internationalization into China. Depending on the level of success they achieved in internationalization with their client support, some participants then choose to branch out and serve other clients. The participants also chose a variety of strategic objectives, which included servicing Chinese customers (both within and outside China), servicing international businesses in China (including Australian organizations in China), and servicing the

Australian market with either a product produced in China, or by purchasing products in China for use or sale in Australia.

These findings demonstrate that both proactive and reactive strategies can lead to successful internationalization into China, that success is more likely with the support of existing customers, and that a range of strategic objectives can be utilized for successful entry into the Chinese market.

CHAPTER 8

Entry Mode and Location Choices in China

The success of an international venture is influenced by the choice of entry mode; different entry modes offer different advantages and disadvantages. Each mode also requires different resources and time commitments and entails different risks. Factors such as culture, the political and business environments, and the skills of the manager in internationalizing all have a bearing on the correct entry mode choice. This chapter discusses the various entry modes the research participants choose when internationalizing to China and describes some of the issues they experienced with those entry modes. This chapter also considers the impact of location on entry mode choice and the success of internationalization. This includes a consideration of whether the selection of the wrong location can significantly disadvantage internationalization.[1]

Why Are Different Entry Modes Chosen?

Entry modes are usually the cornerstone of an organization's market entry strategy to another country.[2] An entry mode is defined as "an institutional arrangement that makes possible the entry of a firm's products, technology, human skills, management, or other resources into a foreign country."[3] The entry mode chosen is a major determinant of the required resources, risks, constraints, types of marketing and production strategies, and the management and control options required.[4] Entry mode choice impacts on the success, performance, and rewards of the international venture.[5] For example, an organization may chose to enter via a WOFE because a JV would require them to share profits and a licensing agreement would only allow an organization to charge a royalty on the sales made. This choice comes at a price, for organizations, as the risks associated with a WOFE are much greater than for a JV or a licensing entry mode.

The different types of entry mode selected will also determine the challenges that the organization will face in that market.[6] For example, an exporter will be faced with challenges around developing the host location marketplace and creating revenue without a strong local presence. A WOFE will involve the challenge of deciding whether to acquire an existing business (which can be risky) or setting up a greenfield operation (which can be expensive and time-consuming).

Entry into a foreign market will also require decisions such as the correct level of vertical integration to adopt. This will require consideration of whether the organization should source from and supply to the market or should it have an ownership stake in both its upstream and downstream suppliers such as raw material suppliers and distributors.[7] Increased levels of vertical integration can provide increased control and certainty however; they can also increase the complexity of the organization, the cost of establishment and consequently increase the level of capital risk.

Risk is an important dimension of entry mode decision choices and all entry modes entail a risk. Even in situations such as joint ventures where the usual risks are reduced by spreading them across several organizations, other unique risks will be introduced by that decision. To date, there are no shortages of cases demonstrating failure due to inappropriate JV partners. For example, when the French food product company Danone partnered with the Chinese organization Wahaha based in Hangzhou, in a JV partnership, they experienced the consequences of an increased IP risk.[8] Danone licensed the JV to produce certain Danone products for the Chinese market. Later, Danone accused Wahaha of producing products covered by this license independently of the JV.[9] Danone took Wahaha to court in China for breach of the licensing contract and has since dissolved the partnership.

Choosing the right entry mode at the start of the internationalization process is important, as changing entry modes is both costly and time-consuming.[10] Low risk entry modes, such as exporting, can be an attractive first stage for these reasons however, they also result in a very slow market development and the loss of any potential first mover advantage. The theories that were found to be particularly relevant to China entry mode choice include transaction cost, Dunning's eclectic (OLI), the resource-based view (RBV) of the firm, and internationalization theory.

These will be briefly reviewed before examining the findings that related to each of these theories.

Transaction cost theory compares operating efficiency with strategic goals, including internationalization and global competitiveness.[11] Prior research in this area has determined that international organizations will frequently select an entry mode that reduces transaction costs.[12] Factors such as the cultural distance between countries, institutional factors, and the business and policy frameworks can incur costs for international organizations. Organizations will react by selecting an entry mode that will minimize those costs.[13] If the intended host country is culturally distant from the organization's home country, a JV entry mode will minimize the costs of not knowing and understanding the new culture.[14] The selection of a JV should be balanced against the risks involved with transferring valuable IP to a partner.

Dunning's eclectic (OLI) theory identifies ownership, location, and internalization factors as important considerations for entry mode choice.[15] An organization intending to enter a particular market must have an ownership advantage that provides a competitive advantage in a foreign market. In addition, an organization will select a country/location for production (or in the case of a large country such as China, the region), which offers the greatest number of operational advantages, such as land, labor and capital costs, availability of skilled staff, technology, government incentives and policies, trade barriers, political risk and transportation costs. In some cases, an attractive market may not offer as many locational advantages as the organization's home country, in which case the organization should choose to export there. Internalization considerations are particularly important when considering internationalizing to China. As discussed in Chapters 5 and 6, it was found that there were weaknesses in the legal system, and IP was not greatly protected. These are sufficiently important internationalization considerations in relation to China. These considerations may cause an organization to internalize production, rather than license, contract or set up a JV, to alleviate the risk of that entity appropriating their technology. Internalization theory provides similar conclusions to transaction cost theory regarding internationalization to China. The costs of creating, monitoring, and enforcing a contract in China will be high if production is outsourced; therefore, the organization should consider internalizing production when operating in China.

It is important to complement the transaction and internalization perspective with the capability perspective of the organization, or with the RBV of the firm.[16] The RBV takes an inside-out approach, which suggests that competitive advantage is determined by the internal strategic resources of the organization, and the organization's ability to deploy those resources.[17] To obtain a competitive advantage an organization needs to have their capabilities and resources configured correctly. The uniqueness, compatibility, and the proper utilization of strategic resources are all important.[18] These resources need to be rare, inimitable, and imperfectly substitutable, and need to create value for the firm.[19] Strategic resources can usually be separated into both tangible and intangible resources.[20] Tangible resources include physical, financial, and HR; intangible resources include intellectual property and reputation. If an organization has a cluster of any of these resources, they will usually have associated core competencies that allow them to achieve a competitive advantage.[21] Utilizing strategic resources will influence internationalization and entry mode choices, particularly in relation to transferring strategic resources to a foreign subsidiary.[22] If an organization concludes that it can transfer its resources and obtain a competitive advantage in the host location, it will perceive an equity investment in that market to be attractive. This will lead to entry mode choice of either a WOFE or JV. If the organization is not confident that it can transfer strategic resources to the host location, it will be more likely select a low investment mode such as contract manufacturing, franchise, or licensing. The decision to transfer resources to either a high or low investment mode will also reflect the organization's strategic capabilities, as these determine its ability to manage and transfer its resources to other locations.[23]

The "Uppsala internationalization model," developed by Johanson and Vahlne,[24] describes internationalization as a developmental process, in which an organization increases its level of international activity over time as it acquires knowledge through experience.[25] This model is also known as internationalization or stage theory. The developmental process predicted by this theory presumes that internationalization commences with a low investment/low-risk entry mode choice such as exporting or licensing. As knowledge of the host location increases, alternative higher investment entry modes will be selected such as a WOFE or JV. Johanson and Vahlne combined many of the major sources of internationalization risk into the term "liability of foreignness." The "liability of foreignness" occurs when an organization first internationalizes to a country, and it is often due to their lack of local credibility and knowledge of the host country market and business conditions. In a global market, foreignness is difficult to define and this term has been updated to the "liability of outsidership," which reflects the importance of [international] network membership for internationalization.[26] This modification makes internationalization theory more compatible with the development of "born global" organizations,[27] which are organizations designed to be global or international from inception.[28]

Many of these theories assume that an organization can choose its entry mode.[29] In practice, however, entry mode choice is constrained by a number of external factors including uncertainty in the market, the availability of expansion capital, and local regulations.[30] The entry mode decision therefore reflects the knowledge, internal resources and external conditions of the organization, making internationalization entry mode choice equivalent to other business level strategy decisions.

Root[31] classifies 15 different entry modes, which can be collapsed into five different areas (Table 8.1).

Table 8.1. Root's Classification of Different Types of Entry Modes[32]

Entry mode	Details
Export	The sale of goods/services produced in the home country, and sold in the host country.
License and franchise	A formal permission or right offered to an organization or agent located in a host country to use a home country proprietary technology or other knowledge resources in return for payment.
Strategic alliance	Agreement and collaboration between an organization in the home country and a firm located in the host country to share activities in the host country.
JV	Shared ownership of an entity located in a host country by two (or more) partners, where one has originated from the host country and the other is from the home country.
Wholly Owned Foreign Entity	Complete ownership of an entity located in a host country by a firm located in the home country to manufacture or perform value adding or to sell goods/services in the host country.

What Entry Modes Do Australian Organizations Use and Why?

The research conducted for this book examined the entry mode choices made by Australian organizations for entry into China. In the study, the organizations had chosen a variety of entry modes, as depicted in Table 8.2. It should be noted that some organizations used a variety of modes.

Exporting

Six of the organizations used an exporting strategy, and some utilized dual strategies of exporting and a JV or WOFE based in China. Organizations in this category included large resources organizations (Resources Co 1 & 2), as well as smaller organizations such as Wool Co (Case 22); who exported small orders after securing contracts at trade shows in China. Wool Co's (Case 22) internationalization capacity was limited by their small size (three employees including the managing directors and limited resources), which made it difficult for them to access sufficient

Table 8.2. Entry Modes Chosen by the Participants

Entry mode	Number	Organization
Exporting	6	Resources Co 1, Import/Export Co, Wool Co, Paint Co, Machine Co, Resources Co 2
Agents and partnerships	5	Hotel Co, Uni Co 1, Uni Co 2, Uni Co 3, TAFE Co
Supplier relationship	1	Retail Co
Representative office	2	Gov Co, Uni Co 1
Licensing	1	Book Co
Fly-in-fly-out mode	8	Lab Co, Marketing Co, Agri Co, Fibre Co, IT Co, Import/Export Co, Medic Co, Trade Finance Co
JV	6	Parcel Co, Resource Co 1, Flower Co, Auto Interior Co, Software Co, TAFE Co
WOFE	13	Bank Co 1, Architect Co, Resources Co 1, Metal Co, Vat Co, Build Co, Auto Components Co, Law Co, Engineering Co, Brake Co, Chain Co, Responsibility Co, Resources Co 2, Bank Co 2, Gambling Co
Exporting assistance	1	Trade Finance Co

resources to develop the market. Paint Co (Case 27) was also an exporter, whose reactive internationalization decision resulted from interaction with Chinese business people wishing to migrate to Australia. The Australian business migration scheme allows Chinese business people who conduct more than AU$300,000 worth of business with Australian individuals or organizations to migrate to Australia.[33] Paint Co was contacted by Chinese property developers wishing to purchase Australian paint for their property developments in China and qualified for this scheme. Exporting has been successful for Paint Co (Case 27) who has been subsequently investigating other entry modes, including acquisitions, but has not yet identified an alternative attractive entry mode.

Paint Co's experience supports internationalization theory[34] as an explanation for internationalization because the knowledge and experience Paint Co gained motivated them to consider other entry modes. In addition, Paint Co's time in the market has enabled it to develop *guānxi* with their clients in China, and increased business. This supports the important role of networks and "insidership"[35] as a driver for increased internationalization.

Agents and Partnerships

Five of the organizations involved in the study used agents and partnerships. For example, the three university and the TAFE college participants used agents based in China to recruit students to travel to Australia to be educated. The universities also had partnerships with other universities to recruit students from Chinese Universities. This entry mode was chosen because higher investment entry modes such as developing campuses in China were perceived to carry too much risk and too little return:

> *The best strategy is to work with partners. They understand the market, probably a lot better than we do. And so, I think the way to enter the China market for a university is to find a few good partners and work with those partners in a serious way, rather than a scattered approach of signing a thousand MOUs all over the country, most of which won't do anything for you and will cause you a lot of aggravation potentially and will take a lot of time to manage with no return.* (Case 3, Uni Co 1)

For universities, the transaction costs of establishing, operating, and managing a campus or WOFE in China are too high, relative to the anticipated return. There have been more recent changes to this trend. For example, Monash University has opened up a JV campus with a Chinese University in Suzhou in 2012.[36] Suzhou is an industrial zone located 110 km west of Shanghai. Hotel Co (Case 5) used a similar strategy and entry mode to the educational providers. They used agents to source customers (tourists) in China to stay at their hotels in Australia. Again, their strategy was not to invest in China and build a hotel, but just to recruit and attract customers. They have chosen this entry strategy because it would be difficult and expensive for them to transfer their resources to China to set up a hotel in China; it is more efficient for them to continue exporting their service.

Representative Offices

Two participants, Gov Co (Case 10) and Uni Co 1 (Case 3), used representative offices in China. The purpose of Gov Co's entry mode was to establish a presence in the Chinese market and to provide services to Australian companies setting up operations in Tianjin, China. They provided the same types of trade and investment advice to Austrade, but focused on businesses located in their constituency:

> I guess the office exists predominantly as a business facilitation office, but because there is so much cultural and government, and I call it public diplomacy activity between the two, they are quite busy on that as well. I don't think you can separate the two, and particularly in China you shouldn't. And if you do, if you're a business that doesn't really focus on the cultural side of things, then you get lost.

Uni Co 1 (Case 12) uses agents and partnerships in addition to its representative office. It found it was able to attract more students through its agents and partnerships and utilized its representative office to support its Chinese agents and prospective students, academic staff visiting China, and to provide university representation in China. Uni Co 1 was not interested in increasing internationalization or developing campuses in China, as they did not perceive them to be profitable.

Supplier Relationships

Transaction cost theory suggests that organizations will choose an entry mode that offers the greatest efficiencies.[37] Therefore, when the costs of obtaining supplies or products from China is lower than obtaining them from Australia or other international locations, organizations will be motivated to find suppliers in China. This relationship reflects the supply availability and production efficiency levels in China, as well as international exchange rates and therefore varies over time.[38] Retail Co (Case 40) chose a supplier relationship (contract manufacturing) entry mode in China because they have traditionally been a retailer and not a manufacturer and the suppliers they dealt with in China were reliable and cost-efficient. They did not have the capacity to set up manufacturing in China and so adopted the same supplier approach that they had utilized in Europe. From a transaction cost perspective, their lack of local market and cultural knowledge, combined with their limited experience in manufacturing would have increased their transaction costs.

Retail Co designed their products in Australia and sent their designs to trusted suppliers in China. They ensured the quality of the manufacturing by placing Quality Control Managers in their suppliers' organizations. Interestingly, they chose to employ individuals of Brazilian nationality for this task as they had a reputation for being good quality control managers in the industry. Placing their own staff in the factory not only decreases the likelihood of low quality products being shipped to Australia, it enabled quality problems to be more quickly dealt with, at the factory. Retail Co did not consider their entry mode to be contract manufacturing, as they did utilize contracts, and relied on the relationships they had with their suppliers. This arrangement gave them the flexibility to switch suppliers if something went wrong. Furthermore, they believed that using contracts was inappropriate for the suppliers and would "*scare the living daylights*" out of them. Retail Co has achieved a sufficient level of familiarity with the Chinese environment from working with their suppliers that they now plan to invest in a WOFE (factory) in China, to provide more control over scheduling and supply. This finding supports the internationalization process described by internationalization theory.[39]

Licensing

Book Co (Case 23) was the only participant to enter the Chinese market through licensing. Licensing was their usual entry mode for new markets. Book Co selected this entry mode so as to be able to learn about the Chinese market and to use an already established publisher in China with extensive distribution networks and market experience. They initially licensed the publisher, an SOE, for a period of 3 years, with a provision to extend the license at the end of the term. They selected their licensee, after approaching 20 different publishers in China, and asking them to submit a proposal. Book Co met with the publishers, who had responded with a proposal, and then choose the publisher best matched to their needs:

> It is a licensing venture, and our revenue is based on a royalty income. So we license them to use our brand and the content to publish in Chinese. And the venture is just a 3-year term. And that's very common to all our partnerships. Any new partnership, we usually enter that for 3 years. It's a bit like a trial. We want to make sure that they're the right partner, for us long-term. I mean, we go into it thinking it will hopefully be very much a long-term venture because, as you can imagine with this business, you can't just chop and change. Once you go with one partner, you're sort of giving them access to the brand and content. If they did a bad job, then often we can't really re-enter that market with somebody else. So, we go in hoping it will be long term. We are looking for a long-term strategic relationship with a key partner. But it's based on 3 years initially and then it may be extended to, the next might be a 5-year term, or in some cases an 8-year term. So, we kind of keep on extending the agreement. (Book Co, Case 23)

Book Co have a long-term plan to establish a JV with their partner if the relationship proved successful, but have not yet decided to move to the entry mode:

> China is a very big market. We have been very happy with the partner. We have been very successful so far. There are other things we want to do in China, and maybe this is one market where we have actually

decided it's worthwhile to put in more effort and funding to actually drive this business. So, it may be in the second term we actually look at a joint venture arrangement. That's what we're actually considering at the moment. So, we are actually going through the process of looking at the pros and cons of continuing the licensing model with this company, or actually opening a joint venture with this company. (Book Co, Case 23)

The second quote is particularly supportive of internationalization theory; identifying the importance of knowledge and experience developed during the licensing term as support for the decision to increase investment in the market.

Fly-in-Fly-out Mode

A number of (mostly) service organizations participants adopted a fly-in-fly-out mode to enable them to service the Chinese market for a short time, including IT Co (Case 20), Marketing Co (Case 9), and Medic Co (Case 31). Once the service period was complete, the representative would return to Australia. This entry mode was selected because the amount of business to be transacted did not justify local market investment and the product could not be exported. They commented on the cost savings they achieved from using this mode:

We use business partners' offices. So, we've managed to get around all the expenses of setting up foreign-owned enterprises, and all the legal bills associated with joint ventures and all that sort of stuff. Basically, our establishment costs are the costs of travel, the cost of phone bills, translators and that sort of stuff. (IT Co, Case 20)

The participants also noted that the business would not grow unless the organization invested in China, but this idea lacked senior management support:

I think it would be fair to say our business doesn't really understand what it's got there. It's at the stage where it probably needs some investment to go any further, and our executive management seem to try to measure things with Western metrics. You can't put an ROI on it, it's a relationship we're building, and it's something I don't think they've really appreciated. And the way in which their life works there, in general, I think they have zero appreciation for it. (IT Co, Case 20)

Marketing Co (Case 9) combined this entry mode with a registered office in Hong Kong, and rented serviced offices when they were in town for meetings to increase their local capacity:

In Hong Kong, we don't have anybody in the office, we just have a serviced office arrangement where we've set up and we've got our entire infrastructure there. So, what happens is that Glen and I, we're the two directors of the company, we go up there every 3 months, have a number of meetings, put proposals together and do that type of stuff. It's just not worth having anybody there. (Marketing Co, Case 9)

Medic Co (Case 31) adopted a similar approach, but were still in the early days of their internationalization to China:

We've actually made three trips now, and we've really narrowed it down to developing a business strategy… What we have given a commitment to is that we want to go at least every 3 months maximum. And we're looking at one of our staff being over there for maybe 9 months. And we've got seminars lined up with major hospitals in China and some linkages with the university. It's sort of all starting to fall into place. (Medic Co, Case 31)

The above evidence suggests that representatives of organizations fly-in and fly-out to provide a service, and they are also looking at developing their business in the Chinese market. In the future, the organizations may do more in terms of setting up an office and providing more services, but it will depend on how successful they are and the amount of resources they are able to devote to the venture. At the moment, some organizations had limited resources, either because their organization does not support their internationalization properly, as per the case of IT Co, or in the case of Marketing Co, they can only see the worth of devoting resources if they have more work there. Others, such as Medic Co, are still in set-up mode.

Joint Ventures

Transaction cost theory suggests that organizations will seek to reduce the costs (usually of information and knowledge) associated with dealing in a foreign culture.[40] Prior research has identified a relationship between cultural distance and the propensity for organizations to form a JV.[41] This suggests that Australian organizations will choose to enter via a JV to manage the cultural divide between China and Australia. Six of the participants chose a JV entry mode, with varying ownership levels: Parcel Co (Case 4) 49%, Auto Interior Co (Case 14) 70%, Auto Interior Co (Case 14) 70% (plus 10% Government and 20% Customer), and Software Co (Case 26) 95%. The wide variety of ownership models suggests that when creating a JV, the ownership levels vary according to each individual situation. Parcel Co (Case 4) said that their ownership requirements were influenced by the Chinese organization that wanted controlling power. Parcel Co considered the JV to be attractive because the Chinese partner could deal with the "*Chinese bureaucracy,*" as the partner was an SOE, although it did take some time to negotiate their agreement:

> *I guess the joint venture detail was thrashed out extensively so that everyone knew what they were agreeing to. As in any joint venture, it's always not perfect in terms of did you think of all the things and did you get them sorted out beforehand. The world changes, the business changes.* (Case 4, Parcel Co)

Auto Interior Co (Case 14) invited the local government to be a 10% owner of the joint-venture, for the following reason:

> *We were prepared to make a significant financial investment and resource investment in China, but we didn't want to be messed around in the process. And so it was very important for us with all the relationships in China to build a relationship with the local government.* (Case 14, Auto Interior Co)

Auto Interior Co referred to the local government's investment into the venture as "a risk mitigation strategy." They also invited their customer, a large Chinese automotive manufacturer, to take a 20% ownership in the joint-venture. Auto Interior Co believed that this would assist them with planning and scheduling the production for this customer. It also ensured that the customer would make decisions in their favor and that the risks and rewards would be shared with the customer.

Software Co (Case 26) decided to adopt a much greater ownership percentage (95%) because "*It's predominantly an IT driven company and business model.*" The reason for it still being a JV was that, "*We wanted to obtain some people and obtain some network in, essentially, a speed-to-market type of approach.*" This participant was concerned about localizing their product to the Chinese market, which is consistent with Bartlett and Ghoshal framework's international strategy typology, which states that where the cultural and legal requirements of a country are influential, it is necessary to adapt strategy to the local conditions[42]; and Software Co decided that it was important to have "*a local office, and local people.*" Flower Co (Case 15) chose a JV entry mode because they had limited financial resources and needed the resources of a [Chinese] partner to achieve a sufficient scale operations in China. They also felt it was important to choose the right partner:

> *The selection of the joint venture partner is the most critical decision anybody will make. When you can find the right partner, that is the most important thing.* (Case 15, Flower Co)

Resources Co had a different objective for establishing a JV; and that was to JV with clients who would invest in their Australian mines, to assist with mining development and exploration. For Resources Co, this assisted with securing the Chinese market place:

> *We have a joint venture in a Western Australian project with 5 Chinese steel mills, and the purpose of this is to give us a base level of guaranteed market.* (Case 3, Resources Co)

Vat Co (Case 8) originally entered the Chinese market through a JV and then changed entry mode to a WOFE. When Vat Co decided to enter the Chinese market, WOFEs were prohibited, and they were compelled to use a JV entry mode. When the WOFE law[43] was introduced in 1986,[44] the organization dissolved their JV and established a WOFE. They were motivated to establish a WOFE because of the problems that they had been experiencing with their JV partner:

> *At the time you couldn't go in … you couldn't establish a wholly foreign-owned business in China. You can today, but you couldn't then. You had to go in as a joint venture so that's what we did. There's a lot of literature and articles on joint ventures in China. It was very nice when we finally ended that.* (Case 8, Vat Co)

Wholly-Owned Foreign Entity

Organizations will frequently choose a WOFE when there is a high degree of technological content in their products.[45] A WOFE is the most efficient method for transferring technological resources to a host country and creating value with those resources. Dunning's eclectic theory and internalization theory also predict that an organization will internalize production when the risk of technology appropriation is high, that is, the technology is a source of competitive advantage. The ease of transferring technological content to a WOFE is consistent with the RBV of the firm.[46] Thirteen participants chose a WOFE mode, for a variety of reasons. Bank Co 1 (Case 2) initially entered China through a representative office and later moved to a WOFE:

> *We had to go through a series of stages where they were increasingly licensed to do more and more business. But at the stage when we opened our Shanghai branch, we were only allowed to do foreign currency transactions for foreign people and foreign companies. So, we were quite restricted in what we could do. But then, over time, we got the license to do more and more things. There is a new form of license that foreign banks can now get in China, which, if you choose to incorporate locally, you can effectively become a local bank, just by being 100% foreign owned. We've not gotten to that yet.* (Case 2, Bank Co 1)

Other organizations, such as Architect Co (Case 3) and Vat Co (Case 8), preferred a WOFE so as to avoid problems with partners (i.e., politics, disagreements). Architect Co initially considered a JV partner, but found it very difficult to find a suitable partner, and opted for a WOFE instead:

We couldn't get them to necessarily sign or agree to things in Australia that we would see as commonplace, because they weren't really interested in being tied down or, the things were, "If you don't honor the agreement you won't get paid." All sorts of things that we have in Australia, that are intended to protect both parties, but they didn't want to come to the table. They're happy going a bit more cowboyish about agreements, rather than being locked down to a 30-page joint venture agreement.

Metal Co (Case 7) also initially planned to enter via a JV, but found it difficult to find a suitable partner:

We did consider a joint venture, and at one point we were going to go for it. But frankly, we found a lack of suitable partners on terms that we would consider acceptable, and the fact that, well, if we could do it ourselves, why don't we do it ourselves?

Responsibility Co (Case 33) entered via a WOFE, and was invited to set up this operation by Chinese academics who were CPC members, which facilitated the registration of their WOFE. Responsibility Co's case is a fairly unusual one, as it is a very small organization in comparison to other Australian WOFE organizations in China, such as Metal Co (Case 7) and Bank Co 1 (Case 2).

In summary, the findings indicate that entry mode selection is influenced by a variety of factors, including the efficiency of the entry mode, ownership advantages, location advantages, protection of IP, whether a firm can effectively transfer their resources to the foreign location to create value, and international experience, learning and market knowledge. This demonstrates how important selecting the correct entry mode is; most of the participants were able to identify a number of reasons for their selection of their entry mode.

Location Choices in China

The correct location is another important choice for internationalization to China, as the location is likely to have considerable influence on the success of the business venture. Prior research identified the location decision as an operational decision,[47] and is a key element of Ownership, Location, and Internationalization (OLI) theory.[48] Foreign organizations in China can usually choose the location of their operations; however, China's Special Economic Zones (SEZs) offer incentives, which usually make these locations more attractive. Chinese SEZs generally provide superior infrastructure and better market conditions for international organizations. Agglomeration theory[49] indicates that co-locating with suppliers, consumers, good quality infrastructure, ports, and major cities will increase the likelihood of success of a venture. Location choices also influence operations and transportation costs. For example, transportation from central China to the eastern seaboard is more expensive than transportation along the eastern seaboard. The participants generally chose locations close to major cities where greater growth and development occurred, where their industry was located or where customers and suppliers were located. Other reasons included locating in SEZs, or regions that had good infrastructure. These decisions will now be discussed in more detail.

Major Cities and Proximity to Growth Areas, Industry, Customers, and Suppliers

The participants initially chose locations with substantial growth and development, mainly around major cities such as Shanghai, Beijing, and Guangzhou. For example, Metal Co (Case 7) located operations where there was a large volume of economic development occurring such as Beijing, Tianjin, Shanghai, and Guangzhou. Build Co's (Case 16) customers were mainly located in high population regions such as Shanghai, Tianjin, Beijing, and Harbin and so it made sense to locate the offices in these regions. Law Co (Case 17) chose Shanghai because it was the commercial center of China and the location of many of their customers. Staffing expectations also influenced the choice of location for some of the participants. For example, Build Co located their main office in Shanghai to service customers, but also because that location suited the managing director and his family. He wanted to provide his wife with access to a Western life-style, and the children with international schools.

In addition to co-locating with customers, co-location with the industry and suppliers was also considered to be important by the participants. For example, Metal Co (Case 7) chose the location for their WOFE, because (a) it was the largest industrial area in China, (b) it was classified as a SEZ, and (c) their customer industries were located there. Retail Co (Case 14), had an entry mode of contract manufacturing in China, and focused their sourcing on Guangzhou, as this was where the best suppliers were co-located. Auto Components Co (Case 18) chose Ningbo to co-locate with their customers, and Auto Interior Co (Case 14) co-located with the other suppliers of their customers:

> [w]hen we went to China in early 2005, we did a very rapid funneling of business development opportunities there. There are more than a hundred vehicle manufacturers. We have four here in Australia if you include Mitsubishi. And very quickly we realized that the opportunities for us were probably not going to be in Shanghai or Beijing where a lot of Western companies already existed.

Auto Interior's decision to locate in a region with less competition indicates that too much industry activity can introduce negative features for a location. Other participants chose locations based on cost. For example, Software Co (Case 26) chose Chengdu for their software development offices because both rent and wages were lower than in Shanghai or Beijing. Also Chengdu was conveniently situated between Shanghai, Beijing and Tianjin, so that they were still able to service all of those cities from this location.

Special Economic Zones

Government incentives are one of the main reasons for foreign organizations choosing to locate in SEZs. Table 8.3 describes the various SEZs in China. Architect Co (Case 3) chose to locate in the Shenzhen SEZ to be eligible for tax breaks. SEZs have become very popular, although the Chinese government has now removed most of the tax incentives

Table 8.3. *Special Economic Zones in China*[53]

Type of zone	Areas
SEZ	Pudong New Area, Suzhou Industrial Park, Shenzhen (including Shekou), Zhuhai, Shantou in Guangdong Province, Xiamen in Fujian Province and Hainan Province, Beihai, Dalian, Fuzhou, Guangzhou, Lianyungang, Nantong, Ningbo, Qingdao, Qinhuangdao, Shanghai, Tianjin, Wenzhou, Yantai, and Zhanjiang.
Coastal open economic zones	Liaodong Peninsula, Shandong Peninsula, Changjiang and Pearl River Deltas, and Southern Fujian, including Zhōngguó and Quanzhou Delta Areas.

associated with SEZs. In January 1, 2008, a new Corporate Income Tax (CIT) was passed, which taxed foreign enterprises in SEZs at the domestic enterprise rate of 25%.[50] There is still preferential treatment for some industries[51] including high-tech industries and industries aligning with China's 12th five-year plan.[52]

The following describes the decision-making process used by the following company:

> *Inside China, we compare province to province. So why did we pick Dalian versus Tianjin, Nanjing, Guangzhou? Why Dalian? Dalian was narrowed down to three. We had Suzhou, Tianjin and Dalian. And of those three, you could have picked any one of them and it would have met all our criteria. But when you get down to the specifics in China, it's new and the provinces can influence businesses. Dalian is a new generation area. So, when we went up there 5 years ago, the first thing I noticed is, yes, I met a communist party member who was the figurehead, but straight behind that is a new generation: young managers, the director is in her 50s and well educated in the UK. She has surrounded herself with young talent. So, to me, this looked very positive.*

This organization selected this location for operations because of the new generation of talent that they could access and also for the human resources that would create value for their organization. They were encouraged by the fact that the region did not reflect a *"communist old style"* work ethic, but had a Western commercial sense of doing business.

Infrastructure and Quality of Partners

The participants chose to locate where infrastructure levels met their needs; in many parts of China, infrastructure is quite limited by Western standards. Resources Co 2 (Case 34) selected their location on the basis of shipping costs; ports further from Shanghai attracted extra shipping costs. For example, ships took an extra 3 days to get to one port north of Shanghai, increasing transportation costs, although Resources Co 2, stated the infrastructure around that port was better than in Shanghai.

Uni Co 1 (Case 12) did not locate on the basis of infrastructure, but based location on the proximity to partners and agents. They chose partners and agents based on their quality, reputation, and the quality of the students they could recruit and considered it important to maintain a local presence. One university chose to locate outside the major cities, such as Beijing, Shanghai, and Guangzhou, because of the large number of universities already operating in the major cities, which created high levels of competition. Medic Co (Case 31) also chose a regional location to where the scale of their customers (hospitals) was not too large for them to be able to properly service. They found that the hospitals in Chongqing were of a suitable size for their operations.

The main factors driving location choices were growth and the development opportunities and proximity to related industry, customers, and suppliers. A number of participants chose cheaper locations, or locations where more suitable partners and customers could be found (e.g., Medic Co and Uni Co 1). Other participants were influenced in their location choice by the government incentives available for foreign organizations located in SEZs, as well as access to more capable staff. The attractiveness of existing commercial centers (such as capital cities), and local infrastructure also influenced the location decisions of some participants.

Conclusion

This chapter considered the entry modes that the participants utilized in their internationalization to China. Popular entry modes included exporting, joint ventures, fly-in-fly-out mode, and WOFEs. The participants offered reasons for their choice of entry mode, which were consistent with those identified in the research literature. Their entry mode choice was dependent on multiple factors including how long the organization had been in China, the specific Chinese regulations that pertained to the industry, the conditions that the industry experienced and the motivation for entry into China.

This range of moderating factors makes entry mode choice a complex decision. The resources allocated to the internationalization determine both the cost and the competitiveness of the operation and are determined by the entry mode choice, so entry mode choice is particularly critical to the success of an internationalization process. The types of resources required for the selected entry mode will also influence the level of risk that the internationalization process is exposed to. Therefore, it is important that organizations should systematically assess and evaluate the various possible entry mode options from the perspective of resources, future benefits, and risk.

It was also found that the participants adopted a range of criteria to assist them with entry location decisions, which included proximity to growing markets, the industry, customers and suppliers, SEZs, infrastructure, and the most suitable partners or agents. This research suggests that a systematic analysis of the correct Chinese internationalization location decision should include local market conditions, financial opportunities, infrastructure, and supporting agents.

CHAPTER 9

Human Resource Management in China

Can You Find Skilled Staff and Retain Them?[1]

Human Resource Management (HRM) in China can be translated as *renli ziyuan guanli*.[2] It is generally thought that organizations internationalizing to China do not pay enough attention to the recruitment and retention of Chinese staff, and yet it is one of the most challenging areas of Chinese business operations because of the "war for talent" that exists between organizations. As such, it is extremely important for foreign businesses internationalizing to China to be aware of the HR issues they will experience. These issues include skill shortage problems, attracting and recruiting staff, training and development (T&D), compensation, and retaining staff. The international staffing preferences that Australian businesses adopt in China exacerbate these issues by leading to a poor understanding of Chinese cultural environment.

The Chinese Context

Workforce management is a critical issue for foreign organizations in China.[3] The workforce issues foreign organizations experience in China includes managing expatriate staff, managing host country national (HCN) staff, and integrating staff from different nationalities. One of the most significant challenges associated with employing HCN staff is the shortage of skilled HCN labor. The Boston Consulting Group[4] predicted that there would be labor shortfalls of 19 million staff in China and Japan and 60 million employees worldwide by 2020. China has undergone significant institutional change since the mid-1980s. Business conditions have changed from the "*tie fan wan*" or "*iron rice-bowl*" system, characterized by SOEs, life-time employment, and high institutional dependency, to diffused ownership and lower institutional dependency.[5] These ongoing institutional changes have important implications for the way foreign organizations manage their Chinese operations. Until 1987, the recruitment process was conducted according to predetermined government quotas.[6] Labor mobility in China was, therefore, not possible prior to 1987. New labor laws introduced on 1 January 2008 significantly extended employee rights[7] and increased protection for workers, increasing business-operating costs.

The limited research into these issues suggests that, as a result of acute managerial talent deficits,[8] talent management (TM) is an emerging key issue in China. The growth in new businesses and increasing FDI in China has meant that demand for managerial staff has outstripped supply,[9] and will do so into the foreseeable future. The Chinese general labor is also being outstripped by demand. China has an almost zero population growth, and an estimated workforce of 790 million, however, Manpower[10] predicted that China will need 1.1 billion workers by 2020.

The impact of the Chinese government's recent efforts to improve management education and training is, as yet, unknown. The Organization for Economic Co-operation and Development (OECD) predicts that by 2020, China will produce 18% of the 200 million graduates produced in the G20 countries.[11] However, not all of these graduates will be suitable for employment in foreign organizations due to a lack of the mix of skills and experience that these organizations seek (English proficiency being a fundamental issue).[12] This is consistent with other research that has determined that, despite the changes, the Chinese educational system remains conservative, outdated, and struggles to provide the required numbers and caliber of graduates.[13] In addition, older managers, and those who grew up during the Cultural Revolution, retain the practices of China's SOEs and have considerable difficulty in understanding or embracing modern business norms such as demonstrating flexibility and showing initiative.[14]

China's workforce is a major challenge for foreign enterprises. The business environment continues to evolve and has become more supportive of foreign investment. It still requires much more development, before the main talent issues that foreign organizations are experiencing are reduced. Managing talent in China is arguably more complex than in most locations because of the interplay between changing political regimes and the social and cultural differences.

International Staffing Preferences of Australian Organizations in China

The literature identifies the importance of international business and managers with distinct global competencies and the desire to work in culturally, socially, and geographically distant countries.[15] The traditional model for multi national enterprises (MNEs) managing overseas operations (i.e., through the location of Parent Country Nationals (PCNs) in senior management positions) is becoming less appropriate because of the difficulties in attracting candidates, and the issues surrounding international assignment success.[16] This is even more the case for Chinese subsidiaries, because of the cultural distance between China and the Western countries from which the staff are normally sourced. The difficulty in attracting sufficient PCNs staff for expatriate assignments in emerging markets such as China is also due to the high levels of FDI in these countries that has created a shortage of suitable PCNs staff.[17]

There are a number of staffing choices available to foreign organizations in China.[18] They include the ethnocentric approach in which subsidiary management positions are staffed with PCNs, the polycentric approach where management positions in a subsidiary are staffed by HCNs, and, finally, the geocentric approach where management positions in a subsidiary are staffed with "the best person" for the job regardless of nationality or origin.[19] In the geocentric approach, the subsidiary could be staffed with PCNs, HCNs, or even third country nationals (TCNs).[20] Most international businesses utilize a combination of these approaches, combining a degree of ethnocentricity, polycentricity, and geocentricity in all firms.[21]

Fourteen of the twenty participants with staff based in China used an ethnocentric staffing model rather than employing HCNs. However, it was often the preference of these firms to use Australian expatriate managers with significant "China experience." For example, the Metal Co's (Case 7) General Manager had 25 years of experience in China. While the use of Australian nationals in senior positions was very common, a solely ethnocentric style was not always pursued. There was a policy in many of the case firms of *"maximizing the number of Chinese nationals"* within their business. The level of utilization of Chinese nationals, however, varied.

The participants generally adopted an ethnocentric model; however, staffed their subsidiaries with locals for specific reasons, including staffing positions where networks and relationships with Chinese institutions were important (e.g., relationship and trade finance managers, as in Case 39, Bank Co 2):

> *So, for me, it's been critical to make sure that I get a Chinese local as my relationship manager and a Chinese local as a trade finance specialist, who speaks good English, but clearly is Chinese and speaks Mandarin, who knows the local marketplace and has a good network of contacts in the local marketplace, knows how local Chinese banks operate—what are the pitfalls, risks, opportunities. So, I am looking for somebody that has got a reasonably real experience, either in a major Chinese bank or in a major international bank in China for some period of time, which can complement my skills.*

Some of the roles in Chinese operations require staff with a detailed knowledge of the Chinese *"way of doing things."* This combines with the pressure to maximize HCN staffing levels due to the difficulties in getting expatriates to work in China. Another cause for the reluctance of PCN's to work in China is the attitude to the working conditions that they would experience:

> *You've got to find people that are willing to go, that are willing to cross the cultural divide, span the cultural issues, even to go offshore. In general terms, I think in my experiences, Australians are more overseas tourists than they are overseas livers. They're much more timid when it comes to living overseas.* (Case 2, Bank Co 1)

This attitude was one of the contributors to the participants need to employ home country based international managers, who travelled from Australia to China between once per month and annually. For example, Build Co's (Case 16) Australian-based director was responsible for their international operations and would fly to China once every month for 2 weeks at a time to manage the overall operations and building projects.

A number of participants used HCNs with Western education or work experience for their managerial positions in China, that is, *Hǎiguī*. They argued that this strategy provided the organization with the benefits of having individuals who understood the Chinese culture and context, as well as having knowledge of a global, Western business world culture. Vat Co (Case 8) experienced an interesting outcome arising when they utilized this approach. This organization selected a Chinese national who had spent a significant amount of his working life in North America as managing director of their Chinese operations. The local staff, however, did not accept him due to the perceived dilution of his Chinese attitudes and values, which demonstrates the impact of Chinese culture on local staff.

> *Their managing director in China is a Chinese-born fellow who, at a relatively young age, moved to Canada and then subsequently to the US, where he became an employee of this company. Now, they've put him in as Managing Director in China because he's Chinese, but I've discussed him with our managing director who was fully Chinese and he's of the view that he's much more American than Chinese. He's lost it.* (Case 8, Vat Co)

Some of the participants with JVs were prepared to select HCNs, but not necessarily those from their JV partner's staff. For example, Parcel Co (Case 4) did not want to utilize JV partner's staff in senior positions because the SOE or communist management practices they utilized were unsuitable for their business. The Chinese context was also important where the regulations imposed by the government prohibited legal firms from employing local lawyers:

> *You can't sign off directly on Chinese law because you can't employ … the Chinese government still has this barrier, which might go in the free trade agreement, that you can't employ Chinese lawyers. So, you can employ people who are fully qualified to be lawyers, but they're*

not actually admitted as lawyers. So, you could do basically every-thing, but the Chinese government sort of won't let you call yourself a Chinese law firm. You're still a foreign law firm. (Case 17, Law Co)

Skills Shortages: A Talent Deficit

The participants found that talent shortages were a key issue, although not as great an issue as has been suggested in earlier research.[22] Seven participants faced considerable problems attracting the right type of talent (Cases 2, 4, 8, 14, 16, 24, and 26). The majority of them cited availability of managerial talent as arguably the biggest, albeit not the only, issue. This was also a key reason behind the common use of PCNs:

> *[T]here's a very tight supply of qualified and experienced labor and that is over the spectrum of employees that you might have, from office administrative people or sales people right through into the workshop.* (Case 8, Vat Co)

In addition, Vat Co's (Case 8) experience indicates that context can affect the process and speed through which the organization can obtain talent, "*[t]here have been some days when you could snap your fingers and have unlimited numbers of whatever you wanted ... they're gone. That's quite a big factor now.*" This is related to the increasing number of foreign companies in China and the growing significance of China's economy. The Chinese workforce now has many employment opportunities.

Auto Interior Co (Case 14) experienced a shortage of skilled employees, with the main issue being the lack of experience of HCN employees, although their aptitude, attitude, and willingness to work were very good. This experience was shared by number of the participants, however, it was not just the skills of the HCN employees, and these organizations also found it difficult to select expatriates with sufficient skills and China-specific experience:

> *It's very hard to find qualified people. There is a real strain on skilled and qualified resources. So, that's a challenge ... You need the right person to lead the job, and we don't employ "guns-for-hire" in a senior*

position like that. Clients now, with the maturity of the Chinese market, clients now expect that person who is leading the project, to have past China experience. You can't just throw in someone who hasn't been there before. (Build Co, Case 16)

The flat global economy may also be having an impact as it was noted by some that they would like to use greater resources, if they could, on recruitment, and T&D, but economic conditions have prevented this. Two participants experienced problems with recruitment in the provincial areas where they were located and had to target first-tier cities to gain better access to qualified, skilled, and experienced staff.

For us it's the people. It's getting experienced, qualified people into your business, which is probably difficult enough in somewhere like Shanghai. It's aggravated by the fact you're in a more provincial area. (Case 28, Brake Co)

How to Recruit and Select Chinese Staff in China?

A key imperative to successful business is to have the right staff, in the right number, the right place, and at the right time.[23] Organizations planning to enter China should consider a number of recruitment questions including: "Should recruitment be conducted in China?" "Who should be recruited?" "Where should they be recruited from?" Foreign organizations operating in China can choose to recruit expatriates for their Chinese operations, however, too many PCN staff will reduce the labor cost advantage of operations in China. Furthermore, the participants found that maximizing the number of HCN increased the likelihood of success. The literature identifies the advantages associated with the use of HCNs as: familiarity with culture, knowledge of language, reduced costs, good public relations, and local connections and contacts.[24] With this conclusion in mind, this section will focus on recruiting Chinese staff in China.

The work force environment in China is changing dramatically and has done so since China's Open Door Policy, and the four modernization policies that were introduced. One the most significant regulations to be passed in recent years is the new labor law, which was introduced in 2008. Previously, recruitment by Chinese enterprises or foreign invested enterprises (FIEs) had to be carried out through a contract hiring system.[25] Now foreign organizations have other recruitment options, including recruitment through a Chinese partner if the foreign organization has entered into a JV, or directly from a WOFE, or via recruitment services.[26] Foreign organizations can now also recruit from SOEs, government departments, or universities.[27] In the late 1990s, some MNEs, preferred not to recruit from SOEs because of the different ways in which they manage their operations.[28] In addition, MNEs may refer not to recruit students from Chinese universities because of the lack of decision-making skills development in the Chinese educational system.

Depending on how an international business structures its subsidiary, its subsidiary may or may not have a dedicated HR resource. Structures will typically range from departments headed by dedicated HR manager to line managers with HR responsibility. Where an HR department exists, it will typically be responsible for the selection of key people (both locals and expatriates).[29] Prior research has indicated that Western MNEs can run into problems when using Western recruitment and selection procedures in China[30] because Western-based techniques are not always transferable to the Chinese context. The use of tests and behavioral interview questions are an example. Analytical questions screen out 50% of applicants in China, whereas the same procedure screens out only 12% of US applicants, because the Chinese applicants do not have the developed analytical skills that Western applicants do.[31] Similarly, assessment centers, where candidates are set a group task under time pressure, may not suit the Chinese context. Chinese staff do not like to work under pressure in a leaderless group, given their hierarchical nature, therefore, assessment centers are not appropriate for their culture.[32]

Prior research has found that MNEs have used recruitment methods where both expatriate and local managers together recruited staff.[33] In this situation, the expatriate manager made sure that the employment selection criteria were met and that the local managers did not recruit solely based on their *guānxi* network.[34] The local managers had the benefit of being able to pick up on the local language and behavior subtleties that an expatriate manager would not recognize.[35]

China's labor reform and expanding labor market offer multiple options for companies that want to recruit new employees from members of the public.[36] A foreign organization may invite applications from the public by using labor service organizations operated by local government bureaus, advertising in newspapers, magazines and online, attending job fairs organized by various labor departments, and directly recruiting from graduates of higher institutions of education.[37] Through this public recruitment, foreign organizations can negotiate employment contracts directly with potential employees.[38] Research by Ding, Fields, and Akhtar proved that most HCN managers in a foreign-owned subsidiary are recruited through the external market, rather than internally through promotion or advancement.[39] External markets are obviously extremely relevant for those organizations going through a growth stage.

A recent study of the selection processes used by Western MNEs in China found that HR managers used a variety of selection practices.[40] These included *guānxi*-based recruitment methods, where priority was given to job offers to qualified family members of current employees, and employee referrals were also a popular practice for recruiting potential applicants.[41] Other practices included hiring graduate students who had internship experience with their companies, or hiring managerial staff recommended by the government. Organizations can also post job advertisements in newspapers, magazines, journals, and radio.[42] Other recruitment methods could include attending job fairs, using the Chinese government's Foreign Enterprise Service Company (FESCO)[43] or using a local recruiting company.

Foreign organizations can employ their Chinese partner's staff, or PCNs sent from their own organization, or recruited in the Chinese market, or new HCNs. As noted previously, Parcel Co preferred not to use their partner's staff. On a positive note, past research has found that HCNs prefer to work for foreign organizations rather than Chinese SOEs or JVs.[44] In China, there are a number of internet-based advertisement boards, where organizations can advertise their positions (Table 9.1). Other methods include external databases, the organization's own direct recruitment approaches, referrals by staff, and agencies.

Table 9.1. Online Recruitment Boards in China

Online recruitment boards in China	Language
www.51job.com	English and Chinese
www.chinahr.com	English and Chinese
www.ceconline.com/hr/	Chinese
www.jobchina.net	English

Training and Development

Prior research suggests that MNEs in China are not investing enough in T&D.[45] The skills shortage in China will challenge the development of foreign organizations and so is important that they invest in T&D. However, foreign organizations also experience retention problems in China, and it is challenging to make this investment when there is a likelihood that they might subsequently lose the trained staff. Despite that, T&D is effective for developing skills in China, as the following quote from Auto Interior Co (Case 14) conveys:

> *I mean, the quality of people, there is no issue with their aptitude, attitude, their willingness. What may be missing is just their experience. And that's something that we can provide and train and develop.*

Prior research conducted on T&D in the Chinese context determined that both technical and general management training are more extensive in WOFEs than in SOEs.[46] Other research conducted on training in 440 foreign organizations in Shanghai, on various ownership types, found that JVs tended to provide more training than other ownership structures.[47] This research found that technical and professional skills training as well as management development programs were commonly used.[48] T&D was more focused on job-related skills and improvement of worker productivity.[49] Technical training appeared to be the most common, followed by training to help employees understand the firm's business and value systems, and low to moderate levels of behavioral training in areas such as team-building and interpersonal skills.[50] This suggests that basic skills requirements are more important to those organizations than soft skills development.[51] This research determined that T&D was an effective staff development tool.[52]

The training programs developed for MNEs must take the Chinese context into account.[53] For example, managers should not assume that basic knowledge exists as the following quote articulates:

You can't turn around 300 people quickly in terms of training, because they've been trained in a particular way of doing things. So, it's not just starting with fresh students or fresh trade people coming into the game. It's starting with all the oldies, and I can say that because I am old. And that doesn't often, unless you've got a very sophisticated training program, it doesn't work. And, therefore, you've got to have at least 10 or 15 people who are trainers in there who are fluent in Chinese doing all this training. Sometimes that doesn't work either. (Case 18, Auto Components Co)

Older employees may lack the English language skills needed to understand more complex training packages and may fail to benefit from standard packages coming from the West. Training Chinese staff using English, as a medium may be difficult if their English language proficiency is weak. Once a basic introductory course has been given, more complex skills can be developed later.[54] This suggests that training needs to be provided at a more basic level than would be provided in the West,[55] and more importantly in Chinese, as the following suggests:

Just training everything from a very low base, even though people have been university-educated etc. A lot of that is by rote and not by intuitive knowledge. Their parents wouldn't have been educated so it wasn't in the family. They don't learn it by association. (Case 26, Software Co)

Western-based practices such as role plays and experiential exercises may not be suitable for Chinese HCNs who are used to traditional dyadic lectures.[56] Also, if a trainer criticizes a trainee in public, or states that they are wrong, this may result in the trainee "*losing face,*" which has implications for that person's relationship with peers. Therefore, trainers need to be careful on how they deliver training in China. It may be better if HCNs do the training together with PCNs to deal with cross-cultural subtleties. In addition, using a combination of Chinese and Western teaching methods may be beneficial.

Prior research has determined that some (larger) MNEs have established their own universities or training centers to train their Chinese staff in the skills that they require.[57] MNEs have also built up partnerships with local universities, to assist in developing the skills that they need for their organization.[58] Past research has found that on-the-job training can be encouraged through coaching by [expatriate] managers.[59] Apart from in-house training, there is a need and role for training bodies in China,[60] as organizations may not be able to provide for all of their own needs.

Other participants preferred not to use PCNs in their operations, employing mainly HCNs. These organizations relied on training to transfer their knowledge from the home country to the subsidiary:

> We go there and we facilitate, assist, train and teach. Teaching business is not the same as training. Teaching business is what makes money, as distinct from how to make money. And so this has been a very steep learning curve for the Chinese, because obviously there are Western influences in the way we do things. So, whilst we're controlling the major decisions for the organization over there, they're controlling the business operations. So, my first objectives are to introduce equipment technology, system technology, financial technology, occupational health & safety, and procedures for them to operate at a higher level. (Case 32, Chain Co)

Book Co (Case 23) experienced complex issues with training of staff in their licensee. They would have preferred the key staff to be trained in Book Co's Melbourne office, but, for financial reasons, this was not possible:

> So, the fact that they can't actually afford to come to our key office for in-depth training has been a bit of an issue. So, through emails and documents, we've been trying to transfer that knowledge from us to them, but it's so much easier if you can do it face-to-face. I think that has been an annoying element for us—having to rely on fax, email and telephone to get across some very complicated ideas.

In conclusion, the training required to transfer important knowledge from a foreign organization to a Chinese operation can be difficult to deliver due to the context of China. Properly understanding and adapting training to the Chinese context will increase its effectiveness.

Compensation Issues

Average wage rates in China are around RMB 3,566 per month for low-skilled workers,[61] which equates to around $548 per month in Australian dollars as of April 2012.[62] Managerial staff and skilled workers earn much higher wages. All wages in China are currently increasing in the range 7%–25% per year, which is creating serious wage inflation and reducing China's labor-based productivity levels.[63] For example, Standard Chartered released a survey in March 2012 of 200 Hong Kong-based companies, and they found wages have risen by 10% in 2011–2012.[64] Foxconn reported wage increases of up to 25%.[65] This wage inflation is likely to continue, causing issues for organizations who have already invested in China, or are considering doing business there. Commentators are suggesting that wage inflation will bring an end to "cheap China."[66] It is likely that continued wage increases in China will make China a less attractive location for investment, and organizations will move their operations to other low cost locations such as Vietnam, India, Pakistan, and Bangladesh, as some are already doing.[67] Wage inflation differs according to regional location as well, with the high-growth SEZs, and those cities located on the eastern seaboard experiencing much higher wage inflation.[68] In addition, salaries tend to vary across cities and provinces.[69] For example, employees in second-tier cities, such as Qingdao and Tianjin, would receive about 80% of the salary earned in first-tier cities, such as Beijing and Shanghai. Employees in third-tier cities, such as Ulanhot and Ankang, would only receive 60%, of the salary level of first-tier cities.

Some foreign organizations in China have chosen to combat retention problems by establishing policies of being among the top 25% in terms of salary levels.[70] Other strategies to deal with retention problems adopted in China include providing housing to employees, with a retainer that if they stay for 15 years they can keep the house, and they will be guaranteed a long-term career in the organization and advancement.[71] The new generation of Chinese managers has different needs compared to previous generations; they are more individualistic, independent, and more likely to take risks to gain higher salaries in comparison to the older, more traditional managers.[72] The move to a market-based system has led to greater preference for material rewards, with the result that employees are more often motivated to change companies for higher pay.[73] Therefore, it will be a challenge for MNEs to retain the new generation of Chinese worker.

Retention

Retention of talent is a major issue for foreign organizations in China. Turnover rates were approximately 13% in 2011.[74] This is a relatively new development, because the labor turnover rate was virtually zero before the 1990s due to state restrictions.[75] Turnover rates further exacerbate the talent deficit that foreign organizations experience in China, and can hinder these organization's growth.

Ten of the participants identified the retention of staff as a critical issue facing their Chinese operations. These firms were developing strategies for retaining their best local employees; however, the effectiveness of these was constrained by the structure of their Chinese operations and the Chinese institutional context.

Participants observed that financial motivation was a particularly important factor in staff retention. The move towards a market-based economy has resulted in employees adopting quite capitalist values where they would move to better paid roles. Parcel Co (Case 4) experienced barriers to increasing the pay for their best employees, because their SOE partner had limits on the level of pay they would provide to employees. This caused them to be uncompetitive in the local labor market. However, some participants stressed that while employees may run off to the next organization for more money, they did not believe just paying them more was a sensible, long-term solution. Brake Co (Case 28) found that both monetary and non-monetary factors affected their ability to retain workers:

If somebody gives them 10 RMB instead of 8 RMB, they'll jump.
And they just don't look at the monetary thing. They also look at the

canteen food, because we provide them free canteen food. We provide them free transport and we also provide them dormitories. They look at all this sort of thing, "Oh, the Hyundai one, look at their dormitory, that's nice."

A number of participants were cautious about spending significant money on T&D activities as a means of retaining employees. They found that their HCN staff would still move to better paying organizations, and the organization would lose the investment made in development activities, as the following quote indicates:

We would probably be third tier, relative to IBM or General Motors or something. So, there is an issue with the unprofessional finance people, they will come in, spend 2 or 3 years getting their training and then they go off somewhere else. (Case 7, Metal Co)

Concerns were also expressed over spending in the context of deteriorating global economic conditions. Auto Interior Co (Case 14) experienced limited loyalty from their Chinese staff and concluded that "Western" methods of motivation and retention were not particularly successful in the Chinese context.

Conclusion

The research participants made it evident that the "war for talent" was very strong in the Chinese context. Foreign organizations compete vigorously with domestic Chinese enterprises for the best talent.[76] The institutional environment of China is a key factor affecting the availability of talent and retention. Foreign organizations in China need to monitor changes to the Chinese institutional context because it represents a major influence on the ability to attract, recruit, and retain highly qualified and skilled local employees.[77] For example, the participants that entered China via a JV experienced many HR issues within the partnership, including not being able to increase their employees' pay because the state-owned partner imposed limits pay rates. Management approaches retained from pre-open door China and the communist background of many was inconsistent with the management practices of the foreign partner. They found these management approaches to be unsuitable for the global business environment. For these reasons, the participants that entered China via a WOFE faced fewer restrictions than those that entered via a JV.[78]

Australian MNEs primarily prefer to employ PCNs in their subsidiaries,[79] but preferred staff with "China experience."[80] PCN staff also needed to be able to demonstrate the capacity to adapt to local conditions to be effective managers in China.[81] There is some evidence that utilizing HCNs in management positions reduces transaction costs, and supports the localization of the subsidiary because of the *guānxi* networks they introduce.[82] This is particularly important in some Chinese industries, such as the banking industry, where HCNs provide important links and networks in the local community.[83] The role of HCNs will also vary with the industry as foreign service organizations focusing on the Chinese market may need stronger links with the local community than manufacturing organizations setting up facilities in China to manufacture for exports. One participant used Chinese, returning from overseas (students or workers termed *Hǎiguī*)[84] to help adapt the foreign organization's preferred management techniques to the Chinese conditions. Employing *Hǎiguī's* also has some drawbacks as the different mindset and values that they possess make it difficult for HCNs to work with them.[85]

Interestingly, the participants found it difficult to get PCNs to take on international assignments in China, which is consistent with other research findings.[86] This was primarily attributed by the participants to the cultural or psychic distance between Australia and China.[87] To overcome this, the participants tended to utilize a range of other staffing options, in addition to employing PCN, TCN, and HCNs. Some participants utilized international commuter assignments, whereby staff commuted from their home country to the host country on a bimonthly basis.[88] The utilization of a multifaceted staffing approach in China, comprising both foreign and HCNs, assisted the MNEs to manage the complexities of global integration while retaining local knowledge.[89] In addition, the use of expatriate managers may facilitate learning and knowledge transfer to host country employees.[90]

Geographical location proved to be an important HRM factor in China for the participants. The organization's location in China had a strong impact on the process of attracting and retaining of talent. While the participants found the availability of talent to be lower in provincial areas, employee retention is more difficult in the first-tier cities due to competition from other employers.[91] This suggests that national level institutions, as well as regional conditions, influence the process of attracting and retaining staff.

The participants offered more attractive remuneration to improve the levels of Chinese staff retention. The suitability of this approach has been confirmed by other research, which has found that the level of compensation affects Chinese staff retention.[92] The participants were of the opinion that a sole emphasis on higher salaries was not sustainable in the long run, and that they needed other options for improving employee retention. Some of the participants utilized nonmonetary retention practices and found that them effective.

The idea of utilizing Western management techniques in China was questioned by some participants, which is also consistent with other research. Chinese job applicants are not comfortable with Western selection procedures, including the use of role-play as a selection method because of their upbringing and education.[93] Therefore, "it may be naïve ... to think that Western managers can enter China with an armory of motivational techniques, which have proved useful back home."[94]

CHAPTER 10

Conclusions

Do You Know What You Need to Enter the Chinese Market?

This book has described and categorized the business environment of China—the Middle Kingdom or *Zhōngguó*—that organizations internationalizing there will experience. It has identified the key features of the environment and their relevance to Australian organizations, comparing these with the experiences of managers who have interacted with that environment.

It is now time to reflect on this and consider what knowledge of the Chinese environment is required to make a venture in China a success? How can knowledge of the trade and investment environment between Australia and China be used to create a competitive advantage? What strategies can be used to reduce the impact of the cultural gap between Australia and China? How important is the political environment important to the business establishment and how can it be navigated? How can the legal system in China be used to support the business establishment and protect business rights? How can valuable IP be protected there? How can IP be kept in-house and does protecting IP really matter in this case? What is the best process for selecting a China entry strategy, how should it be implemented and which are the most important motivations? How can the unique characteristics of the Chinese business environment be incorporated into this plan and how much flexibility is required to adapt to likely changes? What information is required to inform strategy development, which customers should be targeted and which entry mode will be the most suitable? How can valuable resources be transferred from Australia to China and create value? What is the best way of staffing be selected entry approach: will Parent Country Nationals (PCNs) or host country nationals (HCNs) be involved? What are the different concerns each group will possess, and how can they be appropriately recruited, trained, developed, compensated, and retained? What are the most appropriate measures of success for such a venture?

The book has addressed each of these questions in detail, as part of its aim to enable researchers, students, and business executives to better understand the Chinese business environment. This chapter summarizes these findings and presents conclusions for both research and practice. These conclusions will provide a useful framework for researchers investigating this area of international business and for organizations establishing or developing operations in China.

The Key Findings

Since Deng Xiaoping's Open Door Policy in 1978, China's economic growth has been phenomenal; often been referred to as an "economic miracle." The significant increase in FDI and trade tests to the stability of this growth. Australia's rapidly developing trade relationship with China has been due, in part, to China's enormous economic growth and the consequent demand for Australia's natural resources. As result, resources such as iron ore, coal, and petroleum dominate Australia's trade to China, and China has become Australia's top trading partner. Trade with China constituted 23.1% of Australian trade (exports and imports) in 2010–2011.[1] Australia has also been successful in the trade of services to China, particularly education and education-related travel. Other Australian industries that have been successful in China include the automotive, banking, agricultural business, building, construction and engineering, publishing, and logistics industries. In response to this trade and investment success, the Australian government established 14 Austrade offices in China with approximately 100 staff.[2]

There is no doubt that China's economic growth has offered foreign organizations operating in China many opportunities. The window for foreign organizations to enter China and take advantage of this success is still open. The focus of China's current and 12th five-year plan is: (1) rebalancing the economy, a focus on the central and western regions of China, and improving equality between different socioeconomic groups; (2) environment and sustainability, in which organizations that offer products and services in this category are encouraged by the Chinese government; (3) the development of an innovation-based economy; and (4) containing economic growth to sustainable levels. The fourth point means that growth rates in China will drop from 9% + which has been the case for the last 10 years, to growth rates of around 7%–8%. This may have an effect on organizations trading with or operating in China

China's accession to the WTO in 2001 has created an environment that is much more favorable for trade with China, investments and the protection of IP. In general, the participants in the research conducted for this book suggested that China still had more work to do before it fully met its WTO compliance commitments, however, accession had already improved the Chinese business environment for foreign companies. The Australian government has been negotiating a FTA with China since 2005; however, it appears that these negotiations will continue for some time yet. In addition, the research participants were not convinced that the FTA would create further benefits for Australian exporters or investors in China. Most participants had either neutral or negative views regarding the benefits of an FTA with China.

The research participants reported that the environment for FDI in China was positive, due to its economic policies and accession to the WTO. Investment flows into China have increased significantly since 2000 and totaled US$105.7 billion in 2010.[3] Traditionally, FDI in China has focused on manufacturing, but FDI in real estate and services has increased in recent years. Australian investment in China has lagged behind the rate of development of trade and was only US$16.9 billion in 2011,[4] due to the fact that Australia is not traditionally a capital exporter.[5] International organizations can choose a variety of structures for their investment in China, including EJVs, CJVs, WOFEs, holding companies, representative offices and branches. The recent Mergers and Acquisitions (M&A) regulations introduced in China in 2011 means that all foreign M&A's must pass a national security review. The 12th five-year plan has also changed the focus on which industries were encouraged, restricted, or prohibited for FDI. Overall, the FDI environment in China is attractive; however, some industries experience high levels of restrictions. This means that industry level research is important before considering entry in China, so as to identify the regulations, which may affect the entry plan. For this reason, informed legal advice is also critical.

One of the significant findings from the research was that the culture gap between Australia and China had a major impact on the development of relationships with potential Chinese partners, establishing partnerships, contracts, managing operations in general, and the cultural acceptance of specific products and services in the Chinese market. The research determined that the cultural gap between Australia and China was quite significant and larger than most the participants had expected. The cultural gap included language differences and style of communication. For example, Australians tend to be direct, whereas the Chinese tend to be indirect to prevent the loss of "*face*." This caused difficulties for some of the participants when negotiating business plans or proposals, and slowed down the negotiation process. Other significant cultural differences between Australia and China identified in the research related to power distance, collectivity, and uncertainty avoidance, which was consistent with Hofstede's framework of cross-cultural work values.[6] Key cultural values in China, such as *guānxi*, face (*miànzi*), and *rénqing*, are particularly important in Chinese business negotiations. They determine the rules for the development of relationships, showing appropriate levels of respect, ensuring that loss of face is prevented, and the reciprocation of favors.

Whilst these rules have some significance when negotiating business in Australia, they are very important when negotiating in China. Appreciating these values and how they apply in business negotiation is an important component of preparation for Chinese market entry. Relationship-building through hosting dinners, lunches, and banquets, and giving gifts and indulging in social games, such as *gan bei*, are examples of the actions that are appropriate. Engaging in these behaviors will lead to the development of long-term relationships and networks (*guānxi*), and, as a result, trust will be created. Some participants commented on the "priceless benefits" of the development of *guānxi* for future business development.

A number of strategies can be used to reduce the impact of the cultural differences between Australia and China. Culture is a learned behavior[7] and so the best way to respond to this is to learn about the culture. Approaches for learning about the Chinese culture that were successful identified in the research included cross-cultural training, reading books on the subject, employing a bi-cultural consultant, using staff with a Chinese background, learning the language or using employees as translators and learning from experience. Other approaches identified by the research participants included a focus on relationship building, localizing the business, human resource strategies for recruiting Chinese staff with Western knowledge (*hǎiguī*) or Westerners with Chinese experience, and adopting the correct approaches for dealing with Chinese staff.

The political landscape of China is also an important determinant of establishing a successful business there. A suitable framework for internationalizing to China includes investigating and obtaining the support provided by home and host governments, understanding the political environment in China, negotiating opportunities with the Chinese government and understanding and making allowances for the current regulations relating to entry modes. Intervention into business by the Chinese government was found to be much greater than in countries such as Australia. The participants found that the assistance provided by both the Australian and Chinese governments was helpful for establishing networks and providing advice to assist their business establishment.

The legal environment was also found to be a significant factor for both the entry mode selected and for ongoing operations in China. The legal system in China is a civil code, and differs from Anglo-Saxon common law. The effectiveness of China's legal system has been improving, as China introduces laws to improve the business environment for both domestic and international business. The research identified barriers to business success resulting from the legal system which included transparency, enforceability, relying on relationships rather than contracts and political interference/corruption. The most popular dispute resolution procedure for business disputes in China was found to be the arbitration process, China International Economic Trade Arbitration Commission (CIETAC). It is important that organizations have an arbitration clause in their contracts to resolve disputes. Mediation is another alternative for resolving disputes in China that was found to be effective. The respondents were of the opinion that the popularity of arbitration and mediation reflected the weaknesses in the Chinese legal system administration.

The participants suggested that, whilst it was important to understand the legal system and have good legal advice, contracts were generally unenforceable and the legal system could not be relied upon.

The participants found that strong relationships with customers, suppliers, and authorities were an effective approach for managing legal issues. Using local Chinese advisers (who generally had more influence and a better understanding of the rapidly changing regulatory environment) was found to be effective when dealing with the Chinese legal system. Some participants found using a legal company that was represented in both Australia and China to be helpful. The participants perceived corruption to be a major issue, and claimed that it was present in the legal system. They suggested that *guānxi* with people in positions of power and bribes could result in advantageous legal outcomes. This was a disadvantage for foreign companies that lacked the necessary *guānxi* connections with officials, or chose not to pay bribes.

IP protection is an area where support from the Chinese legal system was perceived by the participants to be particularly weak. The participants suggested that IP theft was rampant in China, which is confirmed by global software piracy rates (e.g., software piracy rates were found to be 78% in China, compared to the world average of 42%). Interestingly, the World Intellectual Property Organization (WIPO) rates the laws in China protecting IP as "world class," and that China has complied with WTO regulations in regard to IP by adopting the Trade-related Aspects of Intellectual Property Rights (TRIPS) agreement.[8] Patents, trademarks, and copyright are all protected under Chinese law, and China has signed a number of international agreements pertaining to IP. This indicates that an adequate framework is in place; however, the Chinese government must provide a stronger enforcement of IP regulation to reduce its negative impact upon international business in China. Political and taxation issues currently interfere with the enforcement of IP law in China.

The research participants were found to be motivated to enter China by a number of factors, which could be categorized as either proactive or reactive. A greater proportion of participants demonstrated a proactive behavior (25 out of 40), the most popular motivations being the growth opportunities, strategic drivers such as globalization or internationalization, or having an "Asian focus." Other participants internationalized in order to gain access to lower cost supplies or source components or products. Some of the reactive motivations included a diminishing market in Australia and being led, encouraged, or motivated by clients, customers, or contacts. Participants in industries including the construction, building, and engineering were invited by clients in Australia to provide the same services in China. The majority of participants responding to a reactive motivation also had no strategic internationalization plans, or had ad hoc plans. Some participants preferred to use loose plans because of the rate of change in China and the need for high levels of flexibility. The participants that did not plan were still mostly successful as a result of being able to service their already established customers in China.

The majority of the participants with strategic plans were also successful. In contrast, although four of the organizations in this category perceived themselves to have had limited success, and one organization had failed in 2010, suggesting they had chosen the wrong strategy. The participants generally adopted internationalization strategies for the entry to China, which focused on both Chinese business and retail sales. A number of these participants developed a localized version of their product for their Chinese consumers. Other participants focused on providing services or products to international clients based in China or to local businesses. A third group of participants manufactured products in China to export to Australia and other international markets.

Entry mode choice was an important issue for the participants because it impacted on the resources and time devoted to internationalization, the level of risk, and the rewards that could be expected. Effective entry mode decisions are based on reliable background information and rational decision-making. The participants all utilized a rational decision-making process to identify the correct entry mode. Some planned to change their entry mode once they had increased their market experience. For example, both Book Co and Retail Co initially chose a licensing and a supplier relationship mode and were considering alternative modes as the next stage for their internationalization to China. This suggests a process of internationalization had been adopted[9] in which the participants commenced with lower risk modes, and, after they gained experience and knowledge in the environment, choose higher risk modes entailing FDI. The majority of the modes chosen by the research participants included exporting, JVs, fly-in-fly-out services, and WOFEs. Most of the participants chose to locate in major cities or growth areas where suppliers or customers were located. SEZs were also popular among the participants. Local infrastructure, customer characteristics, or the proximity of suitable business partners were influential location factors.

Despite its huge population, China faces acute skilled and semi-skilled labor shortages, and a talent deficit. As a result, local companies frequently compete for talent. These conditions made it difficult for the participants to attract and retain suitable staff. The participants suggested that Chinese University graduates often lacked the skills and experience that they expected, and that older employees would only work to Chinese SOE work practices and lacked English language capabilities. These workforce skill and flexibility issues were significant contributors to the skills shortages problem for the participants in China. The participants were of the opinion that the new generation of Chinese were more motivated, aspirational, and willing to be flexible. Although they may still lack practical workplace skills, the participants expected to be able to train and develop them into a suitable resource for the future.

The participants indicated a preference for an ethnocentric approach when internationalizing to China. They preferred to have expatriate PCNs as key staff, who would manage, control, and coordinate the venture. It was considered important for these PCNs to have had "China experience" because of their role, and the maturity of the Chinese market. Many of the participants also wanted to maximize the number of skilled HCNs in the business. These participants appointed PCNs to the top management positions at the outset and then replaced these staff with HCNs later on.

The participants recruited staff in China using similar methods to those used in Australia, including newspaper, magazine and internet advertising, recruiting from universities, careers fairs, and agencies. They found, however, that they needed to adapt their training and development (T&D) process to the Chinese context. For example, T&D in China should not assume basic knowledge, and should start off with basic skills, followed by complex skill development. The participants found that providing the program in Standard Chinese (Mandarin) resulted in better outcomes. They also found that it was very difficult to identify the correct remuneration for staff. This was due to China's dramatic wage inflation of 7%–25% pa (across different industries). Although wage rates in China are still low (the average wage rate was RMB 3,566 per month in 2011[10]), wage inflation may eliminate China's low labor cost advantage in the medium term.[11]

The participants also identified retaining talented staff to be a significant issue. The 2011 average staff turnover rate in China was 13%,[12] reflecting the new opportunities for workers resulting from China's

rapid rate of economic development and its high levels of salary inflation. Retaining staff in China requires the development of imaginative
strategies, which may include higher salaries, long-term incentives, and
building up organizational culture and loyalty. China's current high staff
turnover rates are a disincentive for organizations to invest in T&D,
and could affect the overall productivity of the country in the future—
especially as salary levels increase.

Practical Implications for Business

These findings indicate that China trade and investment must be carefully
planned. Although some of the participants were able to successfully enter
China with limited formal planning, internationalizing without sufficient
planning stopped these organizations from taking advantage of, or protecting themselves from, a number of external factors. It is recommended
that an emergent strategy[13] is the best planning approach for China, as it
incorporates more allowance for the significant rate of change in the local
Chinese environment.

The findings also identified a number of specific areas that must be
addressed as part of the development of Chinese internationalization
plans. Each of these areas will now be briefly considered.

Consider the Motivation to Go to China

Entry plans should include an objective identification of the motivation
for entering China. Possible motivations include taking advantage of
the local Chinese market to achieve business growth, seeking new market opportunities, fulfilling an international strategy (e.g., to establish a
presence in China), responding to industry, supplier, customer, or client
pressure to support them in China, becoming globally competitive by
entering China as a key global marketplace or taking advantage of China's
low-cost materials, production, and labor.

Identify Which Customers to Target

Chinese markets are extremely large and the global markets they connect to are even larger. In addition, there are many domestic and international organizations competing in Chinese markets. This makes market

segmentation a critical component of an internationalization strategy for entering China. In addition to identifying the basis of competition, targeting the specific customers will improve the ability to communicate and address customer needs. Market segments in China are likely to include Chinese consumers, business-to-business customers, Australian businesses, and other international/global businesses operating in the Chinese market. Other attractive segments could include Australian or international customers being serviced through China-based production or local Chinese suppliers.

Decide on a Range of Possible Market Entry Modes

There are many entry mode choices available to organizations entering China including exporting, importing, licensing, franchising, FDI (greenfield, M&A, and JV strategies), strategic alliances, representative offices, utilizing agents, and fly-in-fly-out modes. It is important to choose the most appropriate entry mode, based on the advantages and disadvantages of each mode for the organization, industry, and market segment. Influential factors will include the type of business, products, customers, impact of tariffs, FDI rules and regulations, risk tolerance, the resources available, and broader economic factors such as the condition of the Chinese economy. The best choice for a new Chinese market entry will usually be a lower risk mode, which will expose the organization to fewer risks, increase the likelihood of success and provide an important learning opportunity. If the first entry is successful, plans involving greater investments in China and resource commitments can then be considered. If any form of purchase or partnership is involved, it is important to conduct due diligence on the entities being purchased or prospective partners, to ensure that there are no unspecified encumbrances and performance expectations can be met.

Assess the Political Environment in China and the Political Support That the Australian Government Can Provide

This assessment should include the Chinese political system and the impact it may have on the organization's internationalization. Important sources of assistance include home country government assistance, such as the services provided by Austrade in Australia (advice, assistance, information, seminars, trade missions, business leads, and promotional grants), City Offices (e.g., the City of Melbourne has used trade missions in the past to assist business people in getting acquainted with the Chinese environment, to obtain introductions and develop contacts with Chinese government and businesses), and the assistance provided by business councils, such as the Australia China Business Council (ACBC) network and AustCham (information, seminars, contacts, opportunities to discuss how other members entered the Chinese market, and ongoing relational support from members). Some entry modes, such as FDI, may require Chinese government approval and, in this case, it is important that organizational representatives are able to negotiate with relevant members of the Chinese government. Austrade can often provide introductions for these negotiations.

Develop Criteria for Choosing a Location

It is important to develop criteria for choosing a location in China. Attractive features for a location can include being: a major city or commercial center, close to growth areas, an area where other companies in the same industry, suppliers and customers have located, an attractive SEZ, or an area with high-quality infrastructure, high-quality local partners, low-cost labor (labor rates vary across China), skilled labor, or limited local competition.

Manage the Culture Gap

A weakness in preparation for the culture gap between Chinese and most foreign organizations can create problems with negotiations and communications at all levels. Even Singaporean Chinese organizations find there is a significant and unexpected culture gap when they enter China. Although cultural differences are a well-documented feature of international business in China, the participants in this research were still generally unprepared for the impact of these differences. Poor cross-cultural understanding will delay the development of Chinese operations, obscure opportunities, and increase expenses. Consultants can assist organizations entering China with managing the culture gap. Consultants can assist with planning for and training staff who will operate in or with Chinese subsidiaries. Learning about cultural differences through sources such as books and local courses can provide a good background for dealing with likely cultural issues. In addition, employing local Chinese managers with Western experience or Western individuals who have extensive experience in China can also help in managing the impact of the gap.

Invest in Relationship Building

As Chinese business practices are predominantly relationship-based, it is important that foreign organizations operating in China should invest in relationship building. To do this, transparent business proposals, which have broad support from across the organization and which include allowance for 3–4 trips to China each year to meet with clients, partners and regulators, gifts (these do not need to be expensive, but are an important sign of sincerity) and banquet costs (banquets are a traditional context for establishing business relationships in China). If the Chinese host provides hospitality, it is important for the business visitor to repay hospitality to demonstrate their commitment to the relationship.

Understand the Legal System and IP Issues

Conducting an analysis of the legal system used in China, the rules around FDI, and obtaining the support of a local Chinese lawyer to advise on the rules and regulations applying to the particular industry will help to circumvent legal problems later on. Although the legal system in China offers less protection than in Western countries, it is improving in areas that many Western businesses will find important, such as in arbitration. The use of local lawyers is critical as foreign lawyers have limited power in China and find it difficult to keep up with the rate of change in the Chinese legal system. IP protection is still weak and so it is important to find alternative methods for protecting IP, such as quarantining or retaining critical IP outside China or using alternative IP in Chinese-produced products. Relationships with customers, suppliers, governments, and authorities have a significant impact upon legal outcomes, business negotiation, and rights protection in China.

Follow the Changes That May Occur as a Result of the FTA

Free trade agreements affect the opportunities that operating within China provides—making some forms of business more attractive (such as producing for the local market) and others less attractive (such as exporting from China, as more competitors will commence this trade). For example, the FTA that Australia is currently negotiating with China may have a negative impact on companies that export products produced by Chinese businesses to Australia. If so, these organizations could move to FDI in China. It is unlikely that an FTA will have a negative effect on the exports of products produced by Australian businesses in China to Australia.

Understand the Impact of China's Accession to the WTO

China's membership of the WTO has created opportunities for organizations worldwide because of the improvements to China's business environment, particularly the introduction of business regulations that are more easily recognized and managed by Western businesses. It is important to be aware of the effectiveness of the changes the government has made as well as the expected consequences of China's membership of the WTO.

Make Appropriate Staffing Choices

Effective operations in China require well thought-out strategies for recruitment, selection, and to retain appropriately skilled Chinese staff. The shortage of skilled staff can be a major impediment to the establishment of successful operations in China. Deciding on the correct proportion of PCNs to HCNs is a particularly important staffing decision for Chinese operations. It is usually preferable to use PCNs in key positions and use bilingual (where possible) HCNs in most other positions. Maximizing the number of HCNs will simplify operating within the Chinese environment and also reduces staffing costs. Employment and training should be focused on the new generation of Chinese workers who offer potential, motivation, and willingness. It is important that T&D of the HCN staff takes into account their history and commences with basic training, before commencing more complex training, as well as incorporating attractive compensation, frequent reviews, and career development opportunities to retain staff.

Allow a Minimum of Two Years for Market Entry

It is important to ensure that contingency features are incorporated into a Chinese market entry plan. The data collected from the participants indicated that the greatest success was likely to result from commencement with a simple entry plan, learning more about and gaining experience with dealing with the Chinese environment and the subsequent adoption of a more involved, higher risk mode later down the track. The likelihood of a transition to a higher risk and investment entry mode should be allowed for in all internationalization plans. For example, entry via a 3-year license is acceptable, however, entry via a 10-year license may limit future entry opportunities. A 3-year agreement will allow for a reconsideration of the entry mode choice. The participants also strongly recommended the development of an exit strategy as an important component of an entry plan.

It is far better to allow for as many of the features of operating in the Chinese business environment as possible, when developing initial plans for China. This is best achieved through flexibility rather than creating complex plans, which attempts to individually allow for each feature. Dealing with issues once they have developed is generally less effective, more expensive and time-consuming than establishing mechanisms to ensure that they do not occur in the first place. It is these factors that represent the principal risks as well as the attractiveness (such as the rapid growth of the business environment in China) of doing business in China and therefore warrant a well-considered entry strategy.

Conclusion

The findings presented in this book confirm that establishing a business in China presents unique challenges. The results from the research indicates that entry to the China market usually ends up being attractive in more ways than new market entrants expect, due to the high levels of growth, technology, trade, and FDI reforms underway in China.

The findings from this research have also confirmed that the business environment in China is changing rapidly, in almost every area relevant to business. One example is the FTA negotiations between China and Australia. Most of the participants were of the opinion that the effect of the FTA would be limited to providing Australian businesses with the same rights as Chinese businesses in China and that FTA would not reduce tariffs further. By comparison, most respondents viewed China's accession to the WTO very positively and were of the opinion that it would make business conditions more similar to those in Western countries (and therefore facilitate their own operations in China).

The participants in the research were motivated to enter China by a large range of factors. Some of these included: market development, supplying specific market segments, seeking high-growth markets, developing effective agent relationships, increasing backward integration, being invited to China by the Chinese government, developing existing but small markets, and searching for suitable JV partners.

This research has determined that the participant's China selected entry modes were significantly influenced by these factors. While a number of these factors represented impediments for entry into China, generally, the conditions were found to be quite attractive and generally improving from their standpoint. China's global marketplace status, technology, and innovation focus has made it increasingly attractive, even if local salaries are increasing at a substantial rate.

These findings present a number of practical implications for businesses considering operating a business in China, including the importance of strategic planning, preparation, and the constant monitoring of the developing business conditions in China. An investigation of resources, staff, and technology transfer into Chinese subsidiaries should also be incorporated into planning for entry into China. Entry into China without a well-developed plan should only be considered when the company has the support of and demand from preexisting customers with which the organization has a good relationship.

China is a very attractive market for a large range of industries. It is modern, forward-thinking, and fast-paced. It is also a large, high-growth, emerging market, which offers foreign organizations great growth and development potential. These factors are the cause of the development on the new descriptor, the Asian Century.[14] International businesses must find ways to interact, and engage with Asian counterparts, especially with China, to remain successful and relevant. The Chinese market should be a central focus of an Asian market entry plan because of its unique role in the global context. This makes it critically important to prepare thoroughly for market entry to China. This planning should commence with the development of a deep understanding of the Chinese environment and its people. This learning process can commence with the assistance of the organization's local business council, such as the ACBC in Australia, or a Chamber of Commerce, located in China, such as AustCham in Shanghai or Beijing. These organizations can assist by facilitating access to the experiences of other similar organizations, which have already learnt about the Chinese environment at the practical market entry level. Important questions to investigate include, "How did they internationalize to China?" and "What were the issues they faced?"

An organization's success in China will depend on its knowledge of China and its navigation and negotiation skills. Managers will find it helpful to learn how to develop Chinese relationships, develop some knowledge of the language, and to understand the key cultural requirements for doing business in China. With this knowledge, and some well-considered planning, luck and prosperity in the Chinese environment are sure to follow.

Notes

Foreword

1. Ilan Alon is George D. and Harriet W. Cornell Chair of International Business, Director of The China Center at Rollins College, and visiting scholar and Asia fellow at Harvard University.

Chapter 1

1. *The Wall Street Journal* (2011).
2. Rudd (2011).
3. Ernst and Young (2011).
4. Tian (2007).
5. Wang, Zhang, and Goodfellow (1998).
6. Chan (2011); *The Economist* (2012).
7. KPMG (2011a).
8. Anon (2011a).
9. Datamonitor (2010); *The Economist* (2010a).
10. Modi (2012).
11. China Mining Association (2011).
12. Dines (2011).
13. Department of Foreign Affairs and Trade (2011b).
14. Tian (2007).
15. ANZ (2012).
16. Chung (2008).
17. Department of Foreign Affairs and Trade (2005).
18. Department of Foreign Affairs and Trade (2007).
19. Department of Foreign Affairs and Trade (2012a).
20. Australian Bureau of Statistics (2011b).
21. Department of Foreign Affairs and Trade (2007).
22. Department of Foreign Affairs and Trade (2007).
23. Stewart (2011).
24. Austrade (2011).
25. Australia China Business Council (2012).
26. Department of Foreign Affairs and Trade (2012b).
27. Burgess (1987).

28. Australian Bureau of Statistics (2011a). The Australian and New Zealand Standard Industry Classification (ANZSIC) (2011) is used.
29. McCallum (2011).
30. Linong (2006).

Chapter 2

1. CIA Factbook (2011).
2. Department of Foreign Affairs and Trade (DFAT) (2011b; 2012a); KPMG (2011b).
3. Wang, Zhang, and Goodfellow (1998).
4. National Bureau of Statistics China (2006).
5. Ministry of Commerce (2011a).
6. Ministry of Commerce (2011a).
7. CIA Factbook (2011).
8. Harcourt (2002).
9. DFAT (2012c).
10. DFAT (2012a).
11. DFAT (2012a).
12. DFAT (2012a).
13. DFAT (2012a).
14. DFAT (2012a).
15. DFAT (2012a).
16. DFAT (2012a).
17. Stewart (2011).
18. Stewart (2011).
19. Stewart (2011).
20. DFAT (2012c).
21. Stewart (2011).
22. Australian Embassy (2010).
23. DFAT (2011a).
24. DFAT (2011a).
25. DFAT (2012c).
26. World Trade Organization (2001).
27. WTO (2001).
28. WTO (2001).
29. KPMG (2011b).
30. KPMG (2011b).
31. DFAT (2012b).
32. KPMG (2011b).
33. DFAT (2012b).
34. DFAT (2012b).

35. DFAT (2012b).
36. DFAT (2012b).
37. Ministry of Commerce (2012).
38. Ministry of Commerce (2012).
39. Wang et al. (1998).
40. KPMG (2011b), p. 22.
41. KPMG (2011b).
42. Ministry of Commerce (2011b).
43. US-China Business Council (2011).
44. CIA Factbook (2012).
45. Gu (2011).
46. Linong (2006).
47. Ministry of Commerce (2011b).
48. Datamonitor (2010).
49. Datamonitor (2010).
50. Datamonitor (2010).
51. Datamonitor (2010).
52. KPMG (2011b).
53. Larum (2010).
54. Larum (2010).
55. Larum (2010).
56. Tian (2007).
57. Tian (2007).
58. KPMG (2011b).
59. Tian (2007).
60. KPMG (2011a).
61. KPMG (2011a).
62. Australian Bureau of Statistics (2011b).
63. Larum (2010).
64. Chung (2008).
65. Larum (2010).
66. DFAT (2012a).
67. Thirwell (2008).
68. Thirwell (2008).
69. Australian Bureau of Statistics (2011b).
70. The World Bank (2012).
71. The World Bank (2012).
72. KPMG (2011b).
73. KPMG (2011b).
74. Chung (2011a); KPMG (2011b).
75. KPMG (2011b).
76. KPMG (2011b).

77. PricewaterhouseCoopers (PwC) (2011).
78. HSBC (2011).
79. KPMG (2011b).
80. PWC (2011).
81. PWC (2011).
82. KPMG (2011b).
83. KPMG (2011b).
84. KPMG (2011b).
85. Linong (2006).
86. Linong (2006).
87. Linong (2006).
88. British Embassy, Beijing (2011).
89. KPMG (2011a).
90. KPMG (2011a).
91. KPMG (2011b).

Chapter 3

1. This chapter is adapted from the following Journal article: Chung, M., & Menzies, J. L. (2010). Jump over the gorge: Overcoming cultural gap in doing business with China. *Journal of Asian Business and Information Management*, *1*(1), 42–53.
2. Chung (2008).
3. Hofstede (1984), p. 21.
4. Tylor cited in Ferraro (2002), p. 19.
5. Ferraro (2002), p. 19.
6. Kogut and Singh (1988).
7. Ricks, Toyne, and Martinez (1990).
8. Ferraro (2002).
9. Carte and Fox (2008).
10. Chung (2008).
11. Johanson and Vahlne (1992).
12. Kogut and Singh (1988).
13. Johanson and Vahlne (2009).
14. Johanson and Vahlne (2009).
15. Bartlett and Ghoshal (1989).
16. Bartlett and Ghoshal (1989).
17. Tihanyi, Griffith, and Russell (2005).
18. Barkema, Bell, and Pennings (1996); Benito (1997).
19. It should be noted that Hofstede (1984) did not examine China in his original study; further revisions of Hofstede should include China (Goodall, Li, and Warner, 2007).

20. Linong (2006).
21. Linong (2006).
22. Hofstede (1984).
23. Linong (2006), p. 537.
24. Chung (2008).
25. Hofstede (2012a; b).
26. Linong (2006).
27. Linong (2006).
28. Hofstede (1984).
29. Linong (2006).
30. Hofstede (1984).
31. Linong (2006).
32. Hofstede (1984).
33. Ferarro (2002).
34. Ferraro (2002), p. 35.
35. Hall (1976); Wang, Zhang, and Goodfellow (1998).
36. Trompenaars (1993).
37. Hall (1976).
38. Chung (2008).
39. CIA Factbook (2012).
40. Australian Government (2012).
41. DFAT (2008).
42. Linong (2006).
43. Wang et al. (1998).
44. Hunt and Hodgkin (2012).
45. Wang et al. (1998).
46. Chung (2008).
47. Linong (2006).
48. Linong (2006).
49. Tian (2007).
50. Chung (2011a).
51. Linong (2006).
52. Chung (2008).
53. Linong (2006).
54. Ambler and Witzel (2000).
55. Tjoa, Jianyu, and Pykstra (2012).
56. Australian Government (2012).
57. Tjoa et al. (2012).
58. Linong (2006), p. 548.
59. Linong (2006).
60. Linong (2006).
61. Linong (2006).

62. Chung (2008).
63. Chung (2008).
64. Wang et al. (1998).
65. Wang et al. (1998).
66. Wang et al. (1998).
67. Wang et al. (1998).
68. Wang et al. (1998).
69. Wang et al. (1998).
70. Wang et al. (1998).
71. Wang et al. (1998).
72. Wang et al. (1998).
73. Ferraro (2002), p. 104.
74. Linong (2006).
75. Chung (2008).
76. Linong (2006).
77. Zeithammer and Kellogg (2011), p. 2.
78. Chung (2008).
79. Chung and Smith (2007); Gomez (1999).
80. Linong (2006).
81. Beamer and Varner (2001).
82. Mu (1995).
83. Linong (2006).
84. Chen and Tjsovold (2007).

Chapter 4

1. This chapter has been adapted from the following journal article: Menzies, J. L., & Orr, S. (2010). The impact of political behaviors on internationalization: The case of Australian companies internationalizing to China. *Journal of Chinese Economic and Foreign Trade Studies* 3(1), 24–42.
2. Austrade (2011).
3. Business Monitors International (BMI) (2011).
4. China Daily (2012).
5. Datamonitor (2010).
6. Datamonitor (2010).
7. Austrade (2011).
8. Datamonitor (2010).
9. US Department of State (2012).
10. US Department of State (2012).
11. Gregory and Stuart (1995); The State Council (2004).
12. Linong (2006).

13. Gregory and Stuart (1995).
14. Linong (2006).
15. Datamonitor (2010).
16. Political Risk Services (2012).
17. Sundaram and Black (1992); Baysinger (1984).
18. Lenway and Murtha (1994).
19. Kotabe and Czinkota (1993).
20. DFAT (2005).
21. DFAT (2012b).
22. DFAT (2011a); Austrade (2011).
23. Stewart (2011).
24. Stewart (2011).
25. AusIndustry (2007).
26. O'Toole (2001).
27. Chung and Mascitelli (2008).
28. Australia China Business Council (ACBC) (2012).
29. Austcham Shanghai (2012).
30. Vernon (1971); Baysinger (1984).
31. Luo (2001).
32. Chen (2007).
33. Grunig and Hunt (1984).
34. Baysinger (1984).
35. Vernon (1971); Fagre and Wells (1982); Kim (1988); Grosse (1996).
36. Boddewyn and Brewer (1994).
37. Rosenzweig and Singh (1991); Lenway and Murtha (1994).
38. Luo (2002).
39. Linong (2006).
40. Linong (2006).
41. Chung (2008).
42. Tan, Yang, and Veliyath (2009).
43. Tan et al. (2009).
44. Xie and Amine (2009).
45. Oliver (1996).
46. Astley and Sachdeva (1984).
47. Boddewyn and Brewer (1994).
48. Ekeledo and Sivakumar (1998).
49. Merritt (1986).
50. Osland and Cavusgil (1996); Luo (2001).
51. Douglas and Craig (1995).
52. El Kahal (2005).
53. El Kahal (2005).

54. El Kahal (2005).
55. Chung (2006).
56. Baysinger (1984).
57. O'Grady and Lane (1996).

Chapter 5

1. CIA Factbook (2011).
 2. Australian Broadcasting Corporation (2010).
 3. Costello (2009).
 4. O'Sullivan (2009).
 5. Chung and Mascitelli (2011).
 6. Economic Analytical Unit (EAU) (2005).
 7. Allen, Qian, and Qian (2005).
 8. EAU (2005).
 9. EAU (2005).
10. Blackman (2000).
11. Blackman (2000).
12. Datamonitor (2010).
13. Datamonitor (2010).
14. Linong (2006).
15. Organization for Economic Co-operation and Development (OECD) (2003).
16. EAU (2005).
17. CIA Factbook (2011).
18. Mason (2011).
19. Martin (2010).
20. Martin (2010).
21. EAU (2011).
22. EAU (2005).
23. EAU (2005).
24. Halverson (2004).
25. Halverson (2004).
26. EAU (2005).
27. EAU (2005).
28. EAU (2005).
29. EAU (2005).
30. Law Info China (2010).
31. Law Info China (2010).
32. EAU (2005).
33. CIETAC (2011).

34. CIETAC (2011).
35. CIETAC (2011).
36. CIETAC (2011).
37. Political Risk Services (2012); CIETAC (2011).
38. EAU (2005).
39. Datamonitor (2010).
40. EAU (2005).
41. EAU (2005).
42. EAU (2005).
43. EAU (2005).
44. EAU (2005).
45. Guvenli and Sanyal (2003): International Chamber of Commerce (2012).
46. Linong (2006).
47. Lam and Graham (2007).
48. Lam and Graham (2007).
49. Datamonitor (2010).
50. Linong (2006).
51. Linong (2006).
52. Halverson (2004).
53. Linong (2006).
54. Linong (2006).
55. Law China Info (2005).
56. Luming (2010).
57. Luming (2010).
58. Export, Finance, and Insurance Corporation (2010).
59. Economic Intelligence Unit (2010).
60. PricewaterhouseCoopers (2011).
61. PricewaterhouseCoopers (2011).
62. PricewaterhouseCoopers (2011).
63. International Labor Organization (2011).
64. Ministry of Commerce (2007).
65. KPMG (2011b).
66. KPMG (2011b).
67. Luo (2002).
68. Lubman (1995), p.1–21.
69. Blackman (2000).
70. Weldon and Vanhonacker (1999).
71. Blackman (2000).
72. Blackman (2000).
73. Ambler and Witzel (2000).
74. Broudehoux (2004).

75. Broudehoux (2004).
76. Broudehoux (2004).
77. Ambler and Witzel (2000).
78. White (1996).
79. White (1996).
80. Transparency International (2011).
81. Pei (2007).
82. Pei (2007).
83. Pei (2007).
84. Pei (2007).
85. Datamonitor (2010).
86. EAU (2005).
87. US Commercial Service (2010).
88. EAU (2005).

Chapter 6

1. Backman (2007).
2. Backman (2007).
3. Backman (2007).
4. World Health Organization (WHO) (2011).
5. Anon (2011b).
6. Anon (2011b).
7. Economic Analytical Unit (2005).
8. World Intellectual Property Organization (WIPO) (2010).
9. Rudd (2011).
10. *The Economist* (2010b).
11. Organization for Economic Co-operation and Development (2009).
12. Business Software Alliance (BSA) (2010).
13. BSA (2010).
14. BSA (2010).
15. BSA (2010).
16. BSA (2010).
17. BSA (2010).
18. WIPO (2010).
19. WIPO (2010).
20. WIPO (2010).
21. WIPO (2010).
22. Sen (1983).
23. IP Australia (2011).
24. IP Australia (2011).

25. IP Australia (2011).
26. IP Australia (2011).
27. IP Australia (2011).
28. IP Australia (2011).
29. IP Australia (2011).
30. WIPO (2011).
31. See WIPO (2011) for further information and explanation of the Patent Cooperation Treaty (PCT) (1970).
32. HKTDC (2005).
33. IPR in China (2011a).
34. IPR in China (2011b).
35. WIPO (1992).
36. WIPO (2001).
37. WIPO (2001).
38. Hong Kong Trade Development Council (HKTDC) (2005).
39. HKTDC (2005).
40. WIPO (2001).
41. WIPO (2001).
42. Guo and Huang (2010).
43. IP Australia (2011).
44. IP Australia (2011).
45. IP Australia (2011).
46. IP Australia (2011).
47. Australian Broadcasting Corporation (2008).
48. Gupta and Wang (2011).
49. Harris (2011a).
50. Harris (2011b).
51. Irish Exporters Association and Tomkins and Co. (2004).
52. WIPO (2011).
53. Harris (2011a); Gupta and Wang (2011).
54. Gupta and Wang (2011).
55. Harris (2011a).
56. Dunning (1988).
57. Anon (2009).
58. Anon (2009).
59. Gupta and Wang (2011).
60. Department of Foreign Affairs and Trade (DFAT) (2012a).
61. CISCO (2008).
62. Gupta and Wang (2011).
63. CISCO (2008).
64. Gupta and Wang (2011).

65. Australian Broadcasting Corporation (2008).
66. Harris (2011b).
67. Harris (2011b).
68. Harris (2011b).

Chapter 7

1. Zahra, Ireland, and Hitt (2000).
2. Zahra et al. (2000).
3. Czinkota, Ronkainen, and Ortiz (2004); Johanson and Vahlne (1977, 2009).
4. DFAT (2012a).
5. Austrade (2012).
6. Czinkota et al. (2004).
7. Czinkota et al. (2004).
8. Czinkota et al. (2004).
9. Czinkota et al. (2004).
10. Department of Foreign Affairs and Trade (2012a; 2012d).
11. This situation has changed since the completion of this research. The Australian dollar has reached parity with the US dollar and remained relatively high in the past 2 years. It has caused certain changes in the Australian education market.
12. Chung (2011b).
13. Mintzberg (1985).
14. Czinkota and Ronkainen (2006).
15. Mintzberg (1985).
16. Bartlett and Ghoshal (1989).
17. Bartlett and Ghoshal (1989).
18. Dunning (1993).

Chapter 8

1. Dunning (1988).
2. Tse, Pan, and Au (1997).
3. Root (1983; 1994) cited in Sharma and Erramilli (2004), p. 2.
4. Tse et al. (1997).
5. Davidson (1982); Anderson and Coughlan (1987); Klein, Frazier, and Roth (1990).
6. Gillespie, Jeannet, and Hennessy (2007).
7. Lin (2000).
8. Waldmeir and Tucker (2009).
9. Waldmeir and Tucker (2009).
10. Lin (2000).

11. Williamson (1975); Anderson and Gatignon (1986).
12. Anderson and Gatignon (1986); Buckley and Casson (1976); Gatignon and Anderson (1988); Williamson (1975).
13. Lin (2000).
14. Hymer (1976).
15. Dunning (1988).
16. Penrose (1959); Prahalad and Hamel (1990); Rumelt (1991); Barney (1991).
17. Barney (1991).
18. Barney (1991).
19. Barney (1991); Sharma and Erramilli (2004).
20. Peng (2009).
21. Prahalad and Hamel (1990).
22. Sharma and Erramilli (2004).
23. Sharma and Erramilli (2004).
24. Johanson and Vahlne (1977).
25. Johanson and Valhne (1977).
26. Johanson and Vahlne (2009).
27. Knight and Cavasugil (2004).
28. Knight and Cavasugil (2004).
29. Aulakh and Kotabe (1997).
30. Lin (2000).
31. Root (1994).
32. Root (1994).
33. Department of Immigration and Citizenship (2012). Note, the amount required for the Business Migration Scheme, was stipulated by the immigration policies at the time.
34. Johanson and Vahlne (1977); Johanson and Wiedersheim-Paul (1975).
35. Johanson and Vahlne (2009).
36. Monash University (2012).
37. Anderson and Gatignon (1986).
38. Levitt (1983).
39. Johanson and Vahlne (1977).
40. Lin (2000).
41. Gatignon and Anderson (1988); Goodnow and Hanz (1972).
42. Bartlett and Ghoshal (1989).
43. China.Org.Cn (2012).
44. PricewaterhouseCoopers (PwC) (2011).
45. Anderson and Gatignon (1986).
46. Barney (1991).
47. Tse et al. (1997).
48. Dunning (1988).
49. Marshall (1916).

50. HSBC (2011).
51. PWC (2011).
52. HSBC (2011).
53. Ernst and Young (2006).

Chapter 9

1. This chapter is based on and adapted from the following journal article: Menzies, J. L., & McDonnell, A. (2012). Talent in China: Exploring the issues faced by Australian multinational enterprises. *International Journal of Chinese Culture and Management 3*(2), 107–124.
2. Warner (2009).
3. Scullion and Collings (2006).
4. Boston Consulting Group (2003).
5. Braun and Warner (2002).
6. Rovai (2008).
7. *New York Times* (2008).
8. Tu and Jones (1991).
9. MacEachern, Melulis, Roberts, and Tan (2005); Brocket (2006).
10. Manpower (2006).
11. Organization for Economic Cooperation and Development (OECD) (2012).
12. Ma and Trigo (2008).
13. Ma and Trigo (2008).
14. Manpower (2006).
15. Björkman and Xiucheng (2002); Black and Gregersen (1999); Li and Scullion (2006); Scullion (2001); Stroh and Caligiuri (1998).
16. See Scullion and Collings (2006) for an in-depth discussion.
17. Ketter (2008).
18. Perlmutter (1969); Perlmutter and Heenan (1986).
19. Perlmutter (1969).
20. Perlmutter (1969).
21. Perlmutter (1969), p. 11.
22. Tu and Jones (1991).
23. Schuler and MacMillian (1986).
24. Shen and Edwards (2004).
25. Casati (1991).
26. Casati (1991).
27. McEllister (1998).
28. Björkman and Lu (1999).
29. Björkman and Lu (1999).
30. Björkman and Lu (1999).
31. Björkman and Lu (1999).

32. Björkman and Lu (1999).
33. Björkman and Lu (1999).
34. Björkman and Lu (1999).
35. Björkman and Lu (1999).
36. Ding, Fields, and Akhtar (1997).
37. Ding et al. (1997).
38. Ding et al. (1997).
39. Ding et al. (1997).
40. Han and Han (2009).
41. Han and Han (2009).
42. Han and Han (2009)
43. Beijing Foreign Enterprise Human Resources Co Ltd (2012).
44. Izquierdo (2007).
45. McEllister (1998).
46. Björkman and Lu (1999).
47. Zhu (1997).
48. Zhu (1997).
49. Zhu (1997).
50. Zhu (1997).
51. Zhu (1997).
52. Zhu (1997).
53. McEllister (1998).
54. McEllister (1998).
55. McEllister (1998).
56. Melvin (2001).
57. Yu and Björkman (1999).
58. Yu and Björkman (1999).
59. Yu and Björkman (1999).
60. McEllister (1998).
61. Chan (2011).
62. XE (2012).
63. Chan (2011); *The Economist* (2012).
64. *The Economist* (2012).
65. *The Economist* (2012).
66. *The Economist* (2012).
67. *The Economist* (2012).
68. Yu and Björkman (1999).
69. Melvin (2001).
70. Yu and Björkman (1999).
71. Yu and Björkman (1999).
72. Chen and Francesco (2000).
73. Chen and Francesco (2000).

74. Malia (2011).

75. Warner (1995).

76. Ma and Trigo (2008).

77. Rovai (2008).

78. Gamble (2003).

79. Tharenou and Harvey (2006).

80. Wong and Law (1999).

81. Björkman and Xiucheng (2002).

82. Selmer (2005).

83. Rovai (2008).

84. Jiaojiao (2007).

85. Chung and Smith (2007).

86. Compare Scullion, and Collings (2006).

87. Lowe, Downes, and Kroeck (1999).

88. Scullion and Collings (2006).

89. Gamble (2003).

90. Tsang (2001).

91. Björkman and Lu (1999).

92. Chen and Francesco (2000); Xin, Zhou, and Tsui (1998).

93. Björkman and Lu (1999).

94. Jackson and Bak (1998), p. 23.

Chapter 10

1. Department of Foreign Affairs and Trade (2012a).

2. Stewart (2011).

3. US-China Business Council (2011).

4. Australian Bureau of Statistics (2011b).

5. Larum (2010).

6. Hofstede (1984).

7. Ferraro (2002).

8. World Intellectual Property Organization (WIPO) (2010).

9. Johanson and Vahlne (1977).

10. Chan (2011).

11. *The Economist* (2012).

12. Malia (2011).

13. Mintzberg (1985).

14. McCallum (2011).

References

Allen, F., Qian, J., & Qian, M. (2005). Law, finance, and economic growth in China. *Journal of Financial Economics 77*(1), 57–116.

Ambler, T. & Witzel, M. (2000). *Doing business in China* (2nd ed.). New York, NJ: Routledge.

Anderson, E. & Coughlan, A. T. (1987). International market entry and expansion via independent or integrated channels of distribution. *Journal of Marketing 51*(1), 71–82.

Anderson, E. & Gatignon, H. (1986). Modes of foreign entry: A transaction cost analysis and propositions. *Journal of International Business Studies 17*(3), 1–26.

Anon. (2009). Personal communication: Email, June 4, 2009.

Anon. (2011a). Presentation made to the China Study Program 2011, China.

Anon. (2011b). *China shutters fake apple stores, The Age.* Retrieved July 26, 2011, from http://www.theage.com.au/technology/technology-news/china-shutters-fake-apple-stores-20110726-1hxp6.html

ANZ. (2012). *ANZ in China.* Retrieved September 28, 2012, from http://www.anz.com/china/en/about-us/our-company/china/

Astley, W. G. & Sachdeva, P. S. (1984). Structural sources of intra-organizational power: A theoretical synthesis. *Academy of Management Review 9*(1), 104–113.

Aulakh, P. M. & Kotabe, M. (1997). Antecedents and performance implications of channel integration in foreign markets. *Journal of International Business Studies 28*(1), 145–175.

AusIndustry. (2007). *Invest Victoria.* Retrieved March 25, 2008, from http://www.investvictoria.gov.au

Austcham Shanghai. (2012). *Move towards the creation of an Austcham greater China.* Retrieved February 15, 2012, from http://www.austchamshanghai.com/news/chamber-news/2011/move-towards-creation-of-austcham-greater-china.aspx

Austrade. (2011). *China fact sheet.* Retrieved September 8, 2011, from http://www.austrade.gov.au/ChinaProfile

Austrade. (2012). *About us.* Retrieved March 26, 2012, from http://www.austrade.gov.au/About-Austrade/default.aspx

Australia China Business Council. (2012). *Connecting Australia and China.* Retrieved February 15, 2012, from http://www.acbc.com.au/

Australian Broadcasting Corporation. (2008). *Riding on China's success.* Retrieved June 20, 2008, from http://www.abc.net.au/catapult/indepth/s1496179.html

Australian Broadcasting Corporation. (2010). *China's legal system under the microscope*. Retrieved January 1, 2012, from http://www.abc.net.au/world today/content/2010/s2852443.html

Australian Bureau of Statistics. (2011a). *Australian and New Zealand Standard Industry Classification (ANZSIC)*. Retrieved February 11, 2012, from http://www.abs.gov.au/ausstats/abs@.nsf/2f762f95845417aeca25706c008 34efa/7cd8aebba7225c4eca25697e0018faf3!OpenDocument

Australian Bureau of Statistics. (2011b). Foreign investment in Australia, Catalogue 5352. International Investment Position, Australia, Supplementary Statistics, 2011.

Australian Embassy. (2010). *Trade and investment*. Retrieved January 1, 2012, from http://www.china.embassy.gov.au/bjng/relations2.html

Australian Government. (2012). Australia in the Asian Century white paper. Retrieved November 16, 2012 from http://asiancentury.dpmc.gov.au /white-paper

Australian Government, Attorney General Department. (2012). *Australia's international anti-corruption obligations*. Retrieved March 20, 2012, from http://www.ema.gov.au/www/agd/agd.nsf/Page/Crimeprevention_Corrupt ion_Australiasinternationalanti-corruptionobligations

Backman, M. (2007). *China's counterfeit culture is becoming quite an education, The Age*. Retrieved on July 20, 2011, from http://www.theage.com.au/news /business/chinas-counterfeit-culture-is-quite-an-education/2007/03/27 /1174761469475.html

Barkema, H. G., Bell, J. H. J., & Pennings, J. M. (1996). Foreign entry, cultural barriers, and learning. *Strategic Management Journal 17*(2), 151–166.

Barney, J. B. (1991). Firm resources and sustained competitive advantage. *Journal of Management 17*(1), 99–120.

Bartlett, C. A. & Ghoshal, S. (1989). *Managing across borders: The transnational solution*. Boston, MA: Harvard Business School Press.

Baysinger, B. D. (1984). Domain maintenance as an objective of business political activity: An expanded typology. *Academy of Management Review 9*(2), 248–258.

Beamer, L. & Varner, I. (2001). *Intercultural communication in the global workplace*. New York, NJ: McGraw-Hill Higher Education.

Beijing Foreign Enterprise Human Resources Co Ltd. (2012). *About us*. Retrieved March 26, 2012, from http://www.fesco.com.cn/164/index.html

Benito, G. R. G. (1997). Divestment of foreign production operations. *Applied Economics 29*(10), 1365–1377.

Björkman, I. & Lu, Y. (1999). The management of human resources in Chinese-western joint ventures. *Journal of World Business 34*(3), 306–324.

Björkman, I. & Xiucheng, F. (2002). Human resource management and the performance of western firms in China. *International Journal of Human Resource Management 13*(6), 853–864.

Black, J. S. & Gregersen, H. B. (1999, March–April). The right way to manage expats. *Harvard Business Review 77*(2), 52–63.

Blackman, C. (2000). *China business: Rules of the game.* St Leonards, NSW: Allen & Unwin.

Boddewyn, J. & Brewer, T. (1994). International-business political behavior: New theoretical directions. *Academy of Management Review 19*(1), 119–143.

Boston Consulting Group. (2003, February). *India's new opportunity 2020 report.* New Delhi.

Braun, W. H. & Warner, M. (2002). Strategic human resource management in western multinationals in China: The differentiation of practices across different ownership forms. *Personnel Review 31*(5), 553–579.

British Embassy, Beijing. (2011). FCO country updates for business: Inward Investment, May 2011. Retrieved February 2, 2012, from www.ukti.gov.uk/export/countries/asiapacific/.../china/.../139760.html

Brocket, J. (2006, October 26). Talent war in India and China. *People Management 12*(21).

Broudehoux, A-M. (2004). *The making and selling of post-Mao Beijing.* London, Routledge.

Buckley, P. J. & Casson, M. (1976). *The future of the multinational enterprise.* New York, NJ: Holmes-Meier.

Burgess, R. G. (1987). *In the field: An introduction to field research.* London: George, Allen & Unwin.

Business Monitors International. (2011). *China business forecast report.* London: Business Monitors International.

Business Software Alliance. (2010). *Global piracy study 2010.* Retrieved July 20, 2011, from http://www.bsa.org/globalstudy

Carte, P. & Fox, C. (2008). Bridging the culture gap: A practical guide to international business communication (2nd ed.). Philadelphia, PA: Kogan Page Publishers.

Casati, C. (1991). Satisfying labour laws: And needs. *China Business Review 18*(4), 16–22.

Chan, C-Y. (2011). *Keeping track of the changing HR landscape in Shanghai,* Presentation for Bencham, January 13, 2011, Shanghai.

Chen, N. & Tjsovold, D. (2007). Guanxi and leader member relationships between American managers and Chinese employees: Open-minded dialogue as mediator. *Asia Pacific Journal of Management 24*(2), 171–189.

Chen, X. C. & Francesco, A. M. (2000). Employee demography, organizational commitment, and turnover intentions in China: Do cultural differences matter? *Human Relations 53*(6), 869–887.

Chen, Y-R. (2007). The strategic management of government affairs in China: How multinational corporations in China interact with the Chinese Government. *Journal of Public Relations Research 19*(3), 283–306.

China Daily. (2012). *Full text of Xi's speech to the media*, November 17, 2012 from http://www.chinadaily.com.cn/china/2012cpc/2012-11/16/content_1593 4514.htm

China Mining Association. (2011). *Global pig iron output up 9.4 percent in August*. Retrieved February 12, 2012, from http://www.chinamining.org /News/2011-09-23/1316763559d49863.html

China.Org.Cn. (2012). People's Republic of China Law on Enterprises Operating Exclusively with Foreign Capital (1986). Retrieved March 26, 2012, from http://www.china.org.cn/business/laws_regulations/2007-08/02/ content _1219563.html

Chung, M. (2006). *The impact of cultural difference: An Australian business in China*. Unpublished Doctoral Thesis, Melbourne: Monash University.

Chung, M. (2008). *Shanghaied—Why Foster's could not survive China*. Heidelberg, VIC: Heidelberg Press.

Chung, M. (2011a). *Doing business successfully in China*. Chandos Publishing, Oxford, UK.

Chung, M. (2011b). *Doing business in China is a necessity*, The Conversation, Retrieved 24 September, 2012, from http://theconversation.edu.au/doing -business-with-china-is-a-necessity-not-a-choice-3930

Chung, M. & Mascitelli, B. (2008). The role of sister city relationships in the enhancement of trade: Latrobe city (Australia) and Taizou (China). *Refereed Paper Presentation at the Global Business and Technology Association (GBATA)*, Madrid, Spain, July 8–12.

Chung, M. & Menzies, J. L. (2010). Jump over the gorge: Overcoming cultural gap in doing business with China. *Journal of Asian Business and Information Management 1*(1), 42–53.

CIA Factbook. (2011). *China*. Retrieved January 1, 2012, from, https://www.cia .gov/library/publications/the-world-factbook/geos/ch.html

CIA Factbook. (2012). *China*. Retrieved January 10, 2012, from, https://www .cia.gov/library/publications/the-world-factbook/geos/ch.html

CIETAC. (2011). *About us*. Retrieved January 4, 2012, from http://www.cietac .org/index.cms

CISCO. (2008). *Data leakage worldwide: The high cost of insider threats*. Retrieved February 2, 2012, from http://www.cisco.com/en/US/solutions /collateral/ns170/ns896/ns895/white_paper_c11-506224.pdf

Costello, T. (2009, July 15). The view from the east has a very different hue, *The Sydney Morning Herald*. Retrieved February 20, 2012 http://www .smh.com.au/opinion/the-view-from-the-east-has-a-very-different-hue -20090714-dk46.html

Czinkota, M. R. & Ronkainen, I. A. (2006). *International marketing* (8th ed.). Mason, OH: Thomson Higher Education.

Czinkota, M. R., Ronkainen, I. A., & Ortiz, M. (2004). *The export marketing imperative*. Washington, DC: Thomson Learning.

Datamonitor. (2010). *Country analysis report: China: In-depth PESTLE insights*. London: Datamonitor PLC REP.

Davidson, W. H. (1982). *Global strategic management*. New York, NJ: John Wiley & Sons.

Department of Foreign Affairs & Trade. (2005). *China: Bilateral trade and investment factsheet*. Retrieved February 19, 2008, from http://www.dfat .gov.au/geo/china/proc_bilat_fs.pdf

Department of Foreign Affairs & Trade. (2007). *People's Republic of China country brief—August 2006*. Retrieved February 19, 2008, from http://www.dfat .gov.au/geo/china/cb_index.html

Department of Foreign Affairs & Trade. (2008). *Australia—an overview*. Retrieved June 27, 2008, from http://www.dfat.gov.au/aib/overview.html

Department of Foreign Affairs & Trade. (2011a). *People's Republic of China country brief*. Retrieved August 19, 2011, from http://www.dfat.gov.au/geo /china/cb_index.html

Department of Foreign Affairs & Trade (DFAT). (2011b). *China economic fact sheet*. Retrieved July 20, 2011, from http://www.dfat.gov.au/geo/fs/chin .pdf

Department of Foreign Affairs & Trade. (2012a). China economic fact sheet. Retrieved January 8, 2012, from http://www.dfat.gov.au/geo/fs /chin.pdf

Department of Foreign Affairs & Trade. (2012b). *Australia-China free trade negotiations*. Retrieved November 20, 2012, from http://www.dfat.gov.au /fta/acfta/120417_subscriber_update.html

Department of Foreign Affairs & Trade. (2012c). *People's Republic of China country brief*. Retrieved January 6, 2012, from http://www.dfat.gov.au /geo/china/china_brief.html

Department of Foreign Affairs & Trade. (2012d). *Australia economic fact sheet*. Retrieved May 16, 2012, from http://www.dfat.gov.au/geo/fs/aust .pdf

Department of Immigration and Citizenship. (2012). *Business owner (residence) (Subclass 890)*. Retrieved May 16, 2012, from http://www.immi.gov.au /skilled/business/890/eligibility-business-owner.htm#e

Dines, C. (2011). *Discussion of Australia's mining industry: From bust to boom.* Retrieved February 20, 2012, from http://www.rba.gov.au/publications /confs/2011/connolly-orsmond-disc.pdf

Ding, D., Fields, D., & Akhtar, S. (1997). An empirical study of human resource management policies and practices in foreign-invested enterprises in China: The case of Shenzhen Special Economic Zone. *International Journal of Human Resource Management 8*(5), 595–613.

Douglas, S. P. & Craig, C. S. (1995). *Global marketing strategy.* New York, NJ: McGraw Hill.

Dunning, J. H. (1988). The eclectic paradigm of international production: A restatement and some possible extensions. *Journal of International Business Studies 19*(1), 1–31.

Dunning, J. H. (1993). *Multinational enterprises and the global economy.* Wokingham, UK: Addison Wesley.

Economic Analytical Unit. (2005). *Unlocking China's services sector.* Canberra, ACT: Australian Government.

Economic Intelligence Unit. (2010). *Organising an investment in China: Prepare for opportunity: A practical guide from the Economist.* Retrieved March 20, 2012, from http://www.iberglobal.com/Archivos/china_guide_fdi_eiu.pdf

Ekeledo, I. & Sivakumar, K. (1998). Foreign market entry mode choice of service organisations: A contingency perspective. *Journal of the Academy of Marketing Science 26*(4), 274–292.

El Kahal, S. (2005). *Business in Asia Pacific: Text and cases.* Wiltshire: Oxford University Press.

Ernst & Young. (2011). *Responding to a Black Swan: Principles and protocols for responding to unexpected and catastrophic events.* Retrieved September 25 2012, from http://www.ey.com/Publication/vwLUAssets/Principles_and _protocols_for_responding_to_unexpected_catastrophicevents/$FILE /Black%20swan_FINAL.pdf

Export, Finance & Insurance Corporation. (2010). China country profile: December 2010. Retrieved March 22, 2012, from http://www.efic.gov. au/country/countryprofiles/Documents/CP_CHINA_201012.pdf?utm _source=seo&utm_medium=country-china&utm_campaign=seo-efic -country-china-pdf-lk-110811

Fagre, N. & Wells, L. Jr. (1982). Bargaining power of multinationals and host governments. *Journal of International Business Studies 13*(2), 9–23.

Ferraro, G. P. (2002). *The cultural dimension of international business* (4th ed). New York, NJ: Prentice Hall.

Gamble, J. (2003). Transferring human resource practices from the United Kingdom to China: The limits and potential for convergence. *International Journal of Human Resource Management 14*(3), 369–387.

Gatignon, H. & Anderson, E. (1988). The multinational corporation's degree of control over foreign subsidiaries: An empirical test of a transaction cost explanation. *Journal of Law, Economics, & Organization 4*(2), 305–336.

Gillespie, K., Jeannet, J-P., & Hennessy, H. D. (2007). *Global marketing* (2nd ed.). Boston, MA: Houghton Mifflin.

Gomez, E. T. (1999). *Chinese business in Malaysia: Accumulation, accommodation and ascendance.* Richmond, Surrey: Curzon Press.

Goodnow, J. D. & Hanz, J. E. (1972). Environmental determinants of overseas market entry strategies. *Journal of International Business Studies 3*(1), 33–50.

Gregory, P. & Stuart, R. (1995). *Comparative economic system* (5th ed.). Boston, CT: Houghton Mifflin.

Grosse, R. (1996). The bargaining relationship between foreign MNEs and host governments in Latin America. *International Trade Journal 10*(4), 467–499.

Grunig, J. E. & Hunt, T. (1984). *Managing public relations.* New York, NJ: Holt, Rinehart & Winston.

Gu, B. (2011). China's foreign investment laws, Presentation made to the China Study Program November 16, 2011, East China University of Politics and Law, Shanghai, China.

Guo, S. & Huang, H. (2010). China trademark law and cases. Retrieved February 20, 2012, from http://www.ipr2.org/storage/Trademark_Laws_&_Cases -EN-110504-final1006.pdf

Gupta, A. K. & Wang, H. (2011). *Safeguarding your intellectual property in China.* Retrieved July 20, 2011, from http://www.businessweek.com/globalbiz /content/may2011/gb20110520_313022.html

Guvenli, T. & Sanyal, R. (2003). Perception and management of legal issues in China by US firms. *The Journal of Socio-Economics 32*(2), 161–181.

Hall, E. T. (1976). How cultures collide. *Psychology Today 10*, 67–74.

Halverson, K. (2004). China's WTO accession: Economic, legal and political implications. *Boston College International and Comparative Law Review 27*(2), 319–370.

Han, J. & Han, J. I. (2009). Network-based recruiting and applicant attraction in China: Insights from both organizational and the individual perspectives. *International Journal of Human Resource Management 20*(11), 2228–2249.

Harcourt, T. (2002). *Strange castes of commerce and accidental exporters.* Retrieved February 20, 2012, from http://timharcourt.com/adobe/BOY _SpecialEvents.pdf

Harris, D. (2011a). *Protecting your intellectual property in China, Part 1.* Retrieved July 15, 2011, from http://www.chinalawblog.com/2011/06/protecting _your_intellectual_property_in_china_part_i.html

Harris, D. (2011b). *Protecting your intellectual property in China, Part 2.* Retrieved July 17, 2011, from http://www.chinalawblog.com/2011/06/protecting _your_intellectual_property_in_china_part_ii.html

Hofstede, G. (1984). *Cultures consequences.* Abridged edition, Newbury Park, CA: Sage.

Hofstede, G. (2012a). *Australia.* Retrieved October 12, 2012 from http://geert -hofstede.com/australia.html

Hofstede, G. (2012b). China. Retrieved October 12, 2012 from http://geert -hofstede.com/china.html

Hong Kong Trade Development Council (HKTDC). (2005). *Practical guide to IPR protection in China—How to protect your brand?* Retrieved July 20, 2011, from http://info.hktdc.com/chinaipr/ipr.html

HSBC. (2011). *Doing business in China.* Retrieved January 10, 2012, from http://www.hsbc.com.hk/1/PA_1_3_S5/content/greaterchina/pdf/doing _business_CN.pdf

Hunt, K. A. & Hodkin, W. (2012). The criticality of cultural awareness in global marketing: Some case examples. *Journal of Business Case Studies 8*(1), 1–9.

Hymer, S. H. (1976). *The international operations of national firms: A study of direct foreign investment.* Cambridge, MA: MIT Press.

International Chamber of Commerce. (2012). *Welcome to ICC dispute resolution services.* Retrieved February 16, 2012, from http://www.iccwbo.org/court/

International Labor Organization. (2011). *China: From an active employment policy to employment promotion law.* Retrieved February 20, 2012, from http://www.ilo.org/wcmsp5/groups/public/---dgreports/---dcomm/--- publ/documents/publication/wcms_166905.pdf

IP Australia. (2011). *IP passport: China.* Retrieved July 24, 2011, from http:// www.ipaustralia.gov.au/pdfs/factsheets/ippassport_china.pdf

IPR in China. (2011a). *Copyright law to be revised.* Retrieved January 1, 2012, from http://www.chinaipr.gov.cn/lawsarticle/laws/lawsar/copyright/201107 /1239509_1.html

IPR in China. (2011b). *How long is the duration of copyright protection.* Retrieved January 12, 2012, from http://www.chinaipr.gov.cn/guidescopyarticle /guides/civillaw/civilfaq/200607/234509_1.html

Irish Exporters Association and Tomkins and Co. (2004). *Intellectual property management: A guide for exporters.* Retrieved April 8, 2012, from http: //www.tomkins.com/uploads/news/intellectual_property_management.pdf

Izquierdo, J. P. (2007). Five practical strategies for building a Chinese workforce. *Industry Week November 256*(11), 31.

Jackson, T. & Bak, M. (1998). Foreign companies and Chinese workers: Employee motivations in the People's Republic of China. *Journal of Organizational Change Management 11*(4), 282–300.

Jiaojiao, R. (2007). *The turning tide of overseas Chinese, China Daily.* Retrieved October 6, 2010, from http://www.chinadaily.com.cn/china/2007-05/30 /content_883647.html

Johanson, J. & Vahlne, J. E. (1977). The internationalization process of the firm: A model of knowledge development and increasing foreign market commitment. *Journal of International Business Studies 8*(1), 35–40.

Johanson, J. & Vahlne, J. E. (1992). Management of foreign market entry. *Scandinavian International Business Review 1*(3), 9–27.

Johanson, J. & Vahlne, J. E. (2009). The Uppsala internationalization process model revisited: From liability of foreignness to liability of outsidership. *Journal of International Business Studies 40*(9), 1411–1413.

Johanson, J. & Wiedersheim-Paul, P. E. (1975). The internationalization of the firm: Four Swedish cases. *The Journal of Management Studies 12*(3), 306–307.

Ketter, P. (2008). Chinese employers fight retention battle. *Training and Development 62*, 16–18.

Kim, W. C. (1988). The effects of competition and corporate political responsiveness on multinational bargaining power. *Strategic Management Journal 9*(2), 289–295.

Klein, S., Frazier, G. L., & Roth, V. J. (1990). A transaction cost analysis model of channel integration in international markets. *Journal of Marketing Research 27*(2), 196–208.

Knight, G. A. & Cavusgil S. T. (2004). Innovation, organizational capabilities, and the born-global firm. *Journal of International Business Studies 35*(2), 124–141.

Kogut, B. & Singh, H. (1988). The effect of national culture on the choice of entry mode. *Journal of International Business Studies 19*(3), 411–432.

Kotabe, M. & Czinkota, M. R. (1993). State government promotion of manufacturing exports: A gap analysis. *Journal of International Business Studies 23*(4), 637–658.

KPMG. (2011a). *China's 12th Five-Year Plan: Overview.* Retrieved September 28, 2012, from http://www.kpmg.com/cn/en/IssuesAndInsights/Articles Publications/Documents/China-12th-Five-Year-Plan-Overview-201104.pdf

KPMG. (2011b). *Investment in the People's Republic of China.* Retrieved January 3, 2012, from http://www.kpmg.com/cn/en/issuesandinsights /articlespublications/pages/investment-in-china-201111.aspx

Lam, N. M. & Graham, J. L. (2007). *China now: Doing business in the world's most dynamic market.* New York, NJ: McGraw-Hill.

Larum, J. (2010). *Into the dragon's den: Australia's investment into China.* Retrieved November 24, 2012, from http://www.lowyinstitute.org/Publication .asp?pid=1365

Law Info China. (2010). *A brief introduction to China.* Retrieved January 01, 2012, from http://www.lawinfochina.com/Legal/index.shtml

Lenway, S. A. & Murtha, T. P. (1994). The state as strategist in international business research. *Journal of International Business Studies 25*(3), 513–535.

Levitt, T. (1983, March–April). The globalization of markets. *Harvard Business Review 61*(3), 92–102.

Li, S. & Scullion. H. (2006). Bridging the distance: Managing cross-border knowledge holders. *Asia Pacific Journal of Management 23*(1), 71–92.

Lin, H. (2000). Choice of market entry mode in emerging markets: Influences on entry strategy in China. *Journal of Global Marketing 14*(1–2), 83–109.

Linong, Z. (2006). *China business: Environment, momentum, strategies and prospects.* Singapore: Pearson Prentice Hall.

Lowe, K. B., Downes M., & Kroeck, K. G. (1999). The impact of gender and location on the willingness to accept overseas assignments. *The International Journal of Human Resource Management 10*(2), 223–234.

Lubman, S. (1995). Introduction: The future of Chinese law. *China Quarterly 141*, 1–21.

Luming, C. (2010). *China issues new policies to attract foreign investment.* Retrieved February 20, 2012, from http://www.highbeam.com/doc/1G1-226655995 .html

Luo, Y. (2001). Toward a cooperative view of MNE–host government relation building blocks and performance implications. *Journal of International Business Studies 32*(3), 401–419.

Luo, Y. (2002). *Multinational enterprises in emerging markets.* Copenhagen, Denmark: Copenhagen Business School Press.

Ma, S. & Trigo, V. (2008). Winning the war for managerial talent in China: An empirical study. *The Chinese Economy 41*(3), 34–57.

MacEachern, D., Melulis, E., Roberts, P., & Tan. J. S. (2005). Closing China's supply chain talent gap. *Supply Chain Management 3*(9), 46–52.

Malia, J. (2011). *Managing rewards in Asia.* Retrieved March 20, 2012, from http://www.mercersignatureevents.com/global_outsourcing_2011/resources /Managing%20Rewards%20in%20Asia%20-%20FINAL.pdf

Manpower. (2006). *The China talent paradox.* Shanghai: Manpower China.

Marshall, A. (1916). *Principles of economics: An introductory volume* (7th ed.). London: Macmillan.

Martin. M. F. (2010). *Understanding China's political system.* Retrieved February 10, 2012, from http://www.fas.org/sgp/crs/row/R41007.pdf

Mason, A. (2011). *Human rights in China and Hong Kong.* Retrieved January 4, 2012, from http://law.anu.edu.au/cipl/Publications/OccasionalPapers /MasonAug01.pdf?&lang=en_us&output=json&session-id=14f64aa92e34 c390bbc3c2ff56a2c2e7

McCallum, W. (2011). *Asialink: The Asian Century.* Retrieved August 8, 2012, from http://www.chinaconnections.com.au/zh/the-magazine/back -issues/78-novdec-2011/1046-asialink-the-asian-century

McEllister, R. (1998). Recruitment and retention of managerial staff in China. In J. Selmer (Ed.), *International management in China: Cross-cultural issues* (pp. 99–114). London: Routledge.

Melvin, S. (2001). Special report: Human resources retaining Chinese employees. *The China Business Review 43*, 30–35.

Menzies, J. L. & McDonnell, A. (2012). Talent in China: Exploring the issues faced by Australian multinational enterprises. *International Journal of Chinese Culture and Management 3*(2), 107–124.

Menzies, J. L. & Orr, S. (2010). The impact of political behaviors on internationalisation: The case of Australian companies internationalising to China. *Journal of Chinese Economic and Foreign Trade Studies 3*(1), 24–42.

Merritt, G. (1986). Coping with the new protectionism: How companies are learning to love it. *International Management 41*(9), 20–26.

Ministry of Commerce. (2007). *Labor law of the People's Republic of China.* Retrieved March 20, 2012, from http://english.mofcom.gov.cn/aarticle/policyrelease/internationalpolicy/200703/20070304475283.html

Ministry of Commerce. (2011a). *Import export indicators.* Retrieved December 28, 2011, from http://english.mofcom.gov.cn/static/column/statistic/ieindicators.html/1

Ministry of Commerce. (2011b). *Statistics of January–November 2011 on national absorption of FDI.* Retrieved January 10, 2012, from http://english.mofcom.gov.cn/aarticle/statistic/foreigninvestment/201112/20111207889119.html

Ministry of Commerce. (2012). *China FTA network.* Retrieved January 11, 2012, from http://fta.mofcom.gov.cn/english/fta_qianshu.shtml

Mintzberg, H. (1985). Of strategies, emergent and deliberate. *Strategic Management Journal 6*(3), 257–272.

Modi, M. (2012). *World crude steel production share: By country. Bloomberg* Retrieved February 20, 2012, from http://www.bloomberg.com/news/2012-01-23/world-crude-steel-production-share-by-country-table-.html

Mu, D. P. (1995). Culture and business: Interacting effectively to achieve mutual goals. *East Asian Executive Reports 17*(6), 6–17.

National Bureau of Statistics China. (2006). *Total value of imports and exports.* Retrieved February 2, 2012, from http://www.stats.gov.cn/tjsj/ndsj/2007/html/R1803E.HTML

New York Times. (2008). *New labour law introduced in China. New York Times.* Retrieved October 10, 2010, from http://www.nytimes.com/2008/01/01/business/worldbusiness/01iht-chilabor.1.8968456.html

O'Grady, S. & Lane, H. (1996). The psychic distance paradox. *Journal of International Business Studies 27*(2), 309–333.

O'Sullivan, M. (2009). "Stern Hu 'thrown to the wolves'" *The Sydney Morning Herald*. Retrieved February 02, 2012, from http://www.smh.com.au /business/stern-hu-thrown-to-the-wolves-20090710-dg1r.html

O'Toole, K. (2001). Kokusaika and internationalisation: Australian and Japanese sister city type relationships. *Australian Journal of International Affairs* 55(3), 403–419.

Oliver, C. (1996). The institutional embeddedness of economic activity. In J. Dutton & J. Baum (Eds.), *Advances in strategic management* (pp. 163–186). Greenwich: JAI Press.

Organization for Economic Cooperation & Development (OECD). (2003). *China: Progress and reform challenges*. Paris: OECD.

OECD. (2009). *Magnitude of counterfeiting and piracy of tangible products: An update*. Retrieved August 02, 2012, from http://www.oecd.org/industry /industryandglobalisation/44088872.pdf

OECD. (2012). *Education indicators in focus*. Paris: OECD.

Osland, G. E. & Cavusgil, S. T. (1996). Performance issues in US-China joint ventures. *California Management Review 38*(2), 106–130.

Pei, X. (2007). *Corruption threatens China's future*. Retrieved January 4, 2012, from http://www.carnegieendowment.org/files/pb55_pei_china _corruption_final.pdf

Peng, M. (2009). *Global business*. Cinncinatti, OH: Cengage Learning.

Penrose, E. T. (1959). *The theory of the growth of the firm*. New York, NJ: John Wiley.

Perlmutter, H. V. (1969). The tortuous evolution of the multinational corporation. *Columbia Journal of World Business 4*(1), 9–18.

Perlmutter, H. V. & Heenan, D. H. (1986, March–April). Cooperate to compete globally. *Harvard Business Review* 136–152.

Political Risk Services. (2012). *Country data*. Retrieved January 20, 2012, from http://www.prsgroup.com/Default.aspx

Prahalad, C. K. & Hamel, G. (1990). The core competence of the organization. *Harvard Business Review 68*(3), 79–91.

PricewaterHouse Coopers. (2011). *Doing business and investing in China*. Retrieved October 20, 2012, from http://download.pwc.com/ie/pubs /PwC-Doing-Business-and-Investing-in-China.pdf

Ricks, D., Toyne, B., & Martinez, Z. (1990). Recent development in the international management research. *Journal of International Management 16*(2), 219–253.

Root, F. R. (1983). *Foreign market entry strategies*. New York, NJ: AMACON.

Root, F. R. (1994). Entry strategies for international markets. Washington, D.C.: Heath & Company.

Rosenzweig, P. & Singh, J. (1991). Organizational environments and the multinational enterprise. *Academy of Management Review 16*(2), 340–361.

Rovai, S. (2008). Recruiting high-tech managerial talents in China: An institutional perspective. *Journal of Technology Management in China 3*(2), 181–193.

Rudd, K. (2011). *Australia China 2.0 trade mission*, Presentation, July 14, 2011, Grand Hyatt, Melbourne.

Rumelt, R. P. (1991). How much does industry matter? *Strategic Management Journal 12*(3), 167–185.

Schuler, R. S. & MacMillian, I. C. (1986). Gaining competitive advantage through human resource management practices. *Human Resource Management 23*(3), 241–255.

Scullion, H. (2001). International human resource management: An Introduction. In J. Storey (Ed.), *Human resource management: A critical text* (pp. 3–21). Cornwall: Thomson Business Press.

Scullion, H. & Collings, D. G. (2006). *Global staffing*. Abingdon: Routledge.

Selmer, J. (2005). Expatriates' hesitation and the localization of western business operations in China. *International Journal of Human Resource Management 15*(6), 1094–1107.

Sen, A. (1983). Development: Which way now? *Economic Journal 93*(372), 745–762.

Sharma, V. M. & Erramilli, M. K. (2004). Resource based explanation of entry mode choice. *Journal of Marketing Theory and Practice 12*(1), 1–18.

Shen, J. & Edwards, V. (2004). Recruitment and selection in Chinese MNEs. *International Journal of Human Resource Management 15*(4), 814–835.

Stewart, B. (2011). *China 2011*, Presentation made to the China Study Program 16th November 2011, East China University of Politics and Law, Shanghai, China.

Stroh, L. K. & Caligiuri. P. M. (1998). Increasing global competitiveness through effective people management. *Journal of World Business 33*(1), 1–16.

Sundaram, A. K. & Black, J. S. (1992). The environment and internal organization of multinational enterprises. *Academy of Management Review 17*(4), 729–757.

Tan, J., Yang, J., & Veliyath, R. (2009). Particularistic and system trust among small and medium enterprises: A comparative study in China's transition economy. *Journal of Business Venturing 24*(6), 544–557.

Tharenou, P. & Harvey. M. (2006). Examining the overseas staffing options utilized by Australian headquartered multinational corporations. *International Journal of Human Resource Management 17*(6), 1095–1114.

The Economist. (2012). *The end of cheap China: What do soaring Chinese wages mean for global manufacturing?* Retrieved March 20, 2012, from http://www.economist.com/node/21549956

The Economist. (2010a). *Three-way split America, the euro zone and the emerging world are heading in different directions.* Retrieved February 20, 2012, from http://www.economist.com/node/17677746

The Economist. (2010b). *Patents, yes, ideas, maybe*. Retrieved July 20, 2011, from http://www.economist.com/node/17257940?story_id=17257940

The State Council. (2004). *The central people's government of the People's Republic of China*. Retrieved March 28, 2008, from http://www.gov.cn

The Wall Street Journal. (2011). *China overtakes Japan as world's No. 2 economy*. Retrieved October 28, 2011, from http://online.wsj.com/article/SB10001424052748703361904576142832741439402.html

The World Bank. (2012). *Doing business: Economy rankings*. Retrieved January 12, 2012, from http://www.doingbusiness.org/rankings

Thirwell, M. (2008). *Is the foreign review board acting fairly?* Retrieved February 18, 2012, from http://www.lowyinstitute.org/Publication.asp?pid=953

Tian, X. (2007). *Managing international business in China*. Cambridge: Cambridge University Press.

Tihanyi, L., Griffith, D. A., & Russell, C. J. (2005). The effect of cultural distance on entry mode choice, international diversification, and performance: A meta-analysis. *Journal of International Business Studies 36*(3), 270–283.

Tjoa, T., Jianyu, O., & Pykstra, L. (2012). Complying with PRC Antibribery Laws: A clarification of China's criminal and commercial antibribery statutes. *China Business Review*. Retrieved March 20, 2012, from https://www.chinabusinessreview.com/public/0503/wong.html

Transparency International. (2011). *World corruption index*. Retrieved January 01, 2012, from http://www.transparency.org/policy_research/surveys_indices/cpi/2010/results

Trompenaars, F. (1993). *Riding the waves of culture: Understanding cultural diversity in business*. London: Nicholas Brealey Publishing Ltd.

Tsang, E. W. K. (2001). Managerial learning in foreign-invested enterprises in China. *Management International Review 41*(1), 29–51.

Tse, D. K., Pan, Y., & Au, K. Y. (1997). How MNCs choose entry modes and form alliances: The China experience. *Journal of International Business Studies 28*(4), 779–805.

Tu, H. S. & Jones, C. A. (1991). Human resource management issues in Sino-US business ventures. *Akron Business and Economic Review 22*(4), 18–28.

US Commercial Service. (2010). *Doing business in China 2010: Country commercial guide for U.S. Companies*. Retrieved August 20, 2011, from http://www.mwtc.org/uploadedFiles/Doing%20Business%20in%20China%202010.pdf

US Department of State. (2012). *Background note: China*. Retrieved February 20, 2012, from http://www.state.gov/r/pa/ei/bgn/18902.html

US-China Business Council. (2011). *Foreign direct investment in China*. Retrieved January 10, 2012, from https://www.uschina.org/statistics/fdi_cumulative.html

Vernon, R. (1971). *Sovereignty at bay.* New York, NJ: Basic Books.

Waldmeir, P. & Tucker, S. (2009, September 30). Danone to quit joint venture with Wahaha. *Financial Times.* Retrieved March 24, 2012, from http://www.ft.com/intl/cms/s/0/849e7eda-ad87-11de-bb8a-00144feabdc0.html#axzz1q4cUUCab

Wang, Y., Zhang X. S., & Goodfellow, R. (1998). *Business culture in China.* Singapore: Butterworth Heinemen.

Warner, M. (1995). *The management of human resources in Chinese industry.* London: Macmillan.

Warner, M. (2009). 'Making sense' of HRM in China: Setting the scene. *The International Journal of Human Resource Management 20*(11), 2169–2193.

Weldon, E. & Vanhonacker, W. (1999). Operating a foreign-invested enterprise in China: Challenges for managers and management researchers. *Journal of World Business 34*(1), 94–107.

White, G. (1996). Corruption and transition from socialism in China. *Journal of Law and Society 23*(1), 149–169.

Williamson, O. E. (1975). *Markets and hierarchies: Analysis and antitrust implications.* New York, NJ: Free Press.

Wong, L.-S. & Law. K. S. (1999). Managing localization in the PRC: A practical model. *Journal of World Business 34*(1), 26–40.

World Health Organization (WHO). (2011). Medicines: spurious/falsely-labelled/ falsified/counterfeit (SFFC) medicines. Retrieved July 11, 2012, from http://www.who.int/mediacentre/factsheets/fs275/en/

World Intellectual Property Organization (WIPO). (1992). *China: Provisions on the implementation of the international copyright treaties.* Retrieved September 15, 2011, from http://www.wipo.int/wipolex/en/details.jsp?id=6326

World Intellectual Property Organization (WIPO). (2001). *China: Regulations on computer software protection.* Retrieved December 10, 2011, from http://www.wipo.int/wipolex/en/details.jsp?id=840

World Intellectual Property Organization (WIPO). (2010). *China's IP journey.* Retrieved December 10, 2011, from http://www.wipo.int/wipo_magazine/en/2010/06/article_0010.html

World Intellectual Property Organization. (2011). *Summary of the Patent Cooperation Treaty (PCT) (1970).* Retrieved July 20, 2011 from http://www.wipo.int/treaties/en/registration/pct/summary_pct.html

World Trade Organization (WTO). (2001). *WTO successfully concludes negotiations on China's entry.* Retrieved January 13, 2012, from http://www.wto.org/english/news_e/pres01_e/pr243_e.html

XE. (2011). *Currency converter widget.* Retrieved April 7, 2012, from http://www.xe.com/ucc/convert/?Amount=3566&From=CNY&To=AUD

Xie, Y. & Amine, L. S. (2009). Social networks and the internationalization of Chinese entrepreneurs. *Global Business & Organizational Excellence 29*(1), 61–78.

Xin, K., Zhou, S., & Tsui. A. S. (1998). Supply and development of executives and middle managers in China. In J. C. Bartels (Ed.), *Evolution of business practices: China opportunities and risks* (pp. 182–97). Murray Hill, NJ: Dun & Bradstreet.

Zahra, S., Ireland, D., & Hitt, M. (2000). International expansion by new venture Firms: International diversity, mode of market entry, technological learning, and performance. *Academy of Management Journal 43*(5), 925–950.

Zeithammer, R. & Kellogg, R. (2011). *The hesitant Haigui.* Retrieved March 20, 2012, from http://www.anderson.ucla.edu/faculty/robert.zeithammer/HesitantHaigui_Sep2011.pdf

Zhu, C. J. (1997). Human resource development in China during the transition to a new economic system. *Asia Pacific Journal of Human Resources 35*(2), 19–44.

Index

OTHER TITLES IN OUR INTERNATIONAL BUSINESS COLLECTION

Tamer Cavusgil, Georgia State, Michael Czinkota, Georgetown, and Gary Knight, Florida State University, Collection Editors

- *Conducting Market Research for International Business* by S. Tamer Cavusgil, John Riesenberger, and Attila Yaprak
- *Export Marketing Strategy: Tactics and Skills That Work* by Shaoming Zou, Daekwan Kim, and Tamer Cavusgil
- *Born Global Firms: A New International Enterprise* by S. Tamer Cavusgil and Gary Knight
- *Emerging Trends, Threats and Opportunities in International Marketing: What Executives Need to Know* by Michael Czinkota, Ilkka Ronkainen, and Masaaki Kotabe
- *Managing International Business in Relation-Based versus Rule-Based Countries* by Shaomin Li
- *A Strategic and Tactical Approach to Global Business Ethics* by Lawrence A. Beer
- *International Social Entrepreneurship: Pathways to Personal and Corporate Impact* by Joseph Mark Munoz
- *Understanding Japanese Management Practices* by Parissa Haghirian
- *Doing Business in the ASEAN Countries* by Balbir Bhasin
- *Practical Solutions to Global Business Negotiations* by Claude Cellich and Subhash Jain
- *China: Doing Business in the Middle Kingdom* by Stuart Strother

---

Announcing the Business Expert Press Digital Library

Concise E-books Business Students Need for Classroom and Research

This book can also be purchased in an e-book collection by your library as
- a one-time purchase,
- that is owned forever,
- allows for simultaneous readers,
- has no restrictions on printing, and
- can be downloaded as PDFs from within the library community.
    Our digital library collections are a great solution to beat the rising cost of textbooks.
e-books can be loaded into their course management systems or onto student's e-book readers.

The **Business Expert Press** digital libraries are very affordable, with no obligation to buy in future years. For more information, please visit www.businessexpertpress.com/librarians. To set up a trial in the United States, please contact **Adam Chesler** at *adam.chesler@businessexpertpress.com* for all other regions, contact **Nicole Lee** at *nicole.lee@igroupnet.com*.

CPSIA information can be obtained at www.ICGtesting.com
Printed in the USA
BVOW010024080513

320150BV00005B/15/P